OMAR AL-BASHIR
AND
AFRICA'S
LONGEST WAR

Some of Paul Moorcraft's other books on military topics

A Short Thousand Years: The End of Rhodesia's Rebellion (1979)
Contact 2: The Struggle for Peace (1981)
Africa's Superpower (1982)
African Nemesis: War and Revolution in Southern Africa, 1945-2010 (1994)
Axis of Evil: The War on Terror (with Gwyn Winfield and John Chisholm) (2005)
The New Wars of the West (with Gwyn Winfield and John Chisholm) (2006)
Inside the Danger Zones: Travels to Arresting Places (2010)
Shooting the Messenger: The Politics of War Reporting (with Phil Taylor) (2011)
The Rhodesian War: A Military History (with Peter McLaughlin) (2011)
Mugabe's War Machine (2011)
Total Destruction of the Tamil Tigers (2012)

OMAR AL-BASHIR
AND
AFRICA'S
LONGEST WAR

PAUL L. MOORCRAFT

Pen & Sword
MILITARY

First published in Great Britain in 2015 by
PEN & SWORD MILITARY
an imprint of
Pen & Sword Books Ltd
47 Church Street
Barnsley
South Yorkshire
S70 2AS

Copyright © Professor Paul L. Moorcraft, 2015

ISBN 978 1 47382 823 0 HB
ISBN 978 1 47384 252 6 TPB

Typeset in Times New Roman by Chic Graphics

Printed and bound in England
by CPI Group (UK) Ltd, Croydon, CR0 4YY

Pen & Sword Books Ltd incorporates the imprints of
Pen & Sword Books Ltd incorporates the imprints of Pen & Sword
Archaeology, Atlas, Aviation, Battleground, Discovery,
Family History, History, Maritime, Military, Naval, Politics,
Railways, Select, Social History, Transport, True Crime,
Claymore Press, Frontline Books, Leo Cooper, Praetorian Press,
Remember When, Seaforth Publishing and Wharncliffe.

For a complete list of Pen & Sword titles please contact
PEN & SWORD BOOKS LIMITED
47 Church Street, Barnsley, South Yorkshire, S70 2AS, England
E-mail: enquiries@pen-and-sword.co.uk
Website: www.pen-and-sword.co.uk

Contents

About the Author

Professor Paul Moorcraft, an internationally respected expert on crisis communications, especially relating to military and security issues, has worked for *Time* magazine, the BBC and most of the Western TV networks as a freelance producer/war correspondent as well as lecturing full-time (consecutively) at ten major universities in journalism, politics and international relations. He has worked in thirty war zones in Africa, the Middle East, Asia and the Balkans, often with irregular forces. Most recently he has been operating in Afghanistan, Iraq, Palestine/Israel, Nepal, Sudan, Zimbabwe, Syria, Turkey and Sri Lanka.

Dr Moorcraft is a former senior instructor at the Royal Military Academy, Sandhurst, and the UK Joint Services Command and Staff College. He also worked in Corporate Communications in the Ministry of Defence in Whitehall. The Ministry of Defence recalled him for six months during the Iraq War in 2003.

The author of a wide range of books on military history, politics and crime, Dr Moorcraft is a regular broadcaster (BBC TV and radio, as well as Sky, Al Jazeera, etc.) and op-ed writer for major international newspapers (the *Guardian, New Statesman, Washington Times, Canberra Times, Business Day, Western Mail* etc.). One of his recent books is *Axis of Evil: The War on Terror* (Pen and Sword, 2005). An updated version, *The New Wars of the West*, was published by Casemate in the US in 2006. His *Shooting the Messenger: The Politics of War Reporting* (Potomac, Washington, 2008) was co-authored with Professor Phil Taylor. An updated version was released in 2011 (Biteback, London). *The Rhodesian War: A Military History* (with Dr Peter McLaughlin) was first published by Pen and Sword books in 2008. *Mugabe's War Machine* (Pen and Sword) came out in 2011. *The Total Destruction of the Tamil Tigers: A Rare Victory of Sri Lanka's Long War* was released in various editions by Pen and Sword in 2013-14. Three volumes of memoirs have been published, the most recent being *Inside the Danger Zones: Travels to Arresting Places* (Biteback, London, 2010). Dr Moorcraft is an award-winning novelist as well as an author of educational publications related to his charity work (*It Just Doesn't Add Up: Explaining Dyscalculia and Overcoming Number Problems for Children and Adults*, Filament, Croydon, 2014).

Professor Moorcraft has visited Sudan, including all the war zones, especially Darfur, on more than twenty (often extended) occasions since 1996. He has interviewed many of the key players on all sides of the various conflicts while producing a series of documentaries for UK and US TV networks. He was head of mission, for fifty international observers, during the 2010 election. Professor Moorcraft was also given unrivalled access to President al-Bashir. His latest visit to Sudan, and interviews with al-Bashir, was in January 2014.

Paul Moorcraft is the director of the Centre for Foreign Policy Analysis, London, and visiting professor at Cardiff University's School of Journalism, Media and Cultural Studies, Europe's leading journalism centre.

Abbreviations

AMIS	African Union Mission in Sudan
AU	African Union
CAR	Central African Republic
CIA	Central Intelligence Agency
CNPC	China National Petroleum Corporation
COIN	counter-insurgency
CPA	Comprehensive Peace Agreement
CSI	Christian Solidarity International
DPA	Darfur Peace Agreement
DUP	Democratic Unionist Party
EPLF	Eritrean People's Liberation Front
EPRDF	Ethiopian People's Revolutionary Democratic Front
EU	European Union
FCO	Foreign and Commonwealth Office (British)
GNU	Government of National Unity
GoSS	Government of South Sudan
ICC	International Criminal Court
IDP	internally displaced person
IGAD	Intergovernmental Authority on Development
IMF	International Monetary Fund
ISI	Inter-Services Intelligence (Pakistan)
JEM	Justice and Equality Movement
LRA	Lord's Resistance Army
MSF	Médecins Sans Frontières
NATO	North Atlantic Treaty Organisation
NBC	Nuclear, Biological and Chemical
NCO	non-commissioned officer
NCP	National Congress Party
NDA	National Democratic Alliance
NGO	non-governmental organization
NIF	National Islamic Front
NRF	National Redemption Front (Darfur)
NISS	National Intelligence and Security Service (Sudan)
OAU	Organization of African Unity
OLS	Operation Lifeline Sudan

PAIC	Popular Arab and Islamic Congress
PCP	Popular Congress Party
PDF	Popular Defence Force
RCC	Revolutionary Command Council
SAF	Sudanese Armed Forces
SANU	Sudan African National Union
SDF	Sudanese Defence Force
SLA	Sudan Liberation Army
SPAF	Sudan People's Armed Forces
SPLM/A	Sudan People's Liberation Movement/Army
SPLM-N	Sudan People's Liberation Movement-North
SPS	Sudan Political Service
SSDF	South Sudan Defence Force
SSLA	South Sudan Liberation Army
UNAMID	UN-African Union Mission in Darfur
UNMEE	UN Mission in Eritrea and Ethiopia
UNMIS	UN Mission in Sudan
UNMISS	UN Mission in South Sudan
USAID	United States Agency for International Development

Glossary of Terms

abeed	slaves
amir	military commander/tribal leader
Ansar	followers of the Mahdi
awlad al-bahr	the people of the river, riverine Arabs
bayaa	Islamic oath of allegiance
dar	tribal homeland
effendi	originally used to describe Turkish officials, later to describe officials in general
Falasha	Ethiopian Jews
ghazi	tribal warrior
Haj	Pilgrimage to Mecca
haram	forbidden under Islamic law
hudud	Islamic punishment, usually amputation
jabal	hill, mountain
Janjaweed	devil horsemen, pro-government militias in Darfur
Jihadiyya	slave troops under Egyptian rule
Khalifa	steward, Caliph
Khatmiyya	the largest Sufi order in Sudan
marissa	beer
mundukuru	slavers
mujahedeen	holy warriors
mukhabarat	secret police/intelligence service
murahaliin	Baqqara militia
nas	ordinary Sudanese people
Pasdaran	Iranian Revolutionary Guards
sharia	Islamic law
shura	consultative body/practice of consultation
sirdar	commander in chief
Turkiya	Turkish/Egyptian rule
Umma	Islamic community
wadi	seasonal watercourse

Modern Sudanese Timeline

1820	Egypt invades Sudan – Turkish/Egyptian rule.
1881	Mahdist uprising.
1885	Fall of Khartoum; death of Gordon; the Mahdi dies.
1898	Battle of Omdurman; Anglo-Egyptian re-conquest; Fashoda incident.
1899	Anglo-Egyptian Condominium – British rule.
1916	British conquest of Darfur.
1925	Formation of the Sudan Defence Force.
1952	Egyptian army coup.
1954-5	Withdrawal of British forces from Sudan and Egypt.
1955	Mutiny of southern forces in Torit – start of 'First Southern War of Independence' (1955-1972).
1956	Sudanese independence – failure of Anglo-French invasion of Suez.
1958	First military coup led by General Abboud.
1962	Anya-Nya sparks up civil war in the south.
1964	October Revolution – temporary civilian rule.
1966	Sadiq al-Mahdi becomes prime minister.
1969	Ja'afar Numeiri leads the 'May Revolution' – return of military rule.
1970	Joseph Lagu takes over leadership of Anya-Nya.
1971	Communist coup against Numeiri suppressed.
1972	North-south peace agreement at Addis Ababa.
1978	Oil confirmed in Bentiu in southern Sudan.
1983	Numeiri imposes sharia law. Second round of southern war; formation of SPLM/A.
1984	Beginning of severe drought and famine.
1985	Numeiri deposed in military coup.
1986	Civilian government under Sadiq al-Mahdi.
1987	Al-Mahdi government starts arming tribal militias.
1988	Famine in south Sudan.
1989	National Salvation Revolution led by Omar al-Bashir and Hassan al-Turabi.
1991	Osama bin Laden moves to Khartoum.

1993	Al-Bashir becomes president; US adds Sudan to list of states sponsoring terrorism.
1995	Sudan implicated in assassination attempt on Egyptian President Mubarak.
1996	Bin Laden thrown out of Sudan.
1998	US cruise missile strike on Sudan.
1999	Al-Bashir dissolves national assembly, ejects al-Turabi as speaker; oil exported for first time.
2001	Al-Turabi arrested for signing a memorandum with SPLM; US extends unilateral sanctions.
2002	First ceasefire deal with SPLA regarding Nuba Mountains; signing of Machakos Protocol.
2003	Beginning of Darfur war.
2004	US Secretary of State Colin Powell describes Darfur killings as genocide.
2005	Comprehensive Peace Agreement signed; John Garang killed in helicopter crash.
2007	International Criminal Court issues first warrants for Sudanese.
2008	Sudan and Chad sign peace accord; armoured column from Darfur raids Omdurman; north-south fighting in disputed Abyei; ICC calls for arrest of al-Bashir for war crimes.
2010	Al-Bashir wins north and Salva Kiir wins south in internationally supervised elections.
2011	Referendum in south – massive majority for independence; South Sudan gains independence.
2012	South Sudan halts oil production in dispute with Khartoum; border fighting; cost-of-living protests in Khartoum; alleged Israeli air strike on Khartoum; military-intelligence coup suppressed in Khartoum.
2013	Waves of protests in north Sudan about cuts in fuel subsidies; civil war breaks out in South Sudan
2014	Al-Bashir shakes up his party to bring in new faces; offers 'dialogue' to opposition parties.

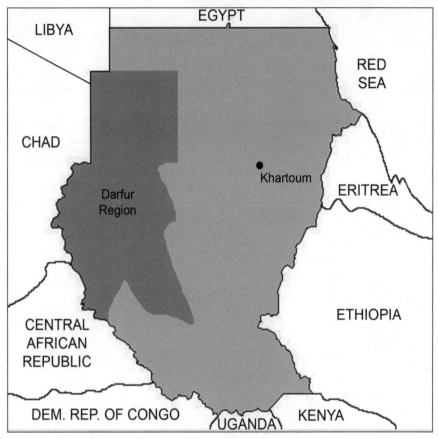

Political map of Sudan – surrounded by nine often hostile neighbours.

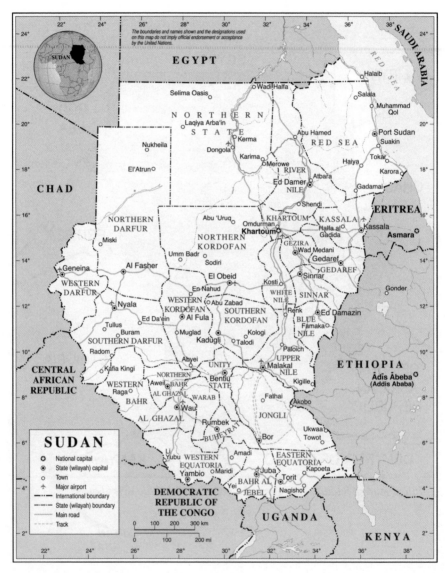

Detailed map of Sudan.

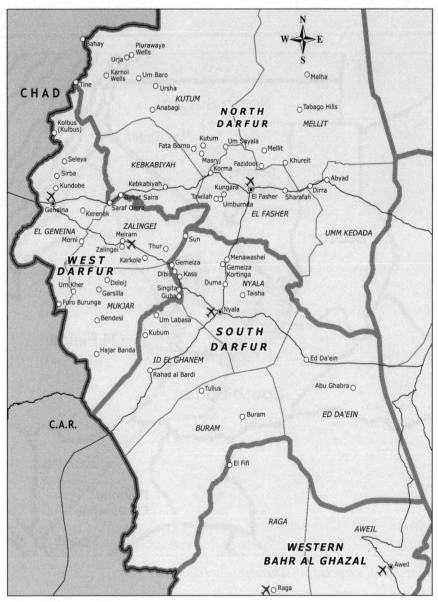

Detailed map of Darfur.

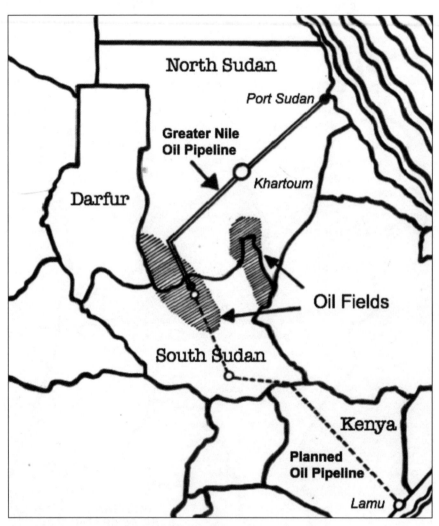

The political terrain of oil. (Designer: Roz Wilson)

List of Illustrations

1. Sudan's pyramids at Meroë are much smaller than their Egyptian counterparts.
2. General Charles Gordon was a religious crank who disobeyed explicit orders to evacuate British and Egyptian officials and troops from Khartoum in 1884.
3. Gordon's death made him a Victorian icon.
4. General Horatio Herbert Kitchener defeated the Mahdists at the Battle of Omdurman in 1898.
5. The leader of the Mahdists was Muhammad Ahmad ibn Abdullah. His tomb in Omdurman. (Picture credit: author)
6. Contemporary picture of the governor's palace where Gordon was killed. After independence it became the presidential palace. (Author)
7. The command vehicle used by General Omar al-Bashir in the 1989 coup. (Author)
8. Al-Bashir greets Sadiq al-Mahdi, the former premier, in early 2014. (Sudan government archives)
9. The Sudanese President greets his old rival, Dr Hassan al-Turabi, during a reconciliation process in early 2014. (Government archives)
10. Dr Hassan al-Turabi was more interested in international jihad rather than the details of domestic governance, but he was a highly gifted intellectual and spiritual leader.
11. For the first years after the revolution of 1989, al-Bashir concentrated on military matters, but eventually he removed al-Turabi from power and became politically dominant by 1999.
12. Bigwigs in the ruling National Congress Party, Dr Ibrahim A Ghandour (left) and Ali Othman Taha, who led Khartoum's team during the peace talks with the south (2002-2005). (Tony Denton)
13. The charismatic but authoritarian leader of the Sudan People's Liberation Army, Dr John Garang.
14. Garang's successor was Salva Kiir, who became the first president of independent South Sudan. (Irwin Armstrong)
15. Riek Machar became Kiir's deputy in the new republic, but rebelled against him in December 2013.
16. In 1998 US President Clinton sent cruise missiles to destroy the Al-Shifa facility in Khartoum. (Author)

17. In 1996 Riek Machar joined Khartoum as part of the 'Peace from Within' policy. In June1996 government troops march as a part of a peace rally in Juba, the southern capital. (Author)

18. Tribal dancer taking part in a peace rally in Torit, June 1996. (Author)

19. Sudan Liberation Army (SLA) insurgents, near El Fasher, Darfur, 2004. (Author)

20. SLA insurgents, Darfur, 2004. (Author)

21. Cameraman Irwin Armstrong with SLA troops, 2004. (Author)

22. Government counter-insurgency forces, Darfur, 2005. (Author)

23. US aid for IDP camp near El Fasher, 2004. (Author)

24. Mosque in Sarasir, the village where al-Bashir grew up. (Tony Denton)

25. Diplomatic duties: al-Bashir at the 12th AU summit. (Government archives)

26. Unlike most heads of state in Africa, al-Bashir is a patient and ready listener, even to Western journalists. (Tony Denton)

27. Al-Bashir's second wife, Widad Babiker Omer. (Tony Denton)

28. Mohammed Hassan, the President's younger brother. (Tony Denton)

29. Hadiya, the President's mother. (Tony Denton)

30. Al-Bashir is very much a family man, seen here with his second wife and stepdaughter, at his farm. (Tony Denton)

31. The President doted on his youngest step-child, Amna. (Tony Denton)

32. Al-Bashir accommodated his three nieces (the children of his brother, Mohammed Hassan) while they studied in Khartoum. (Tony Denton)

33. Salva Kiir voting, in Juba, during the 2010 election. (Irwin Armstrong)

34. SPLA policeman guarding a voting centre in Bentiu, April 2010. (Tony Denton)

35. Author interviewing an election official near Juba during 2011 referendum. (Marty Stalker)

36. In private, al-Bashir was usually a quiet considered man, but he took on another persona in front of crowds. (Government archives)

37. The President at his farm in January 2014. He insisted he wanted to retire to take up farming full-time. (Tony Denton)

38. The Sudanese are famously hospitable to foreigners. On the author's first visit to the country, however, he was arrested by the Minister of Justice himself. On the last visit, nearly 20 years later, he enjoyed a late breakfast with the President at his farm, January 2014. (Tony Denton)

Introduction

Why President Omar al-Bashir's Sudan is important

Sudan occupied a pivotal, if initially largely accidental, role in British imperial history. For centuries it was a backwater ruled by the far-away Ottoman sultans. The 1869 opening of the Suez Canal, a lifeline to the British Raj, subsequently resulted in the de facto occupation of Egypt. Technically, Sudan became an Anglo-Egyptian condominium, but it was still a backwater. Its security was a concern to the British because it was the hinterland of Egypt and because of its precious Nile waters. It was also part of the pink corridor on the imperial map, which linked it to the settler colonies of Uganda and Kenya, and the long-held ambition of a Cape-to-Cairo railway.

The Mahdi rebellion of the 1880s led to the major imperial embarrassment of General 'Chinese' Gordon's death in Khartoum. To avenge this humiliation and, as ever, to deter the French, Sudan was re-conquered a decade later. The British held sway until independence in 1956, although London ran Sudan with a fairly light touch. The colonialists concentrated on the Muslim-Arab triangle around Khartoum, regarded Darfur as a security problem, and dithered about the role of the Christian-animist south, which was inhabited largely by African tribes, ethnically and culturally distinct from the north. In 1956, the new Arab leaders ironically copied much of the political and economic practices of the departed British, although the tone in Khartoum was of course more Islamic.

The Sudan civil service had been run efficiently by a well-bred core of ex-public school English mandarins. At independence the indigenous leaders acquired much of the best of the imperial heritage in law, governance and education. Sudan also inherited the Khartoum-centric view of the country. The peripheries remained largely underdeveloped, and this factor, as well as religion, partly caused the army mutiny in the south just before independence. Underdevelopment, poor governance and the not unconnected constant wars have characterized Sudan's modern history. Brief periods of inefficient democratic rule were constantly interrupted by military coups. The main focus of this book is what followed the Islamist military putsch of 1989, led by the then Brigadier General Omar Hassan Ahmed al-

Bashir in tandem with Dr Hassan al-Turabi, the spiritual mentor of the revolution.

This book concentrates on the al-Bashir period – at the time of writing, the same Field Marshal and President is still in power. Al-Bashir fought a long war in the south as a soldier and later national leader, but technically ended one stage of the conflict in a 2005 peace deal, by offering the right of secession to the southern rebels, the Sudan People's Liberation Movement. South Sudan finally became independent in 2011. Another old conflict, however, had been fired up again in the west, in Darfur, in 2003. It was distinct, but related to the southern struggle. Rebellion also simmered in the east. Meanwhile, all of Sudan's nine contiguous neighbours had stirred the pot, most notably the madcap supremo in Libya, the late and unlamented Colonel Gaddafi.

Under al-Bashir, Sudan became a major oil exporter, and this sucked in international players hungry for mineral resources. China became the dominant influence, which helped to displace Western interests. Western economic sanctions also meant that Beijing had a freer hand. Osama bin Laden was a guest of al-Bashir's government from 1991 to 1996, perhaps not the best way to win friends in the US. Sudan became listed as a terrorist state and was embroiled in the American 'war on terror' after the 9/11 abominations. Khartoum thought that, after Afghanistan and Iraq, it was to be next in line for regime-change treatment. The US stepped up its support for the southern rebels while American lobby groups, and Hollywood stars, became active in the anti-Khartoum movement after 'genocide' was declared in Darfur.

Nevertheless, al-Bashir became an ally of the US, Britain, Norway and African states such as Kenya in finessing the Comprehensive Peace Agreement signed at Naivasha, Kenya, in January 2005. Despite US sanctions, al-Bashir was hailed as a peacemaker. The media firestorm over the savagery, on various sides, in the Darfur war, however, led to the denunciation of al-Bashir as a war criminal, and indictments at the International Criminal Court. Sudan was once more considered a rogue state in much of the West, although the European Union dropped its sanctions.

Al-Bashir's team largely played according to the rules of the 2005 agreement, with an uneasy southern-northern government of national unity in Khartoum, reasonably free elections in 2010, and finally the referendum in 2011 in the south that led to an overwhelming vote for independence. With hindsight, imperial Britain should have grasped the nettle and allowed the south its separate existence after 1945. Many southern leaders, most notably the charismatic but autocratic leader of the Sudan People's Liberation Army (SPLA), Colonel John Garang de Mabior, hoped to create a united Sudan with the democratic participation of the south, and west and east, of what was Africa's biggest country. After Garang's death, just after the signing of the 2005 deal, the southern leadership returned to the preferred option of independence.

When South Sudan emerged as Africa's newest state in the summer of 2011, many outside observers hoped that the main fault-line and cause of Sudan's wars could be resolved. Instead, the south – umbilically connected to the economy of the north – dissolved into ethnic civil war. By 2014 the traditional enemy, al-Bashir, was brought in by the southern president, Salva Kiir, to help forge peace, aided by the neighbouring states. By then, the southern war had emasculated the two countries' oil supplies. South Sudan, already a failed state, slipped into famine and disaster. The north endured riots because of increases in food prices and other staples. A military-intelligence coup almost brought down al-Bashir. He had come to power in a putsch, but now survived one that aimed to topple him. By early 2014 al-Bashir's family members were unanimous in pleading for him to step down. He had been in the army for over twenty-five years and President for twenty-five years. Many in the ruling National Congress Party wanted a new face, but the old guard felt al-Bashir should run again in the scheduled 2015 elections. If he were to step down what would be his national and international legacy?

President Omar al-Bashir has been one of Africa's and, arguably, Arabia's most controversial leaders. He has been in power since 1989, and was the first sitting head of state to be issued with an arrest warrant, for war crimes, by the International Criminal Court. He has been a central personality in Islamic and African politics, as well as a love-to-hate figure for the US in the 'war on terror'. With his 2014 headline role as peacemaker in the southern civil war and other regional conflicts, and Britain threatened with a war crimes indictment by the ICC, al-Bashir's salience is now much greater.

He is a field marshal who has fought and commanded in possibly the world's longest conflict. No authoritative biography has been written on him. Nor has there been a comprehensive military history of Sudan. I have tried to do both and place al-Bashir in the context of the political and military struggles of his country. It is impossible to understand al-Bashir's extended rule without some comprehension of what went before. I have dealt at length with the previous history of ungovernability in Sudan; otherwise, al-Bashir's behaviour makes far less sense. This life and times (some would say crimes) is sometimes close-up and personal, with warts and all. The book covers the military background until independence. Then it dissects the long north-south civil war until al-Bashir's Islamist military coup in 1989 that was supposed to end that enduring conflict. Thereafter, the story covers the wars in the east, south and west (in Darfur). International political and military intervention is also factored in.

This book is based on in-depth one-on-one interviews with al-Bashir himself, and nearly all his family and close political, military and intelligence colleagues, plus my decades-long personal frontline experience of Sudan's many struggles. During nearly twenty years of travels in Sudan, I have met many people; most obstructed me, but some became my friends. It is a paradox that, despite some bad times, mindless bureaucracy, censorship and occasional arrests, I believe the Sudanese reputation for hospitality is generally well-deserved. Khartoum, in the north, is still one of the safest cities in Africa. I was also privileged to receive many acts of kindness, trust and hospitality in the much poorer south, east and west; sometimes in the middle of the fighting. I was often entranced by the desert landscapes, the lushness of the deep south, the sunsets on the Nile, and the ancient history, the pyramids and the archaeological sites. This book is not all bullets and bang-bang.

I have focused on the essence of al-Bashir's life – as a soldier and Islamist. Religion and war have been largely toxic ingredients of the whole country's history. The focus has necessarily been on the man who mainly shaped events, for better or worse, since 1989. I have also tried to reflect the voices of humble farmers or isolated teachers and dedicated doctors I met, as well as the many politicians and military officers. I have also listened carefully to the aid specialists, UN workers and local journalists who know the languages and cultures much better than I do.

Conflict resolution in Sudan is not just obviously important for the 40 million inhabitants of both countries; it is vital in respect of the turmoil in nearly all the neighbouring states: Libya, Chad, Central African Republic, Democratic Republic of Congo, Uganda, Kenya, Ethiopia, Eritrea and Egypt. Sudan's problems are also linked to the ferment in the Maghreb and elsewhere in the Arab world, and it is connected to the incessant war in Somalia. Sudan's ethnic and religious wars have infected Mali and Nigeria. The so-called ungovernable spaces of the Sahel and Sahara as well as the Horn are all potential breeding grounds for al-Qaeda and its franchises that have spread from the badlands of Afghanistan and Pakistan to Yemen and now much of northern Africa, from A-Z, Algeria to Zanzibar. More recently the black flag of jihad has flown defiantly in Syria and Iraq, threatening to spawn a bloody Shia-Sunni catastrophe throughout the Middle East and beyond. Whether Western intervention contains or incites jihad remains a moot point.

I am writing this on the precise anniversary of the start of the First World War. This conflagration destroyed a number of empires, and in particular the Sublime Porte. It is no coincidence that the peripheries of the former Ottoman Empire are today the source of so much conflict or controversy – in Bosnia, Kurdistan and south Sudan, for example. More central Ottoman territories are also tearing up the straight-lined borders drawn up by the haughty cartographers of the British and French victors of the 1914-1918 war. It is surprising that so many artificial states have lasted so long. I expect many others to collapse, not least the Saudi pack of cards. So the far-flung Sudanese fragment of Istanbul's long recessional needs to be understood in historical as well as contemporary context.

This book tells the story of one man in one country – now become two, but Sudan's fate also impacts on the whole continent of Africa, as well as on the vast shifts in the tectonic plates of the Islamic world. Some Arab analysts might portray al-Bashir as an Islamic visionary; Western reporters usually depict him as a traditional African strongman. In our conversations, al-Bashir described himself as a simple soldier who was dedicated to Islam and his country. The West has already condemned the Sudanese President and wants to drag him off to a court in The Hague, but many of his own countrymen and women might well pronounce differently, as they have in (admittedly flawed) elections. It was an unintended consequence of Western pressure that many northern Sudanese who disliked their president reacted as supportive patriots when he was indicted by the ICC.

Sudan – now we must say two Sudans — is a stirring and tragic story that I have tried to tell in a way that is fair to all the many sides in the complex matrix. Yet, sadly, history keeps repeating itself in Sudan. Whether my interpretation can help, even just a little, to end the vicious circle of fighting, I do not know. I have simply done my best. The Sudanese, from north and south, and for that matter east and west, all deserve better than endless war.

Most people gave me a hard time in covering Sudan, but I would like to mention a few who made my many often arduous trips possible, tolerable and sometimes pleasant. Irwin Armstrong was an ever-patient cameraman and friend from the start. Later, Marty Stalker joined the film team. Lindsey Hilsum, a true 'Sudanorak', helped with refining my films for broadcast on the UK's Channel Four News. Pieter Stapel was a Khartoum hotelier who often provided much-needed beverages after exhaustingly dry trips in the desert. Mohamed Salahuddin fixed many things in Khartoum. Uthayla Abdullah-Bray saved me from a series of disasters during the 2010 election observer mission that I tried to lead. Tony Denton also helped on that mission, as well as taking the excellent photographs of the President and his family in 2014, plus helping with the book's design. Heidi Modro was a tower of strength for me at the UN headquarters in Khartoum and later in Juba; and I rarely praise big bureaucracies. Judy Larkin came on the 2010 observer mission and helped with the editing. James Barker checked historical facts. It almost goes without saying that the many mistakes, especially in the Arabic transliteration, are my own. Arabic scholars will no doubt correctly criticize my lack of standardization in translating names and places – I have generally used names more common in English or the system deployed by the BBC.

Paul Moorcraft
Surrey Hills
England
4 August 2014

Chapter 1

The Historical Background

<u>What is Sudan?</u>

Sudan derives its name from the Arabic *bilad as-Sudan* meaning 'land of the blacks' and historically referred to the wider region immediately south of the Sahara; so modern Sudan is just *part* of a region defined by Arabic-speaking North Africans. Separately, *Sudd* (or *Sadd*) is Arabic for 'barrier'; this defines the largest swamp in the world, to be found in the south. The country also boasts the longest river in the world, the Nile; actually it is at least two rivers, mainly the Blue Nile, creamy brown from the mud of the Ethiopian highlands, and the paler White Nile, which merge at Khartoum, the capital of what was Africa's biggest country until the secession of the south.

Topography and climate have pre-conditioned much of the country's history. A glimpse at a relief map will immediately distinguish the dry north from the more tropical south. It is a land of mountains, swamps and jungles as well as unforgiving deserts and interminable savannah. For thousands of years the nature of the terrain made military campaigning difficult, even for modern armies, as the British found in the late nineteenth century, not least contending with the forbidding cataracts on the Nile. Colonialists would talk of MMBA – miles and miles of bloody Africa.

Michael Asher, the historian and explorer, said it was 'the most fascinating country in Africa' and noted that its 'vastness and diversity of cultures qualify it almost for the status of a miniature continent'. Modern Sudan was a land of over 600 ethnic groups and distinct languages and dialects, the heritage of migration and conquest. Nomadic lifestyles based on cattle-herding and camel routes to the Red Sea, including maritime access for the *Haj*, led to conflicts with settled pastoralists, clashes which related to changing weather patterns, not least in today's Darfur. It has also been a land of contending religions, chiefly Islam in the north and Christianity and animism in the south.

For thousands of years the land was subject to invasions and wars, which almost inevitably produced an often venomous cultural racism, based less on colour and ideology and more on ethnic identity and language. An adequate analysis of the Arab tribal groups and southern ethnic distinctions would require a large book on its own. So I will refer to these complex distinctions when they are directly relevant to specific military political events.

For most of my story I will focus on the Ja'aliyyin, Shayqiyya and the Danaqla groups (*awlad al-bahr;* people of the river) that comprise the dominant riverine Arabs, now centred in Khartoum state. These groups have tended to control politics, the civil service and the military since independence. What defines 'Sudanese' has usually been a hard question to answer; the Khartoum elite stressed the Arabic language, claims to Arab ancestry (and sometimes a lineage from the Prophet) and the Islamic religion. This sometimes insecure sense of self-identification was reinforced by the fact that the rest of the Arab world did not always uphold the Sudanese elites' claim to their Arab authenticity. Invasions from the north and, later, Turkish, Egyptian and British occupations reinforced this inferiority/superiority paradox. The mixed 'African-Arab' peoples in the west, in Darfur, although nearly all passionate Muslims, were often looked down on as ill-bred rustics. That feeling extended to many of the peoples in the east, especially the unruly Beja, who were Muslims, though not Arabs. The elite's racism applied in spades to the south, where the majority of the many tribal groups were not Arab and not Muslims. In the modern era many elite Sudanese did not feel entirely comfortable with being identified with 'black Africans' and certainly did not want to be defined as 'blacks' when they worked or travelled in Europe or North America.

What constituted Sudanese identity was still an unanswered question long after independence. The coup of 1989 tried to find a solution: the government was committed to making all Sudanese proper Arabs and Salafist Muslims via a vigorous programme of Arabization and Islamization. This had been tried before by imposing *Sharia* law in the south, but it had triggered ever more resistance among the non-Muslim majority there. After 1989, the Islamist revolutionaries would try again, but they would eventually cause the south to secede. Paradoxically, the northern elite's Khartoum-centric racist behaviour was then replicated in the southern capital of Juba. There, a tiny elite held nearly all the wealth and power; it largely disregarded the peripheries, which exacerbated old and bitter ethnic divisions that in turn fuelled the civil war from December 2013.

Early history

Archaeologists have found evidence of a Neolithic culture along the Nile from the eighth millennium before our common era (BCE). The region of Upper Egypt and Nubia (the latter centred on the confluence of the Blue and White Niles and River Atabara) developed similar systems of kingship – rule by Pharaohs – around 3,300 years BCE. The Nubian Kushite kingdom invaded Egypt in 800 BCE. The Kushite Empire stretched from South Kordofan to the Sinai, until the Assyrians halted the Nubian expansion when they invaded Egypt.

The Nubian capital became Meroë. The kingdom was advanced, among the first to develop iron-smelting technology. The Kushite kingdom of Nubia survived the expansion of Roman power in the region, but eventually collapsed in the fourth century AD. The empire broke up into many small states run by warrior aristocracies based around the Nile in what is now northern Sudan. The princely courts were soon influenced by the growing power of Byzantium, thus coming under the sway of various branches of Christianity after AD 550. In the seventh century, the armed followers of the Prophet Mohammed exploded into one of the most remarkable military expansions in history, which eventually conquered territory from the Pyrenees to the borders of China.The Islamic conquests of Egypt inevitably spread the word of the Prophet south via a mixture of war, trade and intermarriage. The riverine Arabs of today descended from the fusion of Arab and Nubian cultures. During the sixteenth century the Funj people moved from southern Nubia and displaced the surviving Christian kingdoms to establish what became known as the Sultanate of Sennar or the Blue Sultanate.

This Sultanate practised an unusual mix of Islam along with Christian and animist beliefs; for example, many of the festivals involved a great deal of alcohol consumption. Despite conflict with Abyssinia/Ethiopia in the east, and the African kingdoms of the south, for the first hundred years the Sennar armies were very effective. They relied on shock troops of heavy cavalry formed from the nobility, as in Europe; they were armed with long broadswords, rather than lances. The horsemen also wore chain mail. The mass of the army, however, was based on infantry carrying swords. Unusually, the Sennar Sultanate sustained a standing army, the result of a successful gold-based economy. It was the largest standing army in north-east Africa until the early nineteenth century. Forts and castles were set up as permanent garrisons. This centralized and well-trained force meant that neighbouring ad-hoc armies were usually defeated. The empire was finally overcome by a bigger, better-organized and better-armed empire – the Ottoman Turks, via their Egyptian proxy.

The *Turkiya*

Technically, Egypt was ruled as part of the Ottoman empire based in Istanbul, but the Khedive (Viceroy) in Cairo, Muhammad Ali, regarded himself as an independent ruler, one with his own imperial ambitions. Originally an Albanian (or some say Kurdish) general in the Ottoman army sent to drive Napoleon's forces from Egypt, Muhammad Ali wanted to forge an Egyptian empire in Libya, Sudan, Ethiopia and east Africa. He later pushed into Arabia, planning to displace Ottoman rule completely. The gold and slaves he would acquire would pay for his army's conquests. It would also distract his army from meddling in domestic politics. In 1821 the Khedive's third son, Ismail Kamil Pasha, headed a motley force of 4,000 Albanians, Turks, troops from the Maghreb and Egyptian Bedouin, plus, crucially, an artillery unit led by an American officer, into northern Sudan.

They gradually conquered most of the riverine settlements. The locals referred to the invaders in general as 'Turks'. Turkish was the language of the administration, only gradually replaced by Arabic. Sudanese call this period *Turkiya*, although Western historians use the awkward phrase Turco-Egyptian rule. Some Sudanese clans fought back, but their lances and swords – and often determined bravery – were no match for the invaders' firepower. Central administration and irrigation brought improvements, but modernization also meant rigorous taxation. The newcomers attempted to introduce a more orthodox form of Islam to the Sudanese, although the mystical *Sufi* version remained dominant in the rural areas. An extremely onerous system of tax on slaves, cattle and grain, plus a hut tax, eventually prompted a revolt, led by the Ja'aliyyin coalition in Shendi. They burnt to death Ismail Pasha and his key henchmen in their quarters, and the revolt spread.

'Turkish' rule tottered and would have collapsed except for their superior weapons. The survival of the occupiers was aided, as ever, by tribal disunity among the Sudanese. One of the most determined initial resisters to the Turks was the Shayqiyya tribe. They fought so bravely that Ismail Pasha absorbed their cavalry units into his own forces and later sent them to strengthen his garrisons around the country – their widespread influence was to last well into the twentieth century. When the Ja'aliyyin clans rebelled, the armed horsemen of the Shayqiyya remained loyal to their new foreign overlords and helped to suppress the rebellion. Incensed by the death of his son, the Khedive in Cairo ordered his occupying troops to destroy all opposition with 'fire and sword'. So great was the vengeance that it took sixty years for the Sudanese to organize another revolt against the Ottoman system.

The occupiers installed a new 'Governor-General', Uthman Bey, who established, in 1825, a new capital in Khartoum. The origins of the name are disputed. Early British explorers assumed it came from *qurtum*, a flower cultivated extensively in Egypt for its oil. Arab historians prefer to derive the name from the shape of the spit in land in the confluence of the White and Blue Nile that looked a little like an elephant's trunk. The Arabic *khartum* fits this translation better.

Uthman Bey was a middle-aged Mamluk, originally from the Caucasus. The Mamluks, a little like the Janissaries who comprised mainly Christian boys from the Balkans, were originally a warrior class formed from slaves. Their discipline was akin to the Christian military orders, except in this case their loyalty was to Islam. The Mamluks had acquired respect because they had defeated the Mongols and the Crusaders, although the Khedive also had to suppress a Mamluk rebellion in Cairo. True to his own origins, Uthman Bey set about forming a new regular army by capturing slaves from the Nuba Mountains and the upper Blue Nile region. Slavery was believed, by some, to be sanctioned by the Koran, although it was *haram*, forbidden, to enslave Muslims. Other imams argued it was *haram* to enslave anybody. Ordinary slaves could never carry weapons, but the strict discipline and Islamic indoctrination of the new army, called *jihadiyya,* inspired loyalty. They were trained in Aswan by European instructors, although their officers were literate in Turkish, the language of command. This regular force comprised the backbone of the military power of the Turco-Egyptian regime.

The civilian administration, however, did not match the relative efficiency of its army. Eventually the rapacious tax system was reformed, but the slave-raiding economy was not. The Khedive in Cairo, still an ambitious empire builder, urged his administration in Khartoum to explore the White Nile and to traverse the so far impenetrable *Sudd* to reach the imagined riches of the African hinterland. Gold, ivory and slaves were there in abundance, Cairo believed. This expansionism coincided with a growing European interest, especially in France and Britain, in discovering the source of the White Nile. The Khartoum government was encouraged by Cairo to push ever south, but meanwhile the *Turkiya* controlled only the settlements along the river as far as Khartoum and a few so-called 'islands of authority' in regions such as Kordofan. Elsewhere, except for occasional punitive or slave-raiding expeditions by the *jihadiyya,* local warlords and nomads did what they pleased in the vast ungoverned expanses. The *ghazis,* or tribal warriors, carried on their feuds and mini-wars, capturing cattle and women, untroubled by the would-be centralizers and modernizers in the far-away capital.

As Muhammad Ali, the Khedive in Cairo, slipped into senility and paranoia, his empire declined, especially in Sudan. He had become more and more reliant on foreign aid from European Christians, especially bankers, traders and soldiers. When he died in 1849, his successor, his grandson Abbas I, was an ineffective conservative who did his best to exclude Western influence during his brief rule. His successor, however, Muhammad Said Pasha, had been educated by French tutors and welcomed Western investment, not least for the construction of the Suez Canal and the development of the telegraph. He came to rely more and more on foreign loans. As he slipped more deeply into debt, he considered abandoning Sudan.

He stayed, however, and made the weak provincial administrations directly responsible to Cairo, thus enfeebling further the already fragile central government in Khartoum. Influenced by his Western advisers, he ordered his powerless Governor General in Sudan to stop the slave trade in 1854. This incensed Sudanese traders, who regarded the practice as not only a major source of income, but ordained by the Koran. Almost worse for pious Sudanese was the appointment of an Armenian Christian as governor of Khartoum and Sennar. Meanwhile, Western missionaries and traders became more active, often working hand in hand with Europe's great powers who wielded extensive power via their local consuls. The Western traders chased ivory in the south, while the missionaries sought to save souls and prevent slavery. The Muslim elite in Khartoum felt increasingly alienated by Western and Egyptian interventions in their traditional lifestyle.

In 1863 a new more dynamic Khedive, Ismail Pasha, tried to revitalize Egypt and Sudan by extending railways, the telegraph, schools and a postal service – and the final abolition of the slave trade. Railway tracks from Egypt reached Khartoum in 1874 and Suakin on the Red Sea in 1875. The paddle-steamers built in Khartoum improved transportation up the White Nile. Ismail Pasha inherited the dreams of an empire in equatorial Africa. A modernized army could be deployed by the new trains and ships. Krupp artillery was introduced, and repeating Remington rifles from the USA replaced the old muzzle-loaders. At the end of the American Civil War, soldiers from both sides were recruited as military advisers. Most notably, a US Union officer, Brigadier General Charles Pomeroy Stone, served as the Egyptian chief of staff. Stone had enjoyed a chequered career. He was jailed without trial, including a long period in solitary confinement, after being accused of treason after the Battle of Ball's Bluff in October 1861. In perhaps one of the most controversial cases of American military jurisprudence, he was eventually released, without charge or apology. Stone was an innocent victim of political infighting. In partial recompense, the US military recommended him for service in Egypt, where he commanded, very ably, for thirteen years. Ironically, the general who had been accused of treason ended up using his engineering skills to build the foundations and pedestal of the Statue of Liberty.

The Khedive also tried to establish an effective police force from Shayqiyya irregulars. They did little to crush the slave trade, however. The traders usually bribed the police when they were stopped on boats on the White Nile or at inland slave markets. The local corruption and connivance in the slave trade further encouraged the Khedive to appoint more European officers whom he considered incorruptible and also morally committed to abolishing slavery. One of the most colourful of these soldiers with a missionary bent was Sir Samuel Baker. Obsessed, like many other Victorian English adventurers with discovering the source of the Nile, he had reached Lake Albert (Nyanza) in 1864. Baker used to travel with his female companion, Florence, who apparently could outshoot and outride her male colleagues. Baker outraged Queen Victoria herself by 'being intimate with a woman not his wife', as the Sovereign put it. That was true. Nevertheless, perhaps because of the popularity of his travel books, he secured a knighthood, but not complete acceptance in polite society. He possibly romanticized the lady not his wife. Baker claimed he had saved the beautiful blonde from sale in a Balkan slave market. She was en route to the Sultan's harem, he said. This was a typical plot of many Victorian pulp novels, but Baker's lifelong hostility to the slave trade may imply that his story of Florence, whom he eventually married, may have had some credibility.

As an Ottoman Pasha, Baker led an army into the south in 1870. He spoke reasonable Arabic and was an energetic leader who managed to penetrate the *Sudd* and expand the Khedive's equatorial empire. According to one leading historian of Sudan, however, he showed 'colossal insensitivity as an Englishman and Christian leading Turkish, Egyptian and Sudanese Muslims on a mission to end the slave trade'.[1] He fought battles with hostile – sometimes cannibalistic – tribesmen and argued bitterly with his own allies. Frustrated, he left Sudan in 1873 never to return.

Interestingly perhaps for Western historians, but fatal to many Sudanese, Baker was replaced as Governor of Equatoria by another flamboyant military adventurer who, in addition, happened to be a stubborn and self-righteous Christian mystic: Charles George Gordon. He was more commonly known as General 'Chinese' Gordon because he had suppressed the Taiping rebellion in 1864. With a small core of European officers, he restored the morale and discipline of the garrisons along the Upper Nile and introduced armed steamers. To the south he raised the Egyptian flag on Lake Albert, in the Great Lakes region dividing Uganda and the Congo. Khedive Ismail was planning an imperial pincer movement by sending an army along the Red Sea into Ethiopia. London put pressure on the Khedive to abandon his forlorn hopes of a new north-eastern empire. Diplomatic constraints and defeats in the field forced a withdrawal from Ethiopia. The Khedive's troops were more successful in Darfur, where the Fur army was defeated in January 1874. The capital of El Fasher was occupied.

Cairo became the victim of imperial overreach generating military setbacks in Ethiopia and renewed revolt in Darfur and elsewhere in Sudan. General Gordon promised the Khedive that he could restore order in the whole of Sudan and also crush the slave trade. The Khedive agreed to Gordon's ambitious plans in early 1877. The purchase and sale of all slaves was to be terminated by 1880. The Khedive was no humanitarian campaigner; he was keen to use abolition as part of his charm offensive to ensure Western political and financial support for his regime.

Gordon became perhaps *the* British imperial icon, because of the nature of his death which became almost the late Victorian equivalent of a Passion play. Born in London, in 1833, the son of a major general, Gordon was unlike the womanizing Baker, his predecessor. Gordon was a determined bachelor, very awkward with women, and a man who preferred to organize boys' clubs. There is no proof of his homosexuality, but modern psychologists might define Asperger's syndrome because of his obsessive routines (starting with a cold bath every day at the same time), social rigidity and poor personal communications skills. He was a brave soldier, however: Mars without Venus. Commissioned into the Royal Engineers, he saw service in the Crimean War and then led Chinese troops, ruthlessly, in the 1860s during various rebellions against the Chinese emperor. Usually with London's encouragement, he became an imperial trouble-shooter. The Belgians wanted him to sort out the Congo, but he went instead, briefly, to India. He served in Mauritius and then assisted the Cape colonial government in resolving problems in the

British protectorate of Basutoland. He was a religious crank, who held all sorts of eccentric evangelical beliefs, the least of them being reincarnation. Yet he was determined to die for his principles, no matter how much damage he did to the British government. He was lionized in England, though usually detested in China and Sudan. No one actually knows how he died, but it was imagined and romanticized in a popular painting by George William Joy in 1885 as 'General Gordon's Last Stand'. This painting stood alongside Lady Elizabeth Butler's 'Remnants of an Army' that portrayed Dr William Brydon as the sole survivor of the massacre of General Elphinstone's army in Afghanistan. Both depicted, at least in the popular imagination then and now, nadirs of the British imperium. The George Joy painting has, of course, been subsumed by Charlton Heston's depiction of the noble Gordon in the 1966 Hollywood production, *Khartoum*. It is sometimes hard to separate popular imagery from historical events, but Gordon did not resemble Charlton Heston. He was short – about five feet five inches, albeit well-built. Most importantly, he deliberately disobeyed clear explicit orders, thus undermining the career of his prime minister, destroying a London government and, in the Sudanese perspective, causing the unnecessary death of thousands of civilians in Khartoum.[2]

The English Pasha did achieve a great deal in a short time. He curbed, but did not destroy the slave trade. Speaking just a little Arabic, he tended to ignore the concerns of Sudanese, especially the elite in Khartoum, and not just their financial interests in the slave trade. He preferred to rely on his European staff, or his local Egyptian officials. Gordon also liked and trusted the Khedive, but in 1879 Pasha Ismail was deposed because of British and French anxieties over the Khedive's profligacy. London and Paris leaned on the Sultan in Istanbul to sack the Khedive, who cleaned out what remained of the gold in the treasury and sailed away to a comfortable exile. Gordon, exhausted, promptly resigned and sought a long holiday in Europe.

In Cairo, the great powers had helped to install Tewfik, Ismail's son, as the new Khedive. Tewfik was reluctant – he preferred farming to politics. Tewfik also understood that he would be a pawn of Western imperialists, especially Britain and France, although the British were in the driving seat. Tewfik's army rebelled against Western control and the Khedive appealed to his British protectors, who occupied Egypt in 1882, not least to secure the Suez Canal. In the so-called Anglo-Egyptian war of 1882, the Royal Navy bombarded Alexandria, and then the army, led by the Highland Brigade, overwhelmed the Egyptian forces at Tel El Kebir, outside Cairo.

Over 2,000 Egyptian troops were killed for the loss of fifty-seven British. Sir Evelyn Baring (later ennobled as Lord Cromer) had been the aptly named Controller-General in Cairo, as part of the Orwellian-styled 'Control' set up by the British and French to run the finances of the bankrupt country. As Consul-General after 1882 he effectively ruled Egypt until 1906. (British military presence survived until 1954.) It was his decision to withdraw completely from Sudan after 1885, because his austerity budget would not permit any costly military adventures. Baring reformed the Egyptian army, under British officers, to make it a more reliable tool of government. His reforms worked. The new (relatively) efficient army became a national symbol in a failed state; this symbolism played no small part in the dominance of the army, even after the revolutions of the contemporary Arab Spring.

Baring was a true believer in the British imperial mission. According to an Arab historian, he believed that 'subject races were totally incapable of self-government, that they did not really need or want self-government, and that what they really needed was a "full belly" policy which kept it quiescent and allowed the elite to make money and so cooperate with the occupying power'.[3] In what was dubbed a 'veiled protectorate', Baring excluded the French and dominated the Khedives, while improving the economy of Egypt.

The *Mahdiya*

The administration in Khartoum was left in the hands of corrupt and inefficient officials during the turmoil in Cairo. Sixty years after their last revolt against foreign intruders, a national Sudanese uprising began in the nine-mile-long Aba Island, on the White Nile, about 155 miles south of Khartoum. A *Sufi* mystic, Muhammad Ahmad ibn Abdullah, moved there to seek religious contemplation. Born in Dongola in 1845, he received an excellent religious education. Like many Sudanese he disliked the imposition of foreign – to him, less pure – forms of Islam. His ideals were based on religious reform, but they tapped into tribal dislike of alien political rule. He had quarrelled with other religious leaders previously, who disputed his views, but in June 1881 he proclaimed that, in visions, the assembly of previous prophets, headed by Muhammad himself – what the Islamic scholars would call *hadra* – had told him he was the 'Mahdi' (the chosen or guided one). The new Mahdi gathered a small movement, calling his followers the *Ansar* (termed Dervishes by Europeans) and started to establish a local system modelled on the original administration of the

Prophet Mohammad. His armed *Ansar* almost completely annihilated a contingent of Egyptian troops sent to Aba Island to arrest him. The rebellion spread, especially after the *Ansar* defeated two more attempts by the *jihadiyya*, led by the hated 'Turks', in September 1881 and May 1882. Slavers, pious men and disaffected tribesmen flocked to the Mahdi, who proclaimed the Islamic end of days. Such messianic movements were not new in Islamic history, but in Sudan and elsewhere in the Western-occupied Middle East, and then in the twenty-first century, the concept of religious renewal via military jihad caught fire. In Sudan's case, it also meant the possibility of driving out the tax-oppressive Turks. Pragmatism and piety became handmaidens of the tribal warriors' martial proclivities. Thus the Mahdi became a Victorian version of Osama bin Laden.

After four months of siege, the garrison at El Obeid, the new capital of Kordofan, had to surrender, providing more modern weapons for the *Ansar* who had fought with lances and swords and great bravery. This Mahdist victory fuelled a national rebellion that spread west, north and to the Red Sea Hills. Very reluctantly, and despite his ideals of financial stringency, Sir Evelyn Baring and London reluctantly agreed to send Egyptian troops, led by William 'Billy' Hicks, a retired British colonel of the Indian Army. It was raised originally to relieve El Obeid. Hicks Pasha, who was not enthused by the whole operation, quarrelled with Egyptian staff officers as his column made its way south, harassed by the *Ansar*. The Mahdists filled in the wells and, more effectively, used propaganda to persuade the Muslim Egyptian forces that the Mahdi was truly leading 'soldiers of God'. The Kordofan expeditionary force was made up of about 8,000 Egyptian regulars, 1,000 cavalry, 100 tribal irregulars, and around 2,000 camp followers. They carried supplies for fifty days on an immense baggage train consisting of 5,000 camels. The army also boasted artillery, including Krupp field guns and six Nordenfelt machine guns. The Nordenfelt had been patented only a few years before and, although reliable, was soon outclassed and absorbed by the company that produced the famous Maxim guns, but in Sudanese terms it was a super-weapon.

By the time the expedition finally struggled to Kordofan, El Obeid had fallen. The operation was maintained to relieve Slatin Bey, the Austrian-born governor of Darfur. The force was, in the words of Winston Churchill, 'perhaps the worst army that has ever marched to war'. Many of the reluctant soldiers had been freed from Cairo's jails, convicted because they had taken part in the 1882 rebellion against the Khedive. Not only were they unwilling, but they were unpaid, untrained and undisciplined. To quote

Churchill again, 'Its soldiers had more in common with their enemies than with their officers.'

Either by mistake or by design, their guides led them to a plain where they were surrounded at Shaykan, south of El Obeid, on 3 November 1883. Hicks Pasha's force was surprised and some of the Egyptians broke and ran; the majority formed up in a square and fought for two days. The Mahdists eventually overwhelmed them. Some Egyptian troops escaped, but the majority of survivors were taken prisoner. The officers were killed outright, although a handful of Europeans managed to make their way to Khartoum. Hicks' body was never found. It was a great victory for the Mahdi, whose jihadists now had modern artillery.

The Mahdists pushed on into Darfur and eventually captured Slatin Bey. Rudolf Carl von Slatin was one of the most colourful of the European rulers of colonial Sudan. His father had converted from Judaism to Catholicism, and his Catholic son had converted to Islam when his Darfurian troops insisted that he needed to become a Muslim to lead them. His conversion helped when he was taken by the *Ansar*. Most captured infidels were murdered, but he was held in captivity for eleven years, mainly in Omdurman – sometimes treated tolerably (and offered wives), at other times with utmost cruelty. He was also shown Gordon's severed head as an object lesson in good behaviour. After a dramatic escape, he sought absolution from the Pope for his temporary apostasy. He also wrote a remarkable book, *Fire and Sword in the Sudan*, which was later used by many British imperialists to argue for the re-conquest of the country.

In his book, Slatin Bey offers a rare and sympathetic pen portrait of the Mahdi:

> He had a light brown complexion, a sympathetic Arab face on which the marks of smallpox were still traceable, an aquiline nose, a well-shaped mouth, slight moustache, and a fringe of hair on his cheeks, but rather thicker on his chin; he was about middle height, neither thin nor stout, was wearing a jibba covered with small square patches of different colours, and a Mecca takia, or skull cap, around which was bound a cotton turban; he generally spoke with a smile and showed a row of glistening white teeth.[4]

Besides the impact of Slatin Bey's book, the letters of Emin Pasha also caused a sensation in Europe. Born to a middle-class Jewish family in Silesia, Isaak Eduard Schnitzer trained as a doctor, but was later disbarred in Germany. Employed by the Ottoman Empire, the adventurer ended up as a surgeon working for Gordon Pasha. Isaak had converted to Christianity and then, probably, to Islam, always styling himself Mehmed Emin. Gordon put him in charge of Equatoria. After the Mahdist revolution, Emin Pasha retreated south to Lake Albert with his few thousands troops. After the fall of Khartoum, the fate of Emin Pasha became a continuous media event in Europe. The famous Welsh explorer, Henry Morton Stanley, led a relief expedition via an arduous route along the Congo River, and losing two-thirds of his party. Eventually, Stanley met up with Emin Pasha in April 1888 and persuaded him to exit Africa via Zanzibar.

The humiliating defeat of a British general (the Egyptians had promoted Colonel Hicks) was a political blow to British prestige in Egypt and the whole Middle East. And the Islamist nature of the revolt caused anxiety as far away as the British authorities in India. The decision was made, however, not to exact a traditional imperial retribution, but to order the withdrawal from Sudan of all Egyptian troops and administrators and families, especially from Khartoum. The prime minister in London, William Ewart Gladstone, was as reluctant as Baring to get sucked into the expensive wars in Sudan. Sending one man was relatively cheap, however. General Gordon, it was said, had a 'name which was worth an entire army'. Reappointed Governor General, Gordon reached Khartoum on 18 February 1884. His orders were to organize an evacuation of Egyptian and Europeans from the capital.

Gladstone was extremely hostile to further British military involvement in troublesome Sudan. The military occupation of Egypt in 1882 was deemed by his many political opponents a hypocritical betrayal of his principles of non-intervention abroad. The new crisis in Sudan in 1884 was now judged a test of his political sincerity. Ignoring his orders, Gordon decided to stay in Khartoum until he was relieved by forces sent from Egypt. He reasoned that both peace with the Mahdi and total evacuation were impossible. Moreover, he feared that the jihad would spread to engulf Egypt. He did, however, send some women, children and wounded men down the Nile to Egypt. Gordon then set about fortifying the city. The Mahdi himself arrived on the west bank of the Nile opposite Khartoum, in what became known as Omdurman. Gordon showed great courage and charismatic leadership by rallying the frightened citizens of the capital, and its small garrison of 5,000 soldiers. The Mahdi's *shura* (council) argued that it was a trap and the inevitably large force coming from Egypt to relieve the famous general might defeat them. The Mahdi refused to retire to Kordofan.

The final Mahdist assault of 50,000 men came in the early hours of

26 January 1885, when the Nile waters were at their lowest. This exposed solid beachheads around the weakest riverside defences. The Egyptian garrison was overwhelmed, Gordon was killed and the city reduced to ruins. The advance steamers of the relief expedition arrived two days later. 'Too late' screamed the headlines in the British press. To the fury of the British public the death of their hero was not avenged and the large relief force turned around and went back to Cairo.

The leader of the relief force, General Sir Garnet Wolseley, faced much criticism, but it had been a herculean task. Wolseley had served in the lakes of Canada, and arranged for a team of Canadian navigators to help his fleet of small boats overcome the massive obstacles of the six Nile cataracts. This was considered the fastest route through enemy-occupied territory. Eventually, Wolseley divided his 5,000-strong force into an overland camel route (to take a short cut across the big loop of the Nile) while half remained on the river. The internal problems, not least dragging and re-assembling his boats, as well as Mahdist harassment, impeded his progress, although the slow decision in London to permit Gordon's relief was also a factor. The telegraph line had been cut, but Gordon sent out messengers to the north. On 14 December 1884, in the last entry in his journal (which, when published, created a frenzy in the UK) was: 'Now mark this, if the Expeditionary Force, and I ask for no more than 200 men, does not come in ten days, the town may fall; and I have done my best for the honour of our country. Good bye.'

The death of Gordon sent the British popular press into overdrive. The Western media tended to obsess about its own imperial concerns with little understanding about what was happening in Sudan to Sudanese. This bad habit has continued to the present day. Western cultural conditioning tended to portray European Christian heroes fighting either bloodthirsty ignorant Muslims or black pagan savages farther south.

The 317 days of siege spawned a continuous newspaper barrage to send a relief column. Its arrival just two days too late added to the Victorian melodrama. Despite the lack of eye-witnesses, varying – but always lurid – accounts of Gordon's death created a national scandal. In the Hollywood version, over eighty years later, Gordon is beheaded on the steps of the governor's palace. (In the 1990s I had to ascend those same steps to secure rare press passes from another radical Islamic regime; I was never sure whether an implicit warning was intended.) Because it took over a decade to exact imperial retribution, the Gordon saga remained an open wound in the British national psyche.

Queen Victoria addressed Parliament on 14 August 1885 and, unusually for a sovereign, rebuked her own government. She mentioned her 'deep sorrow, which was shared by all my people' and criticized the relief which arrived 'too late' and mourned 'the heroic Gordon'. Gladstone himself usually refrained from defending himself. He did write a private letter at the height of the crisis which said that to have complied with Gordon's demands 'was madness and criminal'. In another private correspondence, Gladstone wrote: 'I must continue to suffer in silence. Gordon was a hero...It was unfortunate that he should claim the hero's privilege by turning upside down and inside out every idea and intention with which he left England and for which he had obtained our approval.' Nearly 130 years later, Gladstone still gets a bad press. To this day the apotheosis of Gordon has been prolonged and almost completely uncritical. His manifest flaws forged a Greek tragedy: hubris leading to nemesis. He wilfully disobeyed his superiors, both civilian and military because he usually held them in contempt. He gravely misread the Mahdist uprising and its tribal and spiritual support and above all its military capacity. The arch-apostle of the Christian imperial mission brought ignominy on his own government and the empire he wished to promote. Gordon's journals as well as bestselling books by Europeans, most notably Slatin Bey, added to the Gordon myth by denigrating and demonizing the Sudanese. Some of these books were secretly funded by British military intelligence in Cairo.[5]

The Mahdi had explicitly ordered that Gordon should not be killed, perhaps because of the superstition that his own death would soon follow that of the British General's. Six months later the Mahdi died, probably of smallpox. The succession inevitably prompted religious and tribal disputes. The Khalifa Abdallahi had the best claim by his title ('the steward' of the *Umma*, Islamic community; Caliph in English). Equally important, his Black Flag division controlled the new capital of Omdurman. Having decisively outmanoeuvred his opponents, the Khalifa now wanted to fulfil his mentor's prophecy by spreading the jihad throughout the world, starting with the rest of Sudan.

Messianic movements had been emulated in the African Fur and Masalit tribes in Darfur. The Khalifa ordered his Baqqara tribesmen to suppress the revolt. The Khalifa's nephew, Mahmuud Ahmad, spent the next five years pacifying the Darfur region, but separatism there was never fully quelled. On the Ethiopian border, the *Ansar* had also been severely thrashed. After crushing a mutiny in the Mahdist army, the Khalifa regrouped his forces and sent them on a successful plundering raid against the ancient Ethiopian capital of Gondor. Retaliation soon followed. The Ethiopian army, massively reinforced, was led by Emperor John IV himself. On the edge of defeat, the *Ansar* army triumphed because a stray bullet killed the emperor and his troops retreated in disarray. Mahdist soldiers also pushed south along the Nile deep into Equatoria. The south, west and east had been largely, if temporarily, pacified, but the success of the universal jihad depended upon a northern conquest: Egypt.

The 'soldiers of God' marched across the Egyptian border in the heat of summer in 1889. On 3 August, at the small village of Tushki, just north of Wadi Halfa, they were destroyed by the Egyptian army led by its new *sirdar* (commander-in-chief)), General Sir Francis Grenfell. Although the British officer had purchased his first two commissions, he proved on merit to be an able soldier, eventually reaching field marshal rank, by the time he retired in 1908. He had fought at Tel El Kebir, and in Sudan, most notably defeating the Mahdist army at the Battle of Suakin the previous December.

The *Ansar* commander, Abdal Rahman al-Nijumi, was killed alongside 1,200 of his men in a five-hour battle. Over 4,000 were captured. The victory demonstrated the improvement of the reformed Egyptian army, which in this battle had a core of only a squadron of British 20th Hussars. The *Ansar* had marched over seventy miles into Egypt, carefully avoiding the Egyptian garrison at Wadi Halfa, but it had not inspired any local popular support, unlikely anyway in such a remote area. The battle ended the Islamist threat to Egypt from the south.

The Khalifa in Omdurman obviously needed to re-valuate the Mahdi's prophecy of universal jihad. The north, populated by millions of Muslims, had been cut off. The far south was less promising: the terrain was tough and very few Muslims lived there. And Emin Pasha's forces continued to resist. In the early 1890s local warrior kingdoms allied with Belgian officers from the Congo Free State defeated Mahdist southern advances. Internal tribal antagonisms were intensified by military defeats as well as drought, famine and epidemics. Many Sudanese began to question Allah's blessings on the *Mahdiya*. Tribal revolts ensued and the Khalifa took years to ensure his dominance. Gradually, he tried to transform the Mahdist theocratic state into a more traditional Islamic monarchy in which the succession would pass to his son.

The re-conquest

For a while it appeared that Sudan was immune to the frenzied European 'scramble for Africa'. Not for long. Baring in Cairo was still determined to concentrate on domestic reforms, but eventually he began to change his mind. The re-conquest of Sudan had little to do with revenge for Gordon or the need to subdue an Islamist state, and had everything to do with European politics. The British Conservative prime minister, Lord Salisbury, an energetic imperialist, decided to stop any other European power from controlling the flow of the Nile waters. The Belgians had shown interest in the region, so had the Germans, but the French, as always, were deemed the primary threat, epitomized later in the 1898 Fashoda crisis, which almost sucked the two imperial powers into war over Sudan. The British in Cairo became thoroughly alarmed by talk of French gunboats on the Nile and their (unlikely) erection of dams.

More immediate prompts for the British re-entry into Sudan were the perennial military difficulties of Italian armies. In March 1896, at Adowa, the Italians had suffered a humiliating defeat at the hands of the Ethiopian army under Emperor Menelik II. The Italian government formally requested a British military diversion in the north of Sudan to prevent a Mahdist assault on the weakened Italian garrison in the border town of Kassala. Lord Salisbury decided that an initial push into northern Sudan to seize Dongola was a suitable reply to the Italians and a convenient warning to the French. Baring had come to the conclusion that Britain had to re-occupy the Sudan to keep out other Europeans, and that he could get the Egyptian treasury to pay. It was a neat solution. This was a second-chance forward policy – on the cheap. Some British officers, however, cloaked their official imperial ambitions and personal sense of grievance over Gordon's death under a veil of humanitarian concerns for the perceived chaos in Sudan and the need to end the slave trade.

This invasion was methodical. A new railway was built into northern Sudan; it was a different gauge from the Egyptian system, a clear signal that the British intended to rule a separate southern state, distinct from Cairo, although the diplomatic niceties would still prevail. Gunboats, in sections, were re-assembled above the fifth cataract. Vast amounts of supplies and ammunition were prepared, all under the watchful eye of the new *sirdar*, General Sir Herbert Horatio Kitchener. He had been the last British officer to have been in contact with Gordon before the fall of Khartoum. So for Kitchener it was personal. Despite his stern and calm appearance, Kitchener was often full of anxiety about the success of his mission. He did not want to become the third British general to face an inglorious death at the hands of the Mahdists. He disguised his inner concerns with meticulous attention to detail.

In January 1897 the big push began. The Khalifa was unprepared – it took months for his western army to get into position. Infighting undermined the resistance, as ever. The western troops had to put down a defiant Ja'aliyyin rebellion with much bloodshed. After minor battles, the main confrontation took place on the Karari plain north of Omdurman, where Islamic end-timers believed that the infidel would suffer a final defeat before a great Islamic sweep through the Middle East.

At dawn on 2 September 1898, over 60,000 *Ansar* threw themselves with immense courage, and futility, against fixed positions, defended by Maxim guns and artillery, plus the supporting bombardments from the gunboats. As the waves of the soldiers of God fell back, the Egyptian army moved efficiently forward. By the late morning, over 11,000 Mahdist troops lay dead and another 16,000 were seriously wounded. The invading army of British, Egyptian and Sudanese brigades suffered around fifty killed. The battle included one of the last cavalry charges of the British Empire. A young Winston Churchill, who had inveigled himself into the campaign as an officer-correspondent – despite Kitchener's avowed dislike of journalists – took part in the charge. Kitchener was a great logistics expert, but not a good strategist: one of his columns was almost overwhelmed by a surprise *Ansar* attack from hidden reserve forces. Eventually, the Khalifa and his bodyguard retreated to the western deserts. Kitchener then led his officers to the ruined governor's palace to hold a memorial service for General Gordon.

Unlike the hapless General Lord Raglan in the poorly administered Crimean War, a media event which helped to topple a British government, Kitchener's personality dominated this war in Sudan. In the fall of Khartoum all European eye-witnesses and photographers had been killed. This time it would be different. Although he made occasional exceptions, Kitchener detested journalists, famously calling them 'drunken swabs'. Churchill had been an exception because he was an extremely well-connected young fighting officer, who had to pay his own way and accept all liabilities. Another exception was the *Daily Mail's* George Warrington Steevens, a 28-year old Balliol man who had described the general in glowing terms: 'His precision is so unhumanly unerring, he is more like a machine than a man.' Because of the massive popular domestic engagement with the war, Kitchener was persuaded to allow a small press contingent. They had to submit very brief reports (200 words per day) to the military censors before these were sent by military telegraph to Cairo. The military censored and manipulated the press to maintain support for the war in Sudan. Many of the journalists, most notably Churchill, who wrote a bestselling book called *The River War,* hardly needed media management because they were usually as jingoistic as the military commanders. Nevertheless, critics in London raised voices of protest at triumphalism following the defeat of the Dervishes, as they were called in Britain. The dissenters noted that the Sudanese had fought a modern army while usually wearing chain mail and using ancient weapons. As Steevens conceded in the *Daily Mail,* 'It was not a battle, but an execution.' In addition, liberals at home excoriated the practice of killing the wounded, even though the military explained, correctly, that the Mahdists fought on even when severely injured. Lieutenant Colonel Charles Townsend, an eye-witness to the final 'Battle of Omdurman' as it was dubbed, noted: 'The valour of those poor half-starved Dervishes in their patched jibbahs could have graced Thermopylae.' Churchill's own account of the famous charge noted that the cavalry fought with equal weapons, the sword and the lance – though Churchill used a Mauser pistol as well. When describing the rest of the battle, he referred to British discipline and machinery triumphing over the most desperate courage and fanaticism of the Middle Ages colliding with the organization of the nineteenth century.

In September 1898 Kitchener completed his act of vengeance by ordering the destruction of the Mahdi's tomb at Omdurman by Gordon's nephew, after which the Mahdi's skeleton was to be thrown into the Nile. Public protests, including murmurings from the Queen, prevented Kitchener from sending the Mahdi's skull to London as a trophy (probably as an inkwell).

Very few photographs survive from the 1884-5 siege period, not least because a small Royal Engineer camera team perished. More than a decade later, many of the officers carried Kodak box cameras that had been developed in America in the 1880s. Seven journalists lost their lives in the second Sudan campaign. Others like Churchill made their name by writing an instant book. Steevens's book, *With Kitchener to Khartoum,* was published within weeks of the end of the war. These books helped to transform the later Lord Kitchener into an imperial icon – despite his professed dislike of the drunken swabs. Steevens's account was not entirely uncritical: he wrote about the eternal complaint of fighting soldiers, namely the poor quality of army boots. Nevertheless, he did play down the killing of wounded *Ansar* on the battlefield. Another eminent journalist, Bennett Burleigh, however, was not so discreet. Thoroughly annoyed by Kitchener's open hostility to him, he published critical stories about the British warrior.

Self-censorship, it seemed, had as much to do with personality, and potential book sales, as patriotism.[6]

Kitchener could not rest on his military or media laurels. He had to face a bigger threat than the Mahdists, a rival modern power: France. If you draw a line west to east of French colonial ambitions in Africa and a similar line from the Cape to Cairo linking British pink on the map, they would intersect approximately at Fashoda on the Upper White Nile. It is now called Kodok in the Republic of South Sudan, and remains a sacred place as the ancient capital of the Shilluk kingdom.

At the tail end of the nineteenth century, Fashoda's significance lay in a small riverside fort. In July 1898 after an epic fourteen-month trek from the south-west, Major Jean-Baptiste Marchand struggled into the isolated outpost. He had set out with just 132 men, including a small core of Belgian and French officers, but many succumbed to disease, not combat. They were supposed to meet another French force marching south from Djibouti (French Somaliland). In the previous vacuum of British imperial power in Sudan, the French wanted to claim the headwaters of the Nile. Out of contact with Paris, Marchand was largely unaware of the extent of recent British victories in Sudan. On 18 September, Kitchener and his gunboats arrived at Fashoda. The British general spoke fluent French (he had disobeyed orders as a young cadet by volunteering to serve in the French ambulance corps in the Franco-Prussian war). So Kitchener sat down and enjoyed an amiable dinner with the French junior officer. The British had the military advantage, and so the French talked. Both men got on very well. After dining on cigars and brandy, they decided to refer the dispute to London and Paris. As they waited for the decision, they agreed amicably to fly British, French and Egyptian flags at the fort. Despite calls for war in Paris, where the British displacement of joint Anglo-French control in Egypt in 1882 still rankled, the peace party prevailed. London conceded to French rights in Morocco, and the British were left to run Sudan and Egypt. What lay behind this unusual piece of Anglo-French cordiality was not just good sense, but also mutual fear of Germany's growing militarism not only in Europe, but also in Africa.

British imperial policy had triumphed. London now controlled the Nile from the great lakes to the Mediterranean. Sudan, Egypt and above all the Suez Canal were safely under their military control. The French left Fashoda; the only sign of their presence today is a small patch of iron crosses where brave French explorers succumbed to disease, not British guns. That is all that remains of the Napoleonic dream for France to bestride the Nile, after the French campaigns of 1798-1801. The final postscript to Kitchener's conquest came on 24 November 1899. Colonel Sir Reginald Wingate cornered the remnants of the Mahdist army near the present town of Kosti. The Khalifa and his bodyguard were killed. Kosti is home today to the El Imam El Mahdi University, established in 1994. It is of course named in honour of the leader of the *Mahdiya* revolution.

The death of the Khalifa spelled the final demise of the *Mahdiya*. Sudanese independence had been snuffed out by imperial decisions taken in London and Cairo. It had taken sixty years for the Sudanese to rise up and throw off the Egyptian yoke by force; it would take just over sixty years for the British to leave and allow the Sudanese, finally, to rule themselves.

Chapter 2

British Rule

Despite the formal description of an 'Anglo-Egyptian Condominium', Sudan was now effectively British territory. Evelyn Baring, raised to the peerage in 1893 as Lord Comer, dreamed up this confection. Thus the colonial power reversed the original ambition of Khedive Mohammad Ali to unite the Nile valley. London had expended much blood and gold to retain Sudan; the imperium was not about to hand it back to Cairo, especially after the martyrdom of Gordon and the Battle of Omdurman. British commentators felt that the Mahdist revolution had been partly the result of long years of Turco-Egyptian misgovernment. Now Britain would provide an honest and efficient administration.

For the next half-century Sudan was left largely to its own devices, except when issues of imperial security were concerned. Several Mahdist pretenders emerged, but they were easily suppressed. Nevertheless, they reinforced a general British mistrust of political Islam. British rule was strongest in the central areas of habitation along the Nile. Peripheral areas remained largely untouched until they posed a threat to the centre. Darfur, for example, was not conquered until May 1916 when Sultan Ali Dinar rose up when the Turks joined the German side in October 1914. In a brief campaign, the British crushed the Fur army just outside El Fasher and the Sultan was killed. The former palace of Ali Dinar in El Fasher is now a run-down museum, with a few artefacts of the sultanate. I last visited the small but charming 'palace' in 2004, when a new war had begun in the region. The museum's curator was a diligent man, but he had not been paid in a while and he had no money to maintain one of the few surviving relics of Darfur's independence.

In the south, the Khartoum government did little except make the *Sudd* more navigable. British officers from the Egyptian army ran a skeleton administration while encouraging British Christian missionaries to spread their religion and language as a bulwark against the advance of Islam. Arabic was actively discouraged as were northern Muslim merchants. Egyptian and northern Sudanese officers and troops were removed and they were replaced by locally raised troops under British officers using English as the language of command. They formed the Equatorial Corps.

The north was administered by a coterie of mainly Oxbridge graduates, fluent in Arabic, who comprised the Sudan Political Service (SPS). By and large, this small elite – about 400 in all in the fifty years of its existence – ran the north with an efficient, independent and honest paternalism. But the SPS had a modicum of central direction. This was not the case in the south where officers contracted from the British army – known as 'Bog Barons' – ruled their vast satrapies through the power of their own often quirky and flamboyant personalities. They learned the local African languages and ruled sometimes as if they were paramount chiefs. As long as they kept order, they were left to their own devices. Collectively, this created a muddle because the British could not make up their minds what to do with the south. This characteristic British style of 'muddling through' lasted for nearly fifty years and it had a terrible legacy. The Arabs in Khartoum were trained by the colonialists to focus on Egypt, the centre of British power. As a consequence a succeeding generation of Arab administrators grew accustomed to ignoring the south and the west. And, historically, neighbouring states held as much sway, if not more, over the east, west and south as Khartoum did. This was a recipe for endless border wars.

The possibility of north-south conflict was not yet on the horizon. The British were initially more concerned not only about the revival of Mahdism, but the possibility of conflicts between the two main Islamic sects, the *Ansar* (which later transformed itself into the Umma Party) and the *Khatmiyya* (which formed later the Democratic Unionist Party). Both sects were hereditary family affairs that were to produce decades of political in-fighting in Khartoum. Eventually a more powerful Islamic group, the Muslim Brotherhood, which morphed into the National Islamic Front/National Congress Party, became dominant. When the British destroyed the Mahdist movement, they scattered the seeds of Islamist regeneration for a century.

Under strong and able Governors General such as General Sir Reginald Wingate (1899-1916) Sudan began to prosper. Wingate had earned his spurs during the Mahdist war as an intelligence officer fluent in spoken and written Arabic. His more famous second cousin, Orde Wingate, also became an Arabic-speaking intelligence officer in the Sudan Defence Force. Both Wingates were highly opinionated and independently minded. Sir Reginald Wingate did less well when promoted to service in Egypt as High Commissioner; characteristically, he refused to go, even when his replacement, Lord Allenby, had already arrived.

Sir Reginald Wingate is remembered now in Sudan for his reforms in education. In 1902 the Gordon Memorial College was set up to educate carefully selected sons of the riverine Arabs as well as some southerners. Much of the funding came from public subscription in Britain, as the Khartoum treasury was still dependent upon parsimonious Egyptian grants. The curriculum was designed to create clerical skills to enable the students to aspire to lower-ranking civil service posts at most. There was no hint yet of training for self-government. Orthodox Islam, not *Sufi* rituals, was encouraged by government-selected imams. A parallel system of orthodox judges was established to settle personal and domestic disputes in *sharia* courts.

In the wake of devastation caused by two decades of war, economic development was a priority. Labour shortages became acute in a population reduced to perhaps only two million inhabitants. The slave trade was outlawed again, but immediate emancipation at a time of manpower shortages would have precipitated a political upheaval. Slavery in a number of forms remained. The major British achievement was the Gezira cotton scheme that soon provided many jobs and eventually a budget surplus for Sudan. This reduced Sudanese dependence on Egyptian government grants.

In late 1914 the British deposed the Egyptian Khedive for his dalliance with the Turks. They installed a pliant replacement, despite nationalist outrage. Some extra employment was created by the war effort, but the abrupt demobilization of the Egyptian Labour Corps in 1918 boosted existing high unemployment rates. In addition, the logistical costs of Egyptian involvement in the Great War, and the principles of self-determination announced by US President Woodrow Wilson, helped to inspire, in 1919, a popular revolt against British rule in Egypt. The nationalists in Cairo demanded independence for both Egypt and Sudan. Egyptian independence as a constitutional monarchy was secured in 1922, except in crucial reserved areas such as foreign affairs and defence. Sudan was explicitly excluded. But how could the tiny Sudanese educated elite be inoculated against the virus of Egyptian nationalism? The British answer, as in much of colonial Africa, was 'Indirect Rule'. The urban educated elite was bound to grow with economic and educational progress. The British sidestepped this problem: in north and south tribal leaders would be co-opted. This suited many traditional leaders in Sudan, and the British SPS officials believed they were reflecting genuine nationalist feeling; the traditional leaders often regarded educated urban Sudanese as *effendi,* a name given to alien bureaucrats in the *Turkiya* and Condominium. Ironically, one of the unintended consequences of indirect rule was to confer more authority on the traditional leaders in the *Sufi* orders and the remaining *Ansar* at the expense of modernizing secular nationalists. Thus, 'Islamism in one country' was boosted.

For a while it seemed to work. During the 1919 Egyptian uprising, the urban Sudanese elite did not rise up to join their brethren in the north. Part of the reason was a splitting of opinion that would undermine Sudanese nationalism until independence: should Sudan aspire to become a solo state or merge with its big brother, Egypt? Tiny organizations began to form advocating both outcomes, but for the time being British vigilance kept their activity and publications limited to cultural assertion. Ali Abdel Latif founded a more explicitly political organization, the White Flag League. He was an unlikely man to become a prototype nationalist leader, especially to the conservative riverine leadership. For a start he was a southern Dinka; moreover, he had been born into a slave family in Egypt. But he was a Muslim with obvious leadership skills, honed at the Gordon College and the Khartoum Military School. He was cashiered from the army for insubordination, said the British; he claimed he was a victim of the extraordinary arrogance of a British officer. Demanding self-determination, not unity with Egypt, he was imprisoned for three years for his political agitation, reduced later to one year. Upon his release, he became a national hero. Egyptian support, both financial and political, encouraged him to recant his original views on Sudanese self-determination and instead advocate the Egyptian nationalist line of 'Unity of the Nile Valley'.

British rule relied ultimately on military force. In 1924 Latif's imprisonment spawned anti-British demonstrations. A revolt by the Railway Battalion of the Egyptian army was suppressed by British troops. Then fifty Sudanese cadets at the Military School in Khartoum also mutinied. They surrendered without a fight, the leadership was imprisoned and the school was closed. The Governor General, Sir Lee Stack, warned of 'drastic action'. Shortly afterwards, on 19 November 1924, he was assassinated in Cairo by an Egyptian nationalist.

Military reform now became imperative. The Egyptian army was repatriated from Sudan, sometimes under the barrels of British machine guns. The troops boarded their trains quietly. Sudanese officers were not so quiescent. They were torn between their formal oath of allegiance to Egyptian King Fuad and the respect many of them felt for their superior British officers. Units of the XIth Sudanese Battalion marched through the streets of Khartoum on 27 November. When they refused to disperse,

British troops opened fire on their comrades. The Sudanese fought back. Over thirty people were killed, including fifteen British soldiers. Three Sudanese mutineers were later executed.

The British had operated on a divide-and-rule principle in Sudan, assisted by the Rubik's Cube of contending religious, political and tribal diversity. The development of central political movements that could challenge imperial rule was suppressed or subverted. Yet, paradoxically, the British now set about fashioning what became a central pillar of national identity for the next ninety years – the Sudanese army. Initially, of course, it was intended as an implement of imperial fiat.

Forging a Sudanese army

The Sudanese Defence Force (SDF) was established in 1925 as a response to the turmoil of the previous year. Until then Sudanese served in separate infantry battalions of the Egyptian army under British and Egyptian officers. These were described as Arab or Sudanese battalions. The Egyptians were recruited through annual conscription, but Sudanese units comprised long-serving volunteers. Now the ejected Egyptians were replaced by Sudanese junior commissioned officers and NCOs. A new cadre of officers was trained in Omdurman, most of them northern Arab Muslims. The command and control still rested upon the shoulders of British officers; 140 Britons were transferred from the Egyptian army. The initial strength of the SDF was around 4,500 to 5,000 volunteers, although it expanded rapidly during the Second World War.

As a precaution, the British always kept a battalion of their own troops in the capital. With the disbandment of the old Sudanese battalions, which were designated by numbers, the new approach tried to develop a regional loyalty, not unlike the traditional British regimental structure based on county affiliations. Now the regional order of battle was:

Equatorial Corps in the south
Eastern Arab Corps
Western Arab Corps
Sudanese Camel Corps
The Shendi Horse

They were supported by specialized branches such as artillery, engineers, armoured car and machine-gun units, as well as the standard medical, signals and transport services. Although English was the language of command,

Turco-Egyptian rank structures for officers and men survived. A major, for example, was still called *Bimbashi*. The SDF's primary initial role was internal security, to support the police and provide garrisons that could fly the flag around the vast country. In the late 1930s, facing threats from the Italians, a Sudanese Frontier Force was established. Also, special irregular units were created later: for example, Gideon Force led by Orde Wingate.

Orde Wingate spent the years 1928 to 1933 in the SDF. His relative, General Sir Reginald Wingate, recommended him, thus cutting across the regulation that British officers had to have held a commission for five years and that a British officer serving in the SDF had to sponsor him. Connections were always important in the British military system. Captain Wingate was promoted to *Bimbashi* (major) and posted to the Eastern Arab Corps to patrol the border with Eritrea. He was based in the Dinder area, a mixture of desert scrubland and thick thorny forests, split by river beds and small streams. It was largely unmapped and unexplored. This is where the future general did the groundwork for his guerrilla theories, by fighting the *shifta* bandits poaching or slaving from Ethiopia. Wingate took part in the regular joint SDF operations with the Royal Air Force, flying Fairey 111Fs of 47 (Bomber) Squadron, not least against another Mahdist uprising in 1928. He took the opportunity to risk his first flight in one of the Fairey biplanes, travelling from Kassala to Khartoum. Wingate enjoyed the sight of hundreds of elephants below him, but he was violently sick – over the pilot. He never liked flying and often had premonitions of death, not least in an aircraft.

During his years in the SDF Wingate developed his theories of small independent strike forces, sometimes operating with air support. Despite his anti-social reputation later in his career, and his usually well-hidden bouts of depression, Wingate was well-respected in the SDF, not least for his polo skills, though he was warned once by his CO not to discuss politics, especially Marxism, in the Officers' Mess. Before Sudan, Wingate was in danger of being booted out of the army, but independent command in a wild country was the making of him. Wingate and T. E. Lawrence are often compared: both men pushed themselves physically beyond normal endurance; both were effectively misfits in their own societies and came to champion 'others' as a chosen people. Lawrence became obsessive about the Bedouin and Wingate risked his career helping the Zionists in Palestine. They probably never met, but Wingate was later scathing about Lawrence, calling him a charlatan, though their very divergent views of Arabs and Jews may have had something to do with that hostility. Wingate was to return to

Sudan during the 1939-45 war, which would test the Sudanese military reforms of the inter-war years. [1]

The military reforms were partly based upon encouraging local identity for the various corps. But the central political process from Khartoum tended to support ethnic rather than regional leadership, which was not always the same thing. The tribal structures in the north were often distinct. It was much more difficult in the south. The most populous tribes were the Nuer and Dinka who tended to avoid formal chief or kingship structures and instead relied more on spiritual leaders or prophets. Frustrated British district commissioners sometimes had to invent chieftains or back nonentities with little following, or even hunt for elusive 'lost tribes'. Education slowly developed in English in the southern missionary schools. In the north, primary schools were expanded, often with more emphasis on orthodox Islamic teaching, with rote learning of the Koran, rather than secular education. Secular nationalists in Khartoum accused the British of a concerted policy of separating north and south via separate language and educational policies. It was more accidental drift and pragmatic adaption to local circumstances rather than devious intent, however. British officials worked with the grain in the areas they administered with little more in mind than to preserve the status quo. 'Disturbances' in the south were often met with punitive raids, especially against the Nuer, who would vanish into the *Sudd* or across the Ethiopian border.

Rising economic prosperity in the north also helped to dampen discontent. Government-funded major projects such as the Sennar Dam increased the area of irrigated land. The Gezira scheme, originally set up in 1913, added to the incomes of tenant famers. Just south of Khartoum, it was one of the biggest irrigation schemes in the world. The cotton was actually managed by a private company, the Sudan Plantations Syndicate, but government kept a benevolent eye on prices and wages. Sudan enjoyed ten boom years courtesy of King Cotton, but the 1929 crash hit the single-crop economy very badly. And effective labour unions were still more than a decade away.

Gradually, in the senior echelons of the Sudan civil service, it was understood that 'native administration' in south and north could not rely upon just enough education to produce clerks and accountants to populate the lower rungs of government. In the south conditions remained backward – the Foreign Office suddenly discovered in 1936 that not a single government school existed. The quality of Christian schools varied enormously. Often, the squabbles between Catholic and Protestants began to match the sectarian schisms in the north, where educational standards improved rapidly in the 1930s. Teacher training colleges, schools of law, engineering, medicine and agriculture were introduced. Even the Gordon Memorial College was reformed, although it was not renamed as Khartoum University until 1951.

Improved education inevitably meant bigger educated elites. In 1938 a Graduates' Congress was formed. By the early 1940s embryonic political parties had been forged. The rising nationalism was spurred by some Sudanese opposition to the country's involvement in what they dubbed a British war in 1939. They wanted emancipation from the British – 'Sudan for the Sudanese' – but still could not decide whether union with Egypt was the answer or, conversely, a return to a different foreign domination. Secular and sectarian rivalry still tore at the heart of Sudanese nationalism. The orthodox fought the more mystical branches, while the *Ansar* and the *Khatmiyya*, one of the largest *Sufi* orders in the Middle East, argued with secular modernisers. Egyptian union or not was the key debate, but other issues such as a theocratic or socialist state were passionately dissected. In 1943 the British set up an Advisory Council to incorporate the limited and polite demands of the moderate urban intelligentsia. But the British were unlikely to make any major concessions until after the Second World War.

The 1939-1945 conflict transformed the Sudan Defence Force. Most of the officers were still British on secondment for two years' probationary period, with a maximum of five years, when officers were expected to return to their own regiments. The attractions in Sudan were a local one-rank promotion, independence of command, and often a more expansive lifestyle including large accommodation and servants as well as desert exploration, archaeology and sport, especially game hunting. Some of the Oxbridge men in the Sudan Political Service were also allowed to join the colours. When Italy declared war on Britain in June 1940, the SDF went on the defensive at first to prevent encroachments from Italian-occupied Abyssinia and Eritrea. The Italians seized various small border towns and villages in Sudan; the most significant was the railway junction at Kassala. In August a small irregular force of Eritrean troops raided as far north as Port Sudan.

The first Italian campaigns in Abyssinia had been a shambles; they had been thrashed at the Battle of Adowa in 1896. Bloodied in the Great War and partially modernized by Mussolini's fascist revolution, the Italian army's second try in 1936 was much better organized. The savagery of the war has tended to be under-estimated partly because of the legacy of perhaps the most famous, and funniest, book on journalists at war, Evelyn Waugh's *Scoop*. Most Western correspondents disliked the bombastic Italian fascist leader, Benito Mussolini, and favoured the underdog, Emperor Haile Selassie. Poison gas was used extensively by the Italians, though the war was shrouded in as much propaganda as gas clouds. One historian claimed that 99 per cent of the photographs were faked. The barbarism on both sides was not. [2]

Waugh and others have tended to create the image that the Italians always fought badly. During the Second World War they fought very hard indeed to retain their East African empire (*Africa Orientale Italiana*). In Abyssinia/Ethiopia alone, fascist officers commanded a force of 250,000 Italian and local troops. After the initial incursions into Sudan, in October 1940 the British foreign secretary, Sir Anthony Eden, convened a major imperial summit in Khartoum: in attendance were British generals from the Middle East and India as well as General Jan Smuts, the South African who was deputizing for Winston Churchill. Before eliminating Italian armies in North Africa, the decision was made to tackle the fascists in the east. A three-pronged attack was devised, from Sudan into Eritrea and Ethiopia and into Ethiopia and Somalia from Kenya in the south.

Although British and Indian army troops (as well as South African and Southern Rhodesian elements) were to take part in this major offensive, manpower was short. The decision was made to beef up the Sudanese forces. The years of training under British officers and experience with the arduous climate and terrain encouraged the top brass to use some of the best Sudanese troops to form what today would be called special forces. Then they were termed irregular units for reconnaissance and strike operations. In October 1940 three mobile machine-gun companies became part of Gazelle Force, led by Colonel Frank Messervy, an Indian Army officer who was later to become the first commander of the Pakistan Army. Elements of the Frontier Battalion were placed under the command of Major Orde Wingate, who had previously served for five years in the SDF. He called this second unit Gideon Force, after the biblical Judge Gideon who commanded a small band of Israelites that vanquished a large army. Wingate always led from the front and was undoubtedly brave, but odd personal habits — such as not bathing, eating raw onions and garlic while attending meetings, or frequently addressing visitors to his quarters while totally naked — did cause disquiet among his commanding officers. He was also an ardent Christian mystic and supporter of Zionism. Wingate had spent much of the 1930s in Palestine, where he had used highly unorthodox methods while leading his Special Night Squads of Jewish and British troops during the Arab revolt of 1936-39.

The controversial apostle of irregular warfare arrived back in Khartoum on 6 November 1940. Wingate famously said, 'A thousand resolute men can paralyse 10,000.' As in Palestine, he chose resolute men as his commanders; one of the most famous was the explorer and Arabist Wilfred Thesiger. Other more conventional units of the SDF, including artillery forces, took part in the big push in January 1941. Gazelle and Gideon Forces proved very effective, not least in linking up with Ethiopian partisans who fought vigorously for their emperor. The major battles of the campaign took place in February and March 1941 around Keren on the road to the capital of Eritrea, Asmara. The Italians often fought as skilfully as elite German paratroopers and inflicted heavy casualties on experienced Indian Army troops and British Highland regiments. Eventually, however, the Italians were overwhelmed.

Sudanese military activity on the eastern front was over except for occupation and border duties. Gideon and Gazelle Forces were disbanded in the early summer of 1941. They had proved their worth and many Sudanese soldiers went on to fight with even more famous units in the main front in North Africa. Wingate continued to develop his original theories of guerrilla war by leading much bigger formations of Chindits in Burma. Many of his colleagues thought him quite mad, but he proved a very effective guerrilla leader in Palestine, Sudan and, finally, Burma, where, as a major general, he died in a plane crash in March 1944. Meanwhile, his small-unit adherents in the SDF had worked closely with the Long Range Desert Group (LRDG) – among the forerunners of the Special Air Service – in south-eastern Libya. The SDF was used to supply the LRDG and Free French outposts in the Italian colony of Libya. French forces under Colonel Phillipe Leclerc had advanced over almost inaccessible desert from Chad in French Equatorial Africa. Anglo-French units took oases and a fort during the battle of Kufra in March 1941. Re-supply was very challenging because of local Italian air superiority. The Libyan-Sudanese border area, largely desert or scrub, was used by the SDF to run supply trucks; later they took over garrison duties at the Kufra oasis. The SDF also engaged in highly secret operations to prevent German commandos infiltrating into Egypt. SDF personnel also worked with British military intelligence to interdict German secret agents hoping to encourage an Egyptian uprising against the British rule.

By the end of the world conflict in 1945 the SDF could boast of 'a good war'. Its seventy Sudanese officers had shown distinguished service in conventional and irregular warfare throughout north and east Africa. As independence hovered on the horizon, more and more local officers replaced their British counterparts. By March 1954 British troops in the Sudan comprised one battalion stationed in Khartoum. The SDF was under British command, but the deputy commander was Ibrahim Abboud. Born in Suakin in 1900, the future Sudanese general served in Egypt and Iraq, as well as in operations in north and east Africa. General Abboud took over as commander in chief of the SDF at independence. Initially, he remained aloof from politics, but he headed the only disciplined and centrally controlled institution in the country. The most enduring legacy of the British was not constitutional democracy, English education or the rule of law, but an effective, battle-hardened national army's pivotal role in Sudanese life.

Moves towards independence

The same could not be said of any of the burgeoning political parties. In June 1947 the British and Sudanese from north and south met in Juba where they agreed on a unified Sudanese state and a future joint assembly in Khartoum. Southerners at the time felt that their lack of educational and political experience left them at a severe disadvantage in these negotiations; later southern historians claimed the Juba meeting was a complete fix. Nevertheless, in December 1948, the British set up the first legislative assembly, comprising seventy-five members – some were elected and others nominated, with thirteen seats reserved for southerners. Encouraged by the British, the dominant Umma party in the Sudanese assembly rejected strong Egyptian pressure for union. In 1951 the Egyptians unveiled a new constitution for a unified Egypt and Sudan, without consulting the Sudanese, which naturally irritated many Khartoum leaders. By 1952 the majority in the Legislative Assembly was pushing for independence.

Enter a new player. The US government deployed its fresh status as a post-war superpower to persuade an exhausted and near-bankrupt Britain to resolve the 'Sudan Question' with a formula that would not antagonize the Egyptian Crown and government. Washington was regularly to intervene against British interests in the Middle East, arguing that the USA had not fought the Second World War to maintain the British Empire.

The international debate on the Sudan Question was dramatically interrupted on 23 July 1952 when the Revolutionary Command Council overthrew King Faruk. The overthrow of the King shook up the Middle East, including Sudan. The revolution was forged by young Egyptian army officers, led by General Mohammed Naguib. He was half-Sudanese and had been educated in Sudan. General Naguib became Egyptian prime minister in September and changed the policy on Sudan. The leading Sudanese parties were consulted and encouraged to demand immediate self-government from the British. Elections were held in Sudan in which the National Unionist Party (NUP), led by Ismael al-Azhari, won a majority of fifty-one seats in the ninety-seven-seat House of Representatives, with the Umma party trailing with twenty-two seats. The Southern Party won ten seats. In the new senate, the NUP did even better. The pattern of voting was strictly along sectarian lines, reflecting age-old disputes about Islam and politics. In the south this did not apply, but the NUP had taken three seats there, partly because of the lack of educated candidates, as well as the generous distribution of cash and hyperbolic but worthless promises. This was to set a template for future north-south relations.

On the surface the NUP victory meant a popular vote for union with Egypt. In reality, however, it reflected the widespread desire for the British to quit as soon as possible, whatever the name of the party that could achieve that goal in the shortest time. Lingering hostility to Egypt was demonstrated in March 1953 during a state visit by General Naguib. Sayyid Abdel Rahman, who led the opposition to the NUP, organized over 50,000 rural *Ansar* to come to Khartoum. They tried to storm the Governor General's palace. Ten policemen were killed including their British commander, who was hacked to death. Troops were called out and more demonstrators were killed. The British authorities persuaded Sayyid Rahman to order the *Ansar* to go home; the forthcoming ceremonial opening of parliament was cancelled and General Naguib quickly flew back to Cairo.

The riots surrounding Naguib's visit forced most Sudanese leaders to accept the need for independence. Naguib's local origins prompted support from some Sudanese, but he was displaced in a coup, led by Colonel Gamal Abdel Nasser, who was far less popular in Khartoum, despite his own (brief) military service in the country. Nasser consolidated his position by ruthless suppression of the communists as well as his erstwhile allies, the Muslim Brotherhood, establishing a pattern of army-Brotherhood antagonism which was to fester for decades and erupt once more in the 'Arab Spring' of 2011, and lead to mass killings and executions by the army in 2013/14.

The revolutionary turmoil in Egypt in the early 1950s heralded the hasty imperial recessional in the region. At the start of 1954 British officials in Sudan were rapidly pensioned off with generous payments, which the Sudanese leadership accepted as much cheaper than an armed insurrection and more peaceful than the chaos in Egypt. Hundreds of civil service posts were Sudanized, but only a handful went to southern officials working in the south. The northerners now parroted the well-worn colonial argument about the lack of qualified southerners. This was true, but racist and religious bigotry underlined the northern domination of the Sudanization process. The future prime minister, Ismael al-Azhari, dismissed the 'childish complaints' of the southerners. Gregoria Denk Kir, a southern businessman, aptly summarized the bitterness felt in the south: 'As it appears, it means our fellow Northerners want to colonize us for another hundred years.'[3] The reluctant and meagre inclusion of southerners in the quick march to independence implied not only northern colonization, it was also a portent of decades of warfare.

Northerners, alien in terms of religion and language, came south to run the 'hewers of wood and drawers of water'. Too late, southern political leaders started agitating for a federal system to protect their interests. In July 1955 a dissident southern MP was arbitrarily sentenced to a long prison term. His followers rebelled and troops had to be called in. At Nazara, a centre of the local textile industry, police killed eight protestors. Widespread revolt in the south appeared imminent and the army was the ultimate guarantor of security. Would the southern troops remain loyal to Khartoum?

Rumours of northern retaliation spread throughout the south. The garrison of the Equatorial Corps, renamed the Southern Corps, based at Torit, was particularly agitated. No. 2 Company was about to be posted to Khartoum in preparation for the independence celebrations, but word spread that on arrival they would be enslaved or massacred. The southern soldiers broke into the armoury on 18 August 1955 and used their weapons to kill northerners in the area – their officers, merchants and women and children. The rebellion spread like a bush fire to Juba, Yei and Mandi. Northern officials were killed indiscriminately. Northern administrators fled from Wau, leaving southern police in control. The British, with hardly any military forces remaining, kept out of the fray. Hundreds of Sudanese were killed in the south, most of them northerners. It took over two weeks for northern troops to be flown in to restore some order. Most of the mutineers fled into the bush, the first nucleus of a guerrilla army. A few surrendered, were tried and executed.

The knee-jerk northern bitterness at the indiscriminate killings soon hardened into a concerted policy of military control in the south, rather than political reconciliation. To southerners the revolt in Torit on 18 August 1955 became D-Day of the southern Sudanese armed struggle. The small town of Torit became the popular focus of the southern cry for freedom. The last

British troops, the 1st Battalion Royal Leicestershire Regiment, had left the country on 16 August 1955. In the British military vacuum, the minority of pro-Egyptian politicians in Khartoum debated whether they should ask for Cairo to intervene during the so-called 'Southern Sudan Disturbances'. Such an option was anathema to nearly all members of the House of Representatives. On 19 December 1955 they voted unanimously to declare Sudan independent. On 1 January 1956, at a hastily organized ceremony, the flags of Egypt and Great Britain were lowered and the flag of the new Republic of Sudan – three horizontal stripes of red, white and black – was raised.

On New Year's Day 1956 the Sudanese took over political and military control (although a few British Army instructors and advisors would remain). Foreign rule was over. In order to maintain unity Sudan would now have to solve its southern problem on its own. Whether this was to be done peacefully or via war depended on the quality of the new rulers in Khartoum. Decolonization was starting to electrify the whole of the continent. So what would independence bring to one of the first African states to assert its freedom?

Chapter 3

Failed Democracy – Failed Coups (1956–1989)

First years of independence

Independent Sudan began with much optimism. The new government was dominated by the National Unionist Party, led by Prime Minister Ismael al-Azhari. Khartoum could now unify the country, not least by ending the conflict in the south, and economic reforms would bring prosperity to a Sudan that could be a beacon in the Arab world and a decolonizing Africa. A similar pattern emerged in many African and Middle Eastern states after their independence. Foreign oppressors had been driven out and, almost by definition, it was believed, the nascent nations could achieve their true potential. Sadly, the soaring rhetoric of freedom, democracy and financial development soon degenerated into military intervention and economic stagnation.

Sudan faced two primary challenges: internal ones which required good governance, and external ones which demanded sound diplomacy. Revolutionary rule under Colonel Nasser in Cairo bolstered the position of the Egyptian army, and enhanced military authoritarianism throughout the Middle East, although Nasser did also flirt with multi-party-democracy, as well as with the communists and the Muslim Brotherhood. His initial obstacles involved the imperial overlord, Britain. Because of disputes with American funding for the planned Aswan Dam, part of Nasser's retaliation was his nationalization of the formerly French company which operated the French-built Suez Canal. Cairo had waited until the last British troops had left the Canal Zone months before. London portrayed Nasser as another Hitler, and Paris was incensed at Egyptian succour of the Algerian insurgency against French rule. Anglo-French forces, in secret collusion with Israel, invaded the Canal Zone in October 1956. It was a military and political fiasco, especially when the Americans threatened a run on the pound if London didn't stop. Britain was humiliated and Nasser was lauded as a hero in the Arab world. While proclaiming non-alignment, Egypt shifted towards the Eastern camp in the cold war, especially because of Nasser's need for Soviet weapons. Sudan could not stand entirely aloof from the cold war tensions, not least because disputes with Cairo over the Nile dams' costs were to play into domestic political tensions in Khartoum.

Sadly, practically anything could play into Khartoum's political tensions. Within six months the Azhari-led government collapsed because of parliamentary defections. Considering the Azhari team too secular, more conservative parties, the Umma and the new People's Democratic Party, formed a government which tottered along for two years. It proved almost incapable of any governance because of sectarian clashes and petty personal squabbling. Adding to the misery, the price of the main export – cotton – tumbled. The country was left with massive stocks of unsold and then unsellable cotton, created by Sudan's rigid pricing policy. The USA made tempting offers to ease the economic crisis and to boost development programmes. The Umma party was eager to accept Western aid, but others in the coalition believed that the US, frustrated by Nasser's tilt to the Soviet bloc, wanted to isolate Sudan from Egypt and other Arab states.

On the international front, Sudan tried to stay aloof from Nasser's grandiose plans for Arab unity. In early 1958 Nasser's advocacy of unity with Syria became reality – the United Arab Republic was formed. Yemen was also brought into the fold. Nationalism, however, was always going to transcend such a flimsy construction. In particular, the Syrian military grew disaffected. The Cairo-Damascus nexus was soon to be dissolved in a delicious scandal. In a gesture of reconciliation Nasser sent Abdel Hakim Amir, his closest friend, vice president and commander of the Egyptian army, to Damascus to settle the grievances. Though popular with the Syrian military, the handsome womanizing Amir was not a natural trouble-shooter. Syrian military intelligence, of course, tracked his every movement and soon realized that he was spending more time carousing with an Algerian singer than resolving the acute Syrian-Egyptian imbroglio. Finally, military intelligence officials roused Amir from his bed in the middle of the night and, in a deliberate act of malice and public ridicule, put both Amir and his paramour, in their night clothes, on a plane for Cairo. (It is not recorded whether Syrian intelligence was malicious enough to arrange for Amir's wife, Berlenti – a beautiful actress famed for her seductive, and fiery, film roles – to meet them at Cairo airport.) A national uprising in Syria soon followed this public humiliation and most Syrians rejoiced at the end of what they dubbed the 'Egyptian occupation'. Nasser's intervention in Yemen

– along with 70,000 troops – also ended badly. His foolish involvement in the civil war made Israel very happy, but it emptied the Egyptian treasury. Nasser later had to withdraw his troops in another humiliating retreat. Such debacles were bound to influence negatively Sudanese leaders, especially those who still nurtured notions of re-union with Egypt.

The first coup

As ever, Sudanese domestic politics were in turmoil. By November 1958 the new breed of politicians had failed. People looked to the army to unpick the domestic and international tangles. On the morning of 17 November 1958, hours before the new parliament was due to meet, the commander in chief, Major General Ibrahim Abboud, ordered his men to occupy the three central and contiguous towns of Khartoum, Khartoum North and the old Mahdist capital, Omdurman. Abboud abolished the trade unions and political parties and locked up government ministers under a state of emergency. Unlike Nasser, however, Abboud was not a political animal. He had a popular fatherly image with no apparent political ambitions, except to reflect the general anger with the squabbling and corrupt political class. The country needed to be governed efficiently, but the freshly minted Supreme Council of senior officers had no ideology and no plan. The Supreme Council did, however, reflect a degree of religious and tribal cohesion. The military rulers were mostly affiliated to the *Khatmiyya* sect and hailed largely from the riverine elite of the Shayqiyya and Ja'aliyyin tribal coalitions. The rank and file, however, were mostly from the peripheral marginalized tribes: the Nuba, Dinka, Fur and Baqqara.

Despite their discipline and smart uniforms, the members of the Supreme Council were not immune to personal squabbling. Troops from the eastern region, whose commanders had not been given a seat in the council, marched on Khartoum in March 1959. They besieged the capital and surrounded the residence of General — now President — Abboud. The chief mutineers were appeased and Brigadier Abdel Rahim Shannan, in particular, was brought into the council. Nevertheless, the dissidents still felt they were being sidetracked. On 22 May Brigadier Shannan led another march on Khartoum. This time, the other council members had had enough of indiscipline. The eastern commanders were arrested and court-martialled for mutiny and sentenced to death; the dissident troops were sent back to barracks. The Supreme Council was unsure of its supremacy or popularity in the country, and it was even more uneasy about its backing in the professional officer corps. In November, Colonel Ali Hamid led a rebellion of radical junior officers, supported by an infantry battalion in Omdurman. This was different. Throughout Sudan's history the peripheral regions had rebelled – sometimes almost in a ceremonial fashion. Appeasement or punishment might be expected. Mutiny in the centre was much more dangerous. The revolt of junior officers was brutally suppressed: they were summarily tried and hanged in public. That was *not* customary in the Sudanese tradition. On the contrary, Sudanese have always prided themselves on bloodless revolutions. It has become a popular myth, extolled with much gusto, and historical inaccuracy, even today.

The years 1958 and 1959 established a pattern: a bunch of incompetent politicians would be replaced by slightly less incompetent military officers, via a coup, followed by another attempted coup or even two. The earliest putsches did promise much. After all, it was a time of coups in Muslim states – in Pakistan, Iraq and Egypt. And they seemed successful at the time. Egypt's example was especially influential on Sudanese events. The style – ideally, initially bloodless – was the same; as was the installation of a popular figurehead. Nasser had used the respected General Naguib, and likewise the Sudanese plotters had paraded the affable fatherly figure of General Abboud as their front man. Sadly, Sudan was soon to teach Egypt a thing or two about how to, and how not to, stage coups.

President Abboud was too honest to be a politician. He believed Nasser's promises about the Aswan dam – 'soldier to soldier', he thought. In 1960 construction began on the long-delayed High Dam at Aswan (and the Sudanese started on smaller dams). The Egyptian dam immediately produced a large displaced and disaffected Nubian population that had to leave their ancestral lands and eventually, decades later, it had created countless tons of Ethiopian sediment which rendered the project unworkable anyway. The relocated Nubians were just one element of immediate national discontent. In the absence of legal political parties, union leaders and university students rallied to the underground communist party, which had been the only political party publicly to oppose the military coup. The Muslim Brotherhood, founded in Egypt in 1928, also developed a small but influential following in Sudan. As in Egypt, the Sudanese Brothers came to regard military rule as thoroughly un-Islamic.

Being practical, if economically illiterate, men, the ruling officers had the common sense to abandon the previous coalition's absurd pricing policy and the cotton mountain soon disappeared. They were also prepared to accept financial assistance from both East and West. Electricity for Khartoum and a railway from Kordofan to Wau, the first modern north-south rail-line, brought economic advance. Wasteful spending on pet projects, poor accounting and graft soon tainted the military's can-do reputation, however.

In October 1961, General Abboud made a state visit to Washington, where he was warmly welcomed by President John F. Kennedy. The young Democrat president was effusive toward the military man who had overturned the embryonic democracy in Sudan. Kennedy talked of Abboud 'setting an example' to Sudan's immediate neighbours. He went even further by saying that Sudan 'set a standard for the continent'. US presidents would rarely praise leaders of future Sudanese juntas, but they did so occasionally when cold war competition demanded.

The military set up a system of regional and urban councils reporting to a central council in Khartoum, but it was mere window-dressing for the regime, not democracy. These modest reforms gave more power to rural conservatives at the expense of more secular urban opinion. The ruling military had done relatively little to improve politics in the north, but they had done *nothing* to resolve the 'Southern Problem'. As the army was the only relatively effective national institution, the Supreme Council assumed that the iron-fisted crackdown following the 1955 mutiny and the continuing Arabization would settle the matter. The broken promises of federation and continued discrimination exacerbated deep-rooted differences while repression merely pushed the resistance underground. Some of the surviving 1955 mutineers had gone into the bush, although their armed opposition amounted to little more than banditry. The military could have dealt with this in their traditional way. But then the ministry of education in Khartoum took over the missionary schools and integrated them into a national Islamic curriculum, in which Arabic was now taught alongside English. The surviving missionary teachers were harassed and then expelled. The secondary schools in Rumbek and Juba, where many of the southern elite had been educated, were closed after a strike against the draconian northern policy. Many students and teachers joined the thousands of fellow refugees in Uganda or Zaire. In 1963 the Sudan African National Union (SANU) was formed in Kampala. Small south Sudanese groups sprang up in London and Khartoum, but effective southern political resistance inside Sudan was sparse.

More promising for a southern fight-back was the establishment by the indigenous Latuka people of a small guerrilla base, Agu Camp, deep in eastern Equatoria; a few hundred men, led by Emedio Tafeng Odongi, a former lieutenant in the Equatorial Corps, started training. They conducted occasional raids on isolated government positions. Gradually, the resistance set up other bases in the forests and bush along the borders with Uganda and Zaire (now the Democratic Republic of Congo). A small group of Latuka priests and teachers in exile in Kampala tried to forge a political leadership for the sporadic fighting inside Sudan. The leading light was Father Saturnino Lohure, who had represented Torit in the Constituent Assembly, but had fled to Uganda after the 1958 coup. They needed a political name. SANU was discredited, less a movement and more a reference to other prominent African groups such as the Rhodesian ZANU (Zimbabwe African National Union). Like ZANU and numerous other anti-colonial groups, south Sudanese dissidents suffered from tribal rivalries that spawned lots of small rival organizations. At first the southerners in Kampala played around with various titles with 'Pan African' or 'Azanian' included in their putative movements, in order to garner support from the Organization of African Unity and other potential financial and military sponsors. They settled eventually on a traditional African name, on the model of Mau Mau in Kenya. They agreed on *Anya-Nya*. This was a combination of the local word for the fatal poison extracted from a river snake and the name for army ants.

The first Anya-Nya raids in Equatoria were small-scale. The insurgency spread to Bahr al-Ghazal, however. In January 1964 Commander William Deng Nhial, a Dinka, sent one of his lieutenants to attack Wau, the provincial capital. Over a dozen government soldiers were killed and a stash of automatic weapons was captured. This was the first major attack of what southerners call 'The First War of Southern Independence'. By mid-1964 the insurgents numbered perhaps as many as 4,000, but they had no centralized command-and-control structure. Nor did they possess a unified political front. In mid-October 1964 various aspiring guerrilla leaders met in Kampala's Silver Spring Hotel. Walks-out and rows from the 'national convention' inevitably ensued. But one result was the emergence of Agrrey Jaden as a leader. He was a former civil servant from the Pojulu ethnic group who had previously presided over the ineffectual SANU. Theoretically, he headed only one political offshoot of the Anya-Nya, but he did appoint 'Colonel' Joseph Lagu as the first overall military commander of the armed resistance. Lagu, from Madiland, south of Juba, had defected from the government army in 1963. He was to play a prominent part in the southern war, not least encouraging the career of the most charismatic of all southern commanders, John Garang, who served (briefly) under Lagu in the first war, also called the 'Seventeen-Year War' (1955-72).

The racism of the north-south divide was ingrained. Northern Arabs contemptuously referred to southerners as *abeed* (slaves), while the southerners often called Arab northerners *mundukuru* – slavers. So far, to Khartoum's generals, the southern rebels were not a military threat, but they were a political embarrassment. The military reluctantly allowed a debate by students at Khartoum University on the 'Southern Question'. It got out of hand, whereupon the authorities prohibited any more public discussion. Predictably, the students went ahead on 21 October 1964 with another debate, and a confrontation with police was ensured. A student was killed. At the funeral cortege tens of thousands of marchers, many wearing university gowns, started shouting anti-government slogans. Rioting ensued throughout the capital that the army and police struggled to contain. A general strike followed, while the banned political leaders looked on in amazement at a popular revolt in which they had played almost no part. The Supreme Council was split – the younger officers were more sympathetic to the popular discontent, while the older officers opted for tanks rather than talks.

Handing power back to civilian politicians

President Abboud, true to form, was reluctant to use force against his civilian compatriots. He had promised to return the country to civilian rule. On 26 October he announced the end of the Supreme Council and therefore the termination of military rule. The population of Khartoum erupted with joyous celebration in which the normally reserved capital witnessed men literally dancing in the streets. The 'October Revolution' entered Arab history as another bloodless intervention. In fact, scores of students and other demonstrators had already been killed by the police and army in the preceding week.

Abboud stepped down after handing over to a transitional government headed by a respected educationalist, Sirr al-Khatim Khalifa. Very few Khartoum leaders had real civilian experience of the south – the men in uniform knew only about keeping order. The new prime minister, however, had worked extensively in schools there. He included two southerners in his cabinet as well as a balanced mix of communists, Muslim Brothers and representatives of the other main political parties. Abboud quietly retired to civilian life with no legal repercussions for his coup. The day after he stepped down, he was cheered in the *souk* as he ambled around doing his own food shopping. His reluctance to use violence against civilians and his hand-over to politicians may well have owed something to his long service in and with the British army. He had learned from the British that politicians, not soldiers, should be in charge – no matter how little the military respected the selfish, squabbling short-termism of their political masters. Abboud settled for a while in England, but died in Khartoum, aged 82, in 1983.

Abboud bequeathed a civilian cabinet that was even more dysfunctional than the previous one. During military rule conventional parties had disintegrated, but the communist party and the Brotherhood had helped to fill the political vacuum by careful underground organization. The communists were also active in the new cabinet; this upset the Islamists. In the new state council of the transitional government a chairman with a vital skill was appointed. Tijani al-Mahi was a medical doctor who was the first Sudanese to specialize in psychiatry. Yet even a highly qualified psychiatrist could not regulate effectively the often self-destructive and occasionally psychotic behaviour of the civilian political leaders. The Umma Party summoned tens of thousands of *Ansar* to chant Mahdist war cries in the streets of Khartoum. Thoroughly alarmed, the cabinet collapsed in February 1965 and the NUP, the Umma and the political front of the Brotherhood dominated the new one. For the next four years coalitions of old and new parties staggered on in a murky haze of sleaze, tribalism and remarkable incompetence. Like the Bourbons, the Sudanese parties seemed to have forgotten nothing and learned nothing.

The Southern Question continued to fester. On 6 December 1964 thousands of southerners in Khartoum had gathered to welcome back Clement Mboro. Universally referred to in the south as 'Uncle Clement' because of his genuine avuncular popularity, he had worked as a civil servant in the condominium in the south, and then became the first southerner to hold an important cabinet post in Khartoum. He had just been on a tour of the south, but rumours spread rapidly that he had been assassinated. Thousands of southerners went on the rampage killing any northern Arab they came across. Nearly a hundred northerners were killed in what was dubbed 'Black Sunday'. From that day on, at any sign of southern revolt in the city, Arabs in Khartoum would reach for their guns and patrol their neighbourhood, just in case the police and army were not up to the job. The army restored order in the evening of Black Sunday. Some northern intellectuals came to the conclusion that the south was irreconcilable and should be allowed to go its own way. The majority, however, either favoured more repression, immediately, or perhaps an olive branch, first.

A round table conference finally convened in Khartoum in March 1965. The southern representatives proved to be as fractious as their northern compatriots. SANU, for example, had two rival delegations called 'Inside' and 'Out', describing those in exile or operating inside the country. Two

ALF parties pitched up – the Azanian Liberation Front and Sudan African Liberation Front, demanding inevitably a comparison with the Monty Python version of the various Judean Liberation Fronts at the time of Christ. It would have been an amusing farce were not the consequences so tragic. Leaders such as Father Saturnino were there, as were the able Clement Mboro, who had *not* been killed on Black Sunday, but merely delayed. Mboro led the Southern Front comprised of educated southerners living in Khartoum. The government also included a group officially called 'Other Shades of Opinion', which most southerners regarded as stooges. For fifty years the northerners were always to deploy the Quisling tactic. The delegates were divided by class, education, ideology and, of course, tribe. One issue they openly disputed was whether the south should secede or create a federal system. More privately, some southerners analyzed the best means of armed struggle, should peace talks fail.

All the northern parties attended. In addition, delegates came from neighbouring African states. The northerners were able to manipulate the chronically disunited southerners. When all the northern party representatives predictably rejected southern independence, Aggrey Jaden flew off to Kampala in a fit of pique, thus removing his SANU-Outside from the game and allowing one of his main rivals, the Southern Front, to move up the pecking order.

The conference failed to reach any consensus. This was probably the last chance for peace, and for unity of Africa's largest country. True, a twelve-member committee, six from the north and six from the south, formed a working group to try to make a deal. It was chaired by a brilliant lawyer from the Muslim Brotherhood who would become the *éminence grise* of Sudanese Islamist politics after 1989: Dr Hassan al-Turabi. He was a ruthless and yet charming man who, intellectually, could run rings around nearly every other politician, north, south, east or west. And al-Turabi could accomplish this as easily in French or English as in Arabic. The lawyer was also an Islamic scholar who believed in the Islamization of the south, not its separation. As any proposal had to be agreed unanimously he used his veto to ensure the southerners did not get their way. Southerners wanted to ensure that the south remained one administrative unit, but northerners regarded this as a step towards independence. The northerners wanted to Balkanize the southern administration. The southerners also wanted a militia loyal to a local southern administration. Utterly frustrated, the southerners gave up eventually. Most concluded that the north would pay attention to their grievances only through armed struggle.

In the 1965 elections other fissures appeared in Sudan's body politic. The Beja Congress won ten seats. Formed in 1957, the Congress was set up to counter the alienation felt in the east of the country. They were committed to a federal system. Seven seats were also captured by independents in the Nuba Mountains. Both political groups represented the anger felt by marginalized peoples.

The premiership changed hands four times in as many years in almost Italian-style rotation. Initially, a clever, pompous politician, Mohamed Ahmed al-Majub, led the Umma-NUP coalition. Learning nothing from the recent southern attempt to negotiate a peaceful solution, the new prime minster intensified Abboud's policy of Arabization in the south. The army went into action against political dissidents among the small educated elite. In July 1965 a soldier and a local argued over a woman in Juba and in the ensuing fight the soldier was killed. On 8 July, officers in the Juba garrison gave the nod for their troops to rampage through the southern capital to exact revenge. Hundreds of southerners were killed and the town was trashed. Four days later troops from the Wau garrison went on a killing spree at a wedding party and murdered over seventy well-to-do southerners attending the celebration.

A new wave of fugitives fled into the cross-border refugee camps, but other angry southerners bolstered the number of fighting men in the scattered Anya-Nya camps, which had recently acquired weapons supplied by Simba rebels fleeing from the war in next-door Congo. Facing a new stage of armed resistance, the army opted for a tried-and-tested method of isolating insurgents from their rural support. The Sudanese set up 'peace villages', what the Americans called 'strategic hamlets' in Vietnam. The British had called them 'concentration camps' during the Boer War, and despite the furore had used them again in Malaya. It was a common method of draining the Maoist sea of peasant supply and support. The rural population of Equatoria was herded into thirty-three collective villages. Hundreds died from malnutrition and disease. This was an extreme counter-insurgency (COIN) technique, partly because Equatoria in the deep south was adjacent to neighbouring guerrilla sanctuaries in Uganda and the Congo. Along the north-south 'border' the army set up government-allied tribal militias to reinforce the centuries-old disputes over land, water and grazing rights. Sometimes tribes based in the north were encouraged to raid south, or Khartoum armed and bribed rival southern tribal leaders, a classic divide-and-rule principle. The policy of creating irregular tribal militias became a main pillar of northern COIN for the next five decades.

In the face of the new containment policy, the southern politicians still failed to co-ordinate properly. The 'boys in the bush' grew to disdain the talkers in comfortable capitals such as Kampala while they fought hard on the ground. At one stage, some commanders insisted on their troops using their local tongues and not English as the language of command and communication. English had long been seen as a symbol of resistance to the enforced use of Arabic. This move by some Anya-Nya commanders was a deliberate rebuff to the failed leaders in exile. In response, the first major rally, the 'national convention', was held *inside* the south, at Angundri, thirty miles south-west of Juba in July 1967. There, leaders such as Aggrey Jaden declared a 'Provisional Government of South Sudan'. This was the first real attempt to forge a united front of insurgents and politicians inside the country. Naturally, this new stage did not include all the fractious southern parties. The provisional government controlled only a small part of central Equatoria — when the army was not around. But it did publish newsletters to rally the faithful and later set up radio stations. The ad-hoc government collapsed when its president, the energetic but erratic Aggrey Jaden, suddenly decamped to the fleshpots of Nairobi. Once more a failure of leadership had scuppered the stuttering attempts at southern unity. Most insurgencies succeed when they are headed by one charismatic leader, but it would take decades for that kind of leadership to emerge among southerners. Agrrey had been frustrated by the clashes of the Equatorians who resented the aggressive intrusion of the most populous and warlike tribe, the Dinka. Tribalism, army reprisals, and sheer logistical challenges had destroyed the embryonic government almost as much as poor leadership.

Back in Khartoum, the southern political remnants of the Round Table Conference were still around, despite the intermittent legal harassment. The most important, Clement Mboro's Southern Front and William Deng's SANU-Inside, squabbled as much as co-operated. At least they got to talk to northern politicians. This played a role in the compromise deal that was finally reached in 1972. Meanwhile, the armed wing continued to fight on, while pleading with the leaders to get their act together. These same leaders could not even agree on what to call their future independent state. Many thought of 'South Sudan' as an imperial legacy and a mere geographical construct. In March 1969 the 'Nile Provisional Government' was set up, at least in name. It was led by Gordon Muortat Mayen Muborjok, who had served as a middle-ranking police officer and who later defected to the rebels. He was one of the few early nationalists who actually reached the promised land by serving in the federal post-2005 government.

It was under Muborjok's leadership that the Israelis were brought into the fray; a handful of Anya-Nya went to Israel for training and occasionally Israeli advisors entered the deep south. Mossad was always looking for peripheral wars to distract Arab foes. The war in Yemen, for example, had engaged 70,000 of Egypt's best troops during crucial stages of the Arab-Israeli conflict. A handful of advisers, as in south Sudan, could set up a lot of distractions for real or potential Arab enemies.

The failure of leadership continued to afflict the north as much as the south. In July 1966 Sadiq al-Mahdi became prime minster and it seemed to many urban secular intellectuals and religious conservatives alike that cometh the hour, cometh the man. He was young (31), the great-grandson of the Mahdi, an author, an imam to the *Ansar* and an Oxford graduate. Moreover, he was decisive, and appeared to have a national vision which transcended all the debilitating prejudices. He transformed the Umma Party from a religious relic into a modern political machine; encouragingly, he appointed younger ministers based on competence and not merely to balance the party or tribal ticket. Even some southern leaders found grounds for optimism in the al-Mahdi coalition. He wanted to ditch the ramshackle transitional constitution that followed the end of military rule. In trying to balance an Islamic with a secular orientation for a new constitution, the Umma split, however. Despite all the promise, al-Mahdi's government fell after ten months. A new makeshift coalition, led again by Mohamed Ahmed al-Majub, soon became mired in familiar tribal and sectarian passions. Rumours spread of another military coup.

Sadiq al-Mahdi had opposed the first round of military intervention in 1958. It was an interesting historical counterpoint that a young officer, Omar al-Bashir, graduated from the Khartoum Military Academy in December 1966, during the apex of al-Mahdi's brief but meteoric rise to power. In later years I spoke to both leaders at length. Al-Mahdi still impressed with his intellectual debate in almost perfect English; his physical height, demeanour and sculpted beard echoed the age of great Arab conquerors. Yet he became a spent force, the early political promise sullied by his own indecision and the sheer intractability of Sudan's many problems. The soldier who toppled him, Omar al-Bashir, was obviously the more practical man, a pragmatic officer and populist who could reach out beyond the religious elites to touch the common man — albeit only in the north. Both men were two key antagonists in the 1989 culmination of the yo-yo years of military and civilian rule.

That tipping point was still to come, however. In May 1967 the ineffectual Mohamed Ahmed al-Majub returned as prime minister, backed by an Umma faction that had deserted Sadiq al-Madhi in favour of an imam who was a relative of the Mahdi's successor, Khalifa Abdullahi. That original succession battle had been fought over eighty years before, a classic example of Sudanese leaders' absorption in bygone struggles. Party politics was dominated by the Umma (and its various wings) and the Democratic Unionist Party (DUP); both were anachronistic feudal movements. Al-Mahdi's influence stemmed from his relationship with the original Mahdist *Ansar* revolt, and much of the party's power base had been in the west. It had become an exclusive family concern, based on hereditary principles. Likewise, the DUP was based on the *Khatmiyyah* sect run by the Mirghani family, whose influence was largely in the east. These two political dynasties and their religious allies took centre stage, while the communists and Brotherhood were usually pushed into the wings.

The prime minister's arrogance propelled him to ignore domestic politics as almost beneath him. Al-Majub had received previous accolades as a foreign minister. He preferred to indulge his taste for international meddling. Some of it was justified: such as countering the communist Derg government in Addis Ababa that was arming the Anya-Nya. Intercession in Eritrea, Chad, the Central African Republic and the Congo seemed less pressing. In the last case, Khartoum's arming of rebels in the Congo could have disturbed one of the Anya-Nya's southern sanctuaries. In later years supporting rebels, such as the Lord's Resistance Army in Uganda, became a convenient counterweight for Khartoum's floundering southern strategy. In the longer term, Khartoum's cross-border stirring undermined its complaints about its neighbours intervening within Sudan's borders. And al-Majub helped to set this trend.

If Khartoum was perhaps overactive in foreign intervention, its handling of economic issues was underwhelming. Benign neglect allowed the traditional tribal and family domination of the riverine trade to flourish. But Sudan needed big foreign investment, not least to satisfy the demands of the marginalized peoples in the east and west. Slow economic growth, political instability and a civil war did not encourage much foreign investment. What plans there were depended on nationalizing private cotton schemes that further deterred foreign money. An antiquated and grossly unfair taxation structure plus reckless borrowing increased the national debt by a factor of ten in the four years of ham-fisted civilian governance.

The events of 25 May 1969 appeared inevitable to all except the members of the Constituent Assembly who were totally engrossed in mutual backstabbing. Colonel Ja'afar Numeiri and his movement of Free Officers ordered the army to seize key installations in the three towns of the capital. The coup was led by a handful of officers and around 500 men, some mere cadets – although two companies of tough paratroopers also took part. Just as in Brigadier Omar al-Bashir's future coup of 1989, the plotters in 1969 fell out about the timing and so only a few of Numeiri's dedicated followers pressed ahead. Under cover of darkness one armoured column seized the main bridges and the broadcasting centre. Another column took over army headquarters and arrested senior commanders and later senior politicians. It was done efficiently and without shedding any blood. Numeiri's peaceful revolution was consciously modelled on the 1952 Egyptian putsch by the Committee of Free Officers, which proclaimed secular Arab socialism. Nobody, not even the religious conservatives, appeared to mourn the abrupt termination of the second round of civilian rule in Sudan.

Visitors to Sudan always comment on the hospitality and warmth of northerners. Sadiq al-Mahdi, once one of the more promising leaders, was an utterly urbane host as was Hassan al-Turabi, another merging leader. I speak personally as a house guest of both these men (and many other Sudanese politicians). Yet until the late sixties no single leader had been able to climb out of the swamp of selfish nepotistic greed or, when a few did, they did not espouse a vision for the whole country. The Sudanese had looked at the 'big men' in Arab politics, such as Nasser, and wondered whether they could do better. Nasser had been humbled by his crushing defeat by the Israelis in the 1967 Six Day War. Ever-optimistic, the elite in Khartoum now hoped that Numeiri, a political soldier unlike the affable and apolitical Abboud, could lead from the front and, above all, end the north-south conflict. Would the so-called May Revolution in 1969 finally deliver on all the aspirations of independence?

The Numeiri years

Numeiri had been a political activist his whole life. He had been expelled from school for organizing a strike against British rule, and later kicked out of the army for his left-wing politics, but was mysteriously accepted back into the officer corps. After a course at the US Army Command and Staff College at Fort Leavenworth, he was appointed to run an army training school, a useful position to groom young cadets in the ideals of his Free Officers' Movement. The son of a postman, albeit with aristocratic forbears in Dongola, he modelled his revolution closely on that of Nasser.

Judith Miller, of the *New York Times*, interviewed him a number of times. She did not appear impressed:

Flabby, black-skinned and tainted in the eyes of many of his racist northern countrymen by his facial scars – inflicted by tribal healers to protect children against the Nile's innumerable eye diseases – he was a poor orator.[1]

He was clever, energetic and ruthless, however. His small band of military acolytes was determined to reshape the social and economic order in a new socialist state that would be avowedly secular. And, like Nasser, Numeiri believed in pan-Arabism. The Revolutionary Command Council would need its sometimes reluctant allies in the Sudan Communist Party to achieve its goal, not least to wipe out the main religious opponents, the Islamists, especially the *Ansar*. After the *Ansar* had staged mass protests in Omdurman, in March 1970 the Free Officers decided to act against the fortified heart of old-fashioned Mahdism. A large flotilla was sent up the White Nile to attack the well-defended Aba Island. Crack army troops killed thousands of *Ansar* after stiff resistance. The land and properties of all the extended Mahdi's family were confiscated and the urbane Sadiq al-Mahdi had to smuggle himself out of the country for a lengthy exile.

Khartoum's radical socialist army government then proceeded to nationalize nearly all the private commercial sector, including large and successful Sudanese-owned companies and banks. Compensation was meagre. Workers were awarded more rights, however, and debt and rent relief was given to the vast army of tenants in the Gezira cotton scheme. School numbers were boosted. Nevertheless, as with nearly all the economic programmes of state socialism, the five-year plans failed. A radical foreign policy accompanied domestic socialist reforms. Loans were sought from the Soviet bloc and Numeiri toured Eastern Europe, China and North Korea, as well as engaging in pan-Arab affairs. Numeiri shifted from the West, especially Britain and the USA, most notably in arms purchases. New Soviet technicians came into Sudan to assist with the expansion of the army from 18,000 to 50,000 men, with an arsenal of Soviet tanks, artillery and aircraft. Egypt also supplied equipment including armoured personnel carriers.

Elements of the communist party had long been wary of the military government, not least because they had wanted to create a large popular revolution of peasants and workers, not one based on a putsch by a small band of *petit-bourgeois* officers. They had also disliked Numeiri's flirtation with Libya and Egypt in the Tripoli Charter, which set up another pan-Arab experiment, the Federation of Arab Republics. Moreover, the ailing Nasser and the erratic Libyan firebrand, Colonel Gaddafi, had eviscerated their communist parties. Numeiri initially purged some of the main pro-communist officers in the Revolutionary Command Council. Believing he was popular with the people, the president had by now alienated all the political parties and movements in the country and his military intelligence thwarted at least ten planned or actual attempts to overthrow him in the first two years of his rule. On 19 July 1971 surviving pro-communist officers, to avoid imminent arrest, staged a hasty coup in Khartoum in broad daylight. Sudanese communist party leaders were on a visit to London and many surviving pro-communist officers had been caught unawares.

So was Numeiri, who was captured. Communist prisoners in the city were freed and encouraged to stage a protest throughout Khartoum, waving red flags and shouting revolutionary slogans. National radio announced even more sweeping agricultural and commercial nationalization. The instinctive conservatism of the Sudanese population, especially in the three towns, was alienated. The Northern Defence Corps based in Shendi remained loyal and moved on the capital, while a tank unit freed Numeiri, after a fierce fire-fight. Egypt's new president, Anwar Sadat, also intervened. Egyptian army units guarding dam installations were ordered into Khartoum and the Egyptian air force helped to fly in loyal Sudanese troops. The hasty communist coup lasted just three days before it was crushed. The main plotters were tried in secret and promptly hanged, including those who had fled to Libya (and quickly returned). Thousands of communists were arrested and detained in a comprehensive crackdown.

The rapid slaughter of the *Ansar* and then the communists may have secured Numeiri's shaky throne, but his blood-soaked reprisals and secret trials and executions offended the Sudanese belief and pride in the civility of their political life. Everybody might squabble and even tolerate coups, but bloodshed among Muslims was generally viewed as *haram.* The attempted communist coup shook Numeiri's confidence and he moved away from his left-wing socialist stance. A few communists were absorbed into Numeiri's new Sudan Socialist Union, but the power of the communist party was broken for ever, though it survived for a long time as a rump. Numeiri's movement was the only legal party in the country, and the press was also strictly controlled. Just to make sure he was genuinely popular, in August 1971 a rigged poll allowed Numeiri to be president, for another six years.

The southern front under Numeiri
That was a temporary band-aid for northern troubles, but what of the civil war in the south? The communist party had argued for a deal allowing

southern autonomy, but the freshly purged and enlarged officer corps wanted even more arms and troops to crush what they still regarded as a 'mutiny', albeit a rather long and extensive one. Nevertheless, a political deal was back on the table. Numeiri had to shore up his options.

In the south, Aggrey Jaden was still trying to achieve the apparently impossible – a political command for the Anya-Nya. The capable Joseph Lagu had been demoted from commander in chief and so refused to operate with the titular commander in chief, the long-serving but illiterate and incompetent Emidio Odongi – that at least was Lagu's view. The fighting commanders still regarded the political leadership as inefficient and often cowardly fat-cats. After the Six Day War Lagu offered to open a unified southern military front for the Israelis. Lagu even made a secret visit to Israel where a more fully supportive Mossad decided to provide extra money and weapons. Israel also decided to drop the pretence of supporting the Southern Sudan Provisional Government to focus on Lagu's determination to unite the southern fighting forces, without pandering to the hapless politicians.

Lagu certainly appeared brighter and more experienced than Odongi. And coming from the small Madi ethnic group, he had soon mastered the main southern languages as well as Arabic and English. After attending perhaps the best secondary school in the South, at Rumbek, he was one of only two southerners to attend the Sudan Military College, where he was commissioned as a lieutenant in 1960. He defected from the Sudanese army and by 1963 was leading the Anya-Nya, where he developed an equal contempt for southern politicians as well as internecine tribal warfare. The Israeli connection, allied to his military skills, finally enabled Lagu to dominate southern military resistance.

Israeli military training and regular air drops of weapons were important to the Anya-Nya, but so was Mossad's adroit diplomacy. Emperor Haile Selassie was easily persuaded to allow a southern training camp to operate on his territory, not least to move forces across the north into the Upper Nile. Khartoum and other Arab capitals had been supporting the Eritrean insurgency in Ethiopia's far north. Israeli support for the Anya-Nya also came via Uganda. From January 1971 small groups of southerners began training, most notably in military communications, in Israel. At the same time Lagu renamed his (relatively) more united forces as the Southern Sudan Liberation Movement. Lagu also gave up on the original political demands to create an integrated army. Logistically it made sense to allow ethnic armies in the various southern states, with a theoretical command centre. This was later to exacerbate tribal divisions.

By 1970 better training, organization, weapons and communications moved the civil war into a more aggressive phase. Major roads were mined leaving the key towns in government hands, but often dangerously isolated. Even Juba, the southern capital, was shelled by artillery. The Sudanese were hard pressed to supply by air, despite the influx of Soviet advisers and new fighter and transport planes and helicopters. Soviet armour was sometimes met by successful use of Israeli anti-tank weapons. In order to regain some control of the Equatorian hinterland of Juba, Egyptian commandos supported the Sudanese army.

The southern rebels now fought better, but it depended partly on the varying quality of commanders' leadership as well as the different terrain. The rugged landscape of forest and hills of Equatoria was ideal for guerrilla warfare, especially during the rainy season, but in the dry season along the border with northern Sudan, the grassland, scrub and desert were easier to patrol and harass from the air or along the Nile and other minor rivers. The Nuer Anya-Nya, with supplies from Ethiopia, began to hit armoured columns and seize large amounts of arms from the government. They also hit columns trying to break the on-off siege of Wau, as well as destroying the railway to the town. Military intelligence in the north put full-time southern fighters at around 13,000, more than double five years previously. The insurgents were much better armed and trained, thanks mainly to foreign support. Some senior army officers in Khartoum, who had been conducting the fighting in the south, felt that their COIN had reached a stalemate. Perhaps a political approach might finally work, at least temporarily, to allow the northern army to regroup.

The first peace deal

With Haile Selassie's blessing, northern and southern leaders as well as church intermediaries met in early February at the Hilton Hotel in Addis Ababa. Preliminary meetings had taken place discreetly for months beforehand. The north ordered a unilateral ceasefire, while the SSLM still wanted outright secession. In later years southern mythology portrayed the Addis talks as a sell-out, but this failed to understand African circumstances at the time. The Ethiopian government was fighting secessionist movements, not least in Eritrea, and the founding shibboleth of the OAU, after the terrible civil wars in the Congo and Nigeria, was to maintain unity – the traditional colonial boundaries – at all costs. Numeiri carefully selected military officers who were prepared to compromise, while Major General Lagu was also determined to reach a deal. Before tackling the main constitutional issues, they agreed on English as the principal language of the south. The borders were to be maintained as of 1 January 1956, the line inherited from the imperial power, and the south would keep its administrative unity. A southern regional assembly would administer, *inter alia*, education, public health and the police, but the national government in Khartoum would control defence, foreign affairs and the currency. Juba would be the site of the regional government.

But the sticking point remained the army. The southern delegation wanted a separate army run by southern officers; the north believed this was the first step to independence. After days of deadlock, the emperor, as host, suggested a compromise. A Southern Command of 12,000 officers and men – half of whom would be southerners – would be set up. The deal was finally signed on 27 February 1972.

Numeiri declared a great victory, made the temporary ceasefire permanent and toured the south, where he was warmly received. So great was the relief at the end of seventeen years of fighting, with hundreds of thousands displaced and thousands killed, that Lagu's concerns that the 6,000 southern troops would all be Anya-Nya were glossed over. The deal could work, but it all relied on goodwill and trust. Despite the lack of trust, some goodwill persisted and the agreement held for eleven years.

Northerners proclaimed Numeiri as the great peacemaker, and rumours spread that he would soon earn the Nobel Peace Prize. Lagu went north and was made a major general in the Sudanese army, but not vice president as he had expected (a mistake which was carefully avoided in the 2005 agreement). The new government in Juba was dominated by mission-educated local Equatorians, while a number of returning educated exiles were generally disappointed, as were the far more populous Nuer and Dinka of Bahr al-Ghazal and Upper Nile. Tens of thousands of refugees had to be repatriated from across the southern borders, while an even larger number of internally displaced persons (IDPs) from north and south had to be re-homed. Led by the United Nations High Commissioner for Refugees (UNHCR), a host of religious and humanitarian NGOs set about the task of repatriation and resettlement. Many of them would be still be there more than four decades later, as the NGOs emerged as a kind of imperial rearguard, covering the Western retreat from Africa.

Progress was soon made with the formation of a more representative police force, but Khartoum could not shake off the legacy of the northern-centric army as the most – perhaps only – effective national instrument. As the maker, breaker and broker of power in Khartoum, how could it be diluted by southerners who might use it to undermine the country's fragile unity? This was the perennial question in the north. And the traditional divisions remained: most of the rank and file of the northern-dominated army were from peripheral areas, mainly the west, while the officer class came from the traditionally powerful riverine elite. Ironically, many officers were prepared to accept secession rather than dilute their beloved national army. The army's power could be destroyed in the north as well as the south, or so some officers feared. After seventeen years of fighting and propaganda, some officers just could not tolerate 'slaves' and 'terrorists' in their army and so resigned. Southerners feared that the Southern Command would soon push out experienced insurgents or otherwise suffer discrimination from the larger and more sophisticated northern army. Perhaps a few southern idealists saw the new dispensation as the chance to create a proper non-tribal southern force. And an even smaller group might even have hoped that a unified democratic Sudan could emerge — eventually.

If the police and prisons were indigenized quite quickly, the army integration was scheduled to last five years. Just over 6,000 insurgents, proportionately from each province, were integrated and retrained. A few were sent abroad, for example, the promising Captain John Garang de Mabior, destined to command the whole southern army, was sent to the USA for advanced instruction. Over half the former fighters were deployed in public works on farms, road and forestry, although the job-creation schemes soon petered out because of lack of funds. Inevitably some frustrated warriors grew unhappy. In late 1974 and early 1975 mutinies erupted primarily in Juba and Wau in attempts to restart the war. But the new regional president, Abel Alier, intervened. Alier was a respected human rights lawyer and judge, a Dinka Bor Christian whom Numeiri made vice president of Sudan. More often the local crises required the authority of Major General Lagu to bring the dissidents into line.

Temporary peace
Surprisingly, the north-south peace deal held for eleven years. After elections in 1973, the regional assembly in Juba stumbled along, despite the ethnic and personal fissures, and the fact that Khartoum still made unwelcome top-down decisions. They also argued about the controversial Jonglei Canal project. At least it proved the northerners wrong – that southerners could make a reasonable stab at a functioning democracy, one far removed from the northern dictatorship. There, the Numeiri government

still struggled to resolve the place of religion in the constitution. On the economic front, following the massive oil-price hikes after the 1973 Yom Kippur/Ramadan war, vast amounts of Arab petro-dollars flowed into Sudan. It was designed to be the breadbasket of the Middle East. The Kuwaitis poured in money for vast agricultural schemes, especially in the sugar industry. And British entrepreneur Tiny Rowland's Lonrho company invested over $25 million to develop, with the Sudanese government, the world's largest sugar plantation near Kosti.

The most important development in this period was the discovery of black gold. In 1978-79 oil deposits were confirmed by the US Chevron company. The oil was mainly to be found in the south. So was this 'southern oil'? The politicians in Juba certainly thought so, and also wanted the refineries to be built in the south. More crucially, southerners demanded the future oil pipelines be built through the south to the Kenyan coast, not via the more accessible northern route to Port Sudan. As in many African countries, oil was to spawn conflict as much as prosperity.

Economic liberalization and Western investments as well as oil development marked a shift in foreign policy, as well as economic advance. As with most military regimes, weapons supplies were a weathervane of such changes. Khartoum's anti-communist crackdowns had helped to sour relations with Moscow, but the Russians still sold their weapons. These supplies dried up when Moscow backed Sudan's Marxist enemies in Ethiopia. China replaced Russian supplies, while Egypt continued to be an important military and diplomatic partner. With the warming of Western economic relations, so too Washington started to sell more weapons, not least to counter Soviet support of Ethiopia and Libya. US arms sales increased until renewed conflict in the south changed the equation.

Some Sudanese historians depict this period of peace in the south, economic growth and (relative) diplomatic success as a golden age. Better relations with Washington were matched by a flurry of economic deals with western European states. In July 1978 Numeiri was elected as chairman of the OAU. Sudan appeared at last to be fulfilling its continental ambitions. Relations with the Arab world were complicated by Numeiri's lonely support for Anwar Sadat's signing of the Camp David accord with Israel in 1978. This pleased Washington, but angered the Arab League.

Numeiri had waged peace with the south and indirectly with Israel and stabilized the economy. Although his military regime was apparently in control, discontent still simmered in the army and Numeiri's long feud with opposition political leaders, especially Sadiq al-Mahdi, had not been ended.

Any accommodation would need a decision on the role of Islam in the state. The earlier compromises of 'freedom of religion' could not be enough for the Islamists. Ultimately, a political settlement in the Muslim north would mean tearing up the deal in the south.

It is a recurring pattern in military interventions worldwide that coup leaders often fail to understand that what they did, others could do to them. In Africa, military dictators often pampered their officer corps and indulged their rank and file, while beefing up military intelligence to ensure that the bribes are working. Often they don't, and history is repeated, again and again, until a charismatic and able civilian politician could sometimes break out of the vicious circle. Numeiri was a long-term army professional, but he failed to concentrate on his army's concerns, despite all the shiny new weapons. Gradually, he became over-confident, boosted by a manic sense of divine mission, a common psychotic trait of leaders after a lengthy term in power.

Numeiri had paid careful attention to the security requirements in the south, but failed to appreciate that this perceived favouritism would fire up the ancient sense of grievance in the west. On 5 September 1975, elite paratrooper units, mostly disgruntled westerners, mounted a coup. They did the usual – arrested some senior loyal officers, and seized the broadcast facilities in Omdurman. They made the mistake of prematurely announcing the capture of Numeiri. But the president had, by chance – or divine providence, as he later put it – shifted his overnight location. Numeiri did not rally his loyal troops, but fled from Khartoum and hid in a friend's house in the capital's outer suburbs. Loyal troops, led by the tough chief of staff, General Muhammad al-Baghir, managed to crush the mutiny in a few hours. It was a small event in the crowded history of Sudanese coups, but it was significant because it helped to persuade an increasingly deranged Numeiri that he had a divine right to rule Sudan. It was then a short step to believing that he alone was destined to carry on the Prophet's mission on earth.

Another coup attempt against Numeiri

At 05.00 on 2 July 1976 a more concerted *coup de main* was planned. It was long customary in Sudan to greet incoming visitors at the airport, no matter what the hour. This was even more elaborately organized when a president returned. General Baghir and a whole posse of ministers were scheduled to greet Numeiri on his flight back from Europe. Numeiri, in another one of his imagined divine intercessions, arrived early and the entourage was dispersing when a wall of fire raked the runway outside the main airport reception. The president was bundled into a car into a hideaway and General Baghir swung into his coup-crushing operation again. But he had few forces in the capital. He needed to summon units from around the country, with the nearest being Shendi. Communications were down and he used the Sudan News Agency wire services. Troops poured into the three cities on the Friday and allowed loyalist troops to win the day. Surviving rebel soldiers were pursued into the desert and shot out of hand.

Despite its prompt destruction, this coup had been well planned. It might well have worked if Numeiri had arrived on time and been conveniently assassinated at the airport. The man behind the coup was Numeiri's old enemy, Sadiq al-Mahdi. He had formed the National Front in exile in Libya. Under its banner, al-Mahdi had assembled representatives of the traditional parties, all banned under Numeiri's rule. Colonel Gaddafi was a man with a small power base and big ideas, and he had lots of oil money to nourish his dreams of creating a regional empire, which included Sudan, with the first chunk being the occupation of Darfur. The highly volatile Libyan leader later planned to create a pan-African empire. But in the mid-1970s he was focusing on toppling Numeiri. The Sudanese president diagnosed Gaddafi as 'a split personality – both evil'. The Ethiopians connived in Libya's coup plans because Addis Ababa believed that the Eritrean insurgency would collapse without Khartoum's support. The Soviet Union was also in on the plot, disturbed by Numeiri's crackdown on communists, ejection of Soviet advisors and Khartoum's recent tilt to the West. Gaddafi had formed an Islamic Legion to implement his plans, but in his training camps in the southern Libyan desert he had also arranged the training of Sudanese, many of them traditional A*nsar* loyal to al-Mahdi. Some of the *Ansar* had already infiltrated the three cities and had stashed arms ready for the military component whose action at the airport would spark the coup. Some estimates suggest that 3,000 were killed in the brief but bitter putsch. Almost 100 rebels were subjected to show trials and promptly executed. Sadiq al-Mahdi was tried *in absentia* and sentenced to death.

The extent of popular support for the exiled politicians prompted Numeri to offer what was then called 'national reconciliation'. The president was a master manipulator and hoped to entice some exiles to return under a general amnesty, thus weakening the exiled forces. Some communists and *Ansar* returned, as did Sadiq al-Mahdi, who soon left the country, unconvinced of Numeiri's sincerity. Exiled leaders of the Muslim Brotherhood also came back. The most prominent was Hassan al-Turabi, whom Numeiri elevated to the position of attorney general. Al-Turabi set about re-forging the power base of the Brotherhood and revived the issue *of sharia* law being enforced throughout the country. Southerners believed this concept had been buried at the 1972 peace talks. Numeiri also preached national reconciliation to the disaffected regions in northern Sudan, including Darfur and the Nuba Mountains. He promised a degree of regional self-government comparable with the south, although the centrifugal pull of Khartoum – and especially the national economic plans – were to prove too strong for much regional assertion in the north.

Despite the apparent national reconciliation and vaunted northern regionalization, power was held not in the single ruling party, the Sudan Socialist Union, but increasingly in a palace cabal, headed by a certain Dr Bahauddin Muhammad Idris. Sacked from the University of Khartoum for allegedly leaking examination questions to a favoured female student, Dr Idris had somehow ingratiated himself into Numeiri's court. Idris became in effect the president's PA, and introduced him to some dubious characters, the most infamous being Adnan Khashoggi. The flamboyant arms dealer was born in Mecca in 1935 and educated in the US. Said to be the richest man in the world, he certainly owned the world's then largest yacht, which was featured in the James Bond movie *Never Say Never Again*. Khashoggi enjoyed extensive influence and contacts in the Middle East and America, despite his involvement in numerous scandals, most notably the Iran-Contra affair. Equally at home in austere Bedouin tents or in wild champagne- and starlet-fuelled parties in London, Washington and Monaco, his sophistication charmed Numeiri. The shrewd Saudi made millions, if not billions, out of schemes in Sudan that sounded grand, but didn't quite work or were not built. Many of the able technocrats whom Numeiri had originally set up to run petro-dollar projects were sidelined by the corrupt cabal inside the Palace.

The south: going backwards

The south was generally peaceful, although Juba was inevitably a hothouse of political infighting and even plans to return to war. Some military plotters were amnestied by Numeiri under the terms of the national reconciliation deals. The exiled opposition in Libya, and some who had returned to Khartoum, had also reached out to the southerners, in a pattern which was to repeat itself over the next three decades. Major General Lagu had kept some of his options open by talks with, and cash from, Sadiq al-Mahdi. In response Numeiri manoeuvred Lagu out of the army and into parliamentary life, as the southern president, thus removing his powerbase. A good soldier and a bad politician – as with nearly all the prominent soldier-statesmen in southern history – Lagu overpaid his favourites and helped to widen the Equatorian v Dinka rift, thus empowering Numeiri's game of divide and rule. In February 1980 Numeiri engineered the sacking of Lagu and the dissolution of the assembly. Abel Alier, much better at working with Khartoum, or a stooge to some southern radicals, returned as president. His mandate was to use some of the Arab petro-dollars to develop southern agriculture and oil projects. Despite his diplomacy, the returned southern president had a short tenure. A report by Alier condemning plans to re-divide the south was treated as a personal insult by Numeiri because it implied that he had been saved from his own cowardice when southern troops rescued him during the 1976 failed coup. Furious, the president simply dissolved the southern assembly and set up a transitional government led by a Muslim southern officer, General Gismallah Abdullah Rasas.

Numeiri's plans for re-dividing the south into powerful regions did appeal to many tribal groups who feared the domination of the populous, statuesque and warlike Dinka. Others saw it as an obvious divide-and-rule tactic by which Khartoum could re-impose Arabization. In December 1982 Numeiri toured the south and was met by unresponsive crowds, unlike his previous tours where he was hailed as a peacemaker. In particular, he was jeered at by hostile students at the well-known Rumbek secondary school. The famously thin-skinned president lost his temper, closed the school and later arrested politicians who opposed the plan to divide the south into three provinces. In June 1983 Numeiri suddenly announced on television that the south would be divided into three provinces: Bahr al-Ghazal, Equatoria and the Upper Nile, with three separate capitals at Wau, Juba and Malakal. This removed Juba as the central hotbed of dissident views and potential southern unity. He also set about Arabizing and Islamizing the south to unify Sudan. Numeiri had in effect torn up the Addis agreement.

In what was termed Republican Order Number One, a chilling Orwellian title, Khartoum set up three provinces with emasculated powers. The regional assembly in Juba was dead. Governors would be appointed by the president in Khartoum. Most of the previous local fiscal authority vanished. Arabic would be the main official language. The carefully balanced security arrangements in the south were also ditched and the newly integrated troops in the south would be sent on garrison duty in the north and west. Most of these proposals had been discussed secretly for some years among northern politicians in the national reconciliation process. Sadiq al-Mahdi and the Muslim Brotherhood were adamant that real northern agreement depended upon ending southern autonomy and Islamizing the whole constitution – north and south.

Numeiri had steamrollered all opposition previously and now expected southerners to submit meekly. But he had sown the dragons' teeth, not least by creating a cadre of experienced southern officers in his own army. They wanted freedom for the south and an end to Numeiri, not least for the betrayal of his promises. The inevitable result was the resumption of the southern war. This time the rebels were much better led and armed. Yet it would take two decades to force Khartoum to return to the negotiating table.

The Second War of Independence
Some of the integrated battalions of the First Division of the Southern Command went very reluctantly to garrisons in Darfur. The 105th Battalion at Bor refused to go. The integration process into the new SPAF – the Sudan People's Armed Forces – had produced patchy results. Some southerners felt that their training had not brought them up to the standards of the more experienced professional army. This would be true, however, of any integration of irregulars with professionals, as the Zimbabwean and South African experiences were later to demonstrate. A small minority of officers had been carefully selected and trained in the northern military colleges, but it was a maximum of 13.5 per cent, not the 33 per cent agreed at Addis. The intrinsic military grievances and general anger at Khartoum's cavalier treatment of the Addis deal came to a head in May 1983. The 105th Battalion at Bor, the Jonglei state capital, was already on the point of mutiny. The mood was exacerbated by late pay and food shortages. The Dinka major in command, Kerubino Kuanyin Bol, refused to allow a steamer carrying a company of northern troops to land at the dock in Bor. A week later northern troops from the Armoured Division returned to storm the town. The Bor garrison retreated into the bush, as did troops in Pibor. They and other garrisons crossed into Ethiopia with their weapons.

The Bor mutiny and the Republican Order Number One a month later marked the onset of the new war. Thousands of southern troops retreated to Ethiopia while others further west created camps in isolated bush. Some of the hold-outs in Anya-Nya, who had rejected the Addis agreement, now linked up with the defectors from the integrated army. Most of the new dissidents congregated in the Gambella region of Ethiopia. Besides mutineers from the regular army and Anya-Nya diehards, a third element, the Students Revolutionary Group, led by Pagan Amum Okiech, joined them. Okiech was later to become secretary general of the Sudan People's Liberation Movement (SPLM).

Who would lead the new southern rebellion? Numeiri had deliberately siphoned off some of the brightest and best of southern officers to promote them into loyalty in the integrated army. The president had specifically intended to use Colonel John Garang, a Twic Dinka, to defuse the Bor mutiny. Unfortunately for Khartoum, Garang was party to the mutiny he was supposed to suppress. If Sadiq al-Mahdi was Numeiri's political nemesis, John Garang became his prime military enemy. The difference was that Garang was by far the most decisive, ruthless and, ultimately, most successful opponent.

Garang was born into a poor family in 1945 in Twic East in Jonglei state. Orphaned at ten, a kindly uncle ensured the studious young man a good secondary education, first in South Sudan and then in Tanzania. He later secured a scholarship in the US at Grinella College in Iowa, and was then offered a further scholarship at the University of California, Berkeley, but decided to return to the University of Dar Es Salaam. While in America he is said to have been impressed by the success of the melting pot of US society and this helped to secure his belief in a united – democratic and non-racial – Sudan. For his later doctorate he studied the ill-fated Jonglei Canal, first proposed by the British in 1907 and finally begun in 1978. By the outbreak of the second southern war, two-thirds of the 223-mile canal had been built. Today one of the giant German earth-moving machines lies rusting as a symbol of one of the biggest development projects killed off by the war.

After his initial studies, Garang made a second, successful, attempt to join the southern rebels six months before the Addis agreement. The first time he had been judged too young to fight. Quickly promoted because of his education, some of the seasoned Anya-Nya commanders resented his lack of battlefield experience. This is what attracted his northern commanders in the new post-Addis army. He rapidly rose from captain to colonel, and was sent on both civilian scholarships in America and training at the US Army's advanced infantry training school at Fort Benning, Georgia. He also lectured in agriculture in Khartoum University, clearly a man of many parts. Garang had become the best educated and trained southerner in the army, and had kept out of the political intrigues in Sudan, or so the northern generals thought.

A month before the Bor mutiny, Colonel Garang was planning the new war and drew up a programme for the formation of the Sudan People's

Liberation Movement. Garang joined his fellow defectors in Ethiopia and set about forming the armed wing of his new SPLM – the SPLA, the Sudan People's Liberation Army. New defectors and hardline existing rebels soon swelled the ranks of the initial 3,000 mutineers. Some commanders still resented Garang's lack of bushfighting skills and were jealous of his education and rapid promotion, courtesy of Khartoum. Nevertheless, his obvious leadership skills won the day, and the question of Sudanese unity versus southern independence was glossed over in the interests of establishing the SPLM, but above all defeating the great betrayer in Khartoum: Numeiri. Moreover, the vital sanctuaries in Ethiopia dictated a diplomatic silence on the question of secession. Under the old emperor and the dour communist leader, Mengistu Haile Mariam, who replaced the Emperor in 1974, the northern Sudanese support for Eritrean secession had made southern secession an awkward subject.

Garang wrote the new SPLM manifesto himself, and it was personally approved by the great Afro-Stalinist, Mengistu. It was radical, clichéd and anti-separatist, to match the dictates of the OAU as well as the Derg. In Garang's manifesto, and the accompanying penal code, it was clear that the army, not the people, was the fundamental source of authority. Garang later toned down the broadcasts on the SPLM radio – gone were the Marxist rants of the initial manifesto. An inclusive, democratic and secular 'New Sudan' would appeal to some northerners. Garang also toned down anti-Muslim rhetoric, although the propaganda was often anti-Arab. He wanted to reach the African Muslims in Darfur and the Nuba Mountains who formed a large part of the northern regular army. Garang, a good strategist, also could not ignore potential backers in the US, although Washington's later support was predicated on the principle of southern independence to weaken the Islamist regime in Khartoum.

Remnants of the old rebel groups, renamed Anya-Nya 2, still resisted inclusion in the SPLA. Some of the resistance also came from Nuer groups, which the northern army started arming to disrupt SPLA supply lines into Ethiopia. In Equatoria, militias also supported Khartoum in operations against what many Equatorians dubbed the 'Dinka army', the SPLA. In May 1984 the Derg had encouraged Garang to order the assassination of the leader of Anya-Nya 2, Gai Tut. Paulino Matip then led the Anya-Nya survivors to western Upper Nile where he did a deal with Numeiri. Salva Kiir, an internal critic of Garang, often said that the first bullets of the SPLA were used to kill separatists. Kiir never broke with his boss; Lam Akol did – on a number of occasions. Akol claimed that from 1984 to 1989 more

SPLA were killed by rival southern militias than in fighting between the SPLA and the northern army.[2]

The first SPLA attacks launched from Ethiopia in 1983 were directed against the Nasir area inside Sudan. Eventually Garang established a permanent base in eastern Equatoria on the Boma Plateau near the Ethiopian border. The SPLA sometimes allied with other Anya-Nya 2 Nuer to hit the Chevron oil sites near Bentiu, in the Nuer heartland. Khartoum had promised the Americans the army was more than capable of defending the oil installations. Three foreign oil workers were killed and a small number injured in a rebel raid on 3 February 1984. Chevron, dissatisfied with Khartoum's response, pulled out of the oilfield. The US would later impose sanctions on US oil exploration, but the original Chevron concession proved to be the heart of the Sudanese oil bonanza, which benefited the Chinese and Malaysians (and a few Sudanese). The SPLA had previously captured seven French workers on the Jonglei Canal project. Garang had a personal animus about the canal, but attacks on the few big economic projects in the south, while admittedly embarrassing Khartoum, were bound to undermine economic development in a south that had precious little infrastructure or employment. In the next two decades of fighting, it was often hard to make economic sense of the north-south attrition, and even less when fighting spread to the east and west of the massive but fragile country.

Numeiri's endgame

Throughout most of his military career Numeiri had been a conventionally observant Muslim, not distinguished by Islamic zeal. In fact, the whisky-drinking and cigar-chomping leader had publicly preached a secular state and often cracked down on the Brotherhood. Gradually, he moved towards a more exaggerated belief in his personal Islamist mission. He interpreted his escape from a number of coups and assassinations as divine intervention. He also believed he had survived various heart operations as a sign of Allah's munificence (though cynics whispered that it had more to do with the quality of his American doctors and their hospitals). He started pronouncing on religious matters and published a book in 1980 on spiritual reform. He enacted secret Brotherhood plans, devised by al-Turabi, by announcing in September 1983 that *sharia* law would apply in all of Sudan, including the south. Many southerners regarded the September Laws as a declaration of war, although the rural *nas* (ordinary people) in the north welcomed the harsh laws that would clear out what they perceived as the fleshpots in Khartoum. Numeiri finally declared himself a religious leader with the title of Imam.

The *hudud* punishments such as amputations for theft and stoning for adultery were not only enforced, but publicized. Ministers were compelled to attend public executions and amputations. Even the hard-line attorney general, Hassan al-Turabi, fainted at the sight of his first amputation. Radio and television reported the punishments in gruesome detail. Conservative northerners may have had some sympathy with the crackdown on law and order and would tell foreigners that *sharia* meant that the city streets were the safest in Africa, which was probably true. The law-and-order argument was a little undermined by Numeiri's release of over 10,000 common criminals from Khartoum's Kober Prison. The president claimed that he had acted mercifully in the same manner as the Prophet, who had forgiven the people of Mecca. That unsubtle comparison between himself and Mohammed was enough to make ardent members of the Brotherhood a little concerned about their president's mental state. They wondered if absolute power or illness had turned his brain or whether he was genuinely a late convert to radical Islamism. Many ordinary Sudanese were suffering acutely from the decline in the economy. Now they could not seek psychic balm in their traditional beer. Early travellers in Sudan always marvelled at the joyous and copious rural consumption of vast quantities of traditional *marissa* alcohol, even in religious heartlands such as Darfur. And if they could enjoy Western spirits, they would usually extol its medicinal value. Whisky became the favourite of many middle-class professionals in the capital. Now thousands of gallons of best Scotch were poured into the Nile (prompting lots of local jokes about drunken fish) or crushed by bulldozers; all the stunts were heavily publicized. Whether the politicians and civil servants could now make better decisions while being continuously stone-cold sober was yet to be proven. The well-to-do kept their whisky hidden even more carefully and were much more selective about very good friends with whom they could share their Western 'medicine'.

Numeiri started indulging in long religious rants on the radio, blaming everyone but himself for the economic meltdown. He attacked 'profiteers' in foul-mouthed tirades which conservative Sudanese radio listeners were not used to hearing from an imam. He continued to compare himself with the Prophet so that accusations of heresy and insanity grew apace. Any opposition was crushed, martial law and states of emergency were imposed and emergency courts handed out fines and floggings as well as executions and amputations.

The reign of terror reached a height with the execution of Mahmud Muhammad Taha, the leader of a small mild-mannered group called the

Republican Brothers. There were also Sisters, because Taha advocated women's equality as well as religious reforms based on his *Sufi* ideals. Most people in the three towns treated the Brothers' polite distribution of leaflets advocating peaceful co-existence, not just between north and south but with the Israelis, with tolerance and occasional amusement. But they were never seen as any kind of threat. It is true that Taha had been accused of religious sedition as far back as the 1960s, but in the 1980s and aged 76 he was generally considered as a gentle intellectual with odd views. Taha published an innocuous leaflet in December 1984 that criticized the imposition of *sharia* law in the south and called for the return of civil liberties throughout the country. Numeiri decided to make an example of Taha. He and four of his followers were rapidly convicted of apostasy. By this stage the president appeared to believe he had a hot line to God, and promptly hanged Taha, while allowing his four followers to recant, and live. Taha's body was dumped in the desert and a traditional burial was denied.

The Muslim Brotherhood had grown much stronger under Numeiri's religious mania, mainly because of Hassan al-Turabi's organizational genius, though it was a tragedy that his legal training and position as attorney general did not restrain the presidential reign of injustice and terror. In fact, Numeiri's perversion of Islam had caused grave disquiet among the Brothers, but al-Turabi had enforced a rigid discipline upon them. The time was not yet right to strike, they were told. Slowly, they built up their influence – modelled on Leninist cells – in the professions, schools and universities, but above all in the army. They also constructed an extensive financial network in the Gulf and among Sudanese in exile. Wealthy Sudanese businessmen abroad could now believe that they could serve Allah and their commercial interests, not least via the new Islamic banks.

Despite banking reforms, the Sudanese economy continued to deteriorate and ensuing government austerity led to strikes. A railway strike was called treasonable and Numeiri's inevitable response was to deploy the army to crush the industrial action. It was more difficult to send in the army to stamp out strikes by judges, doctors, engineers and university professors. Foreign debt mounted and debt servicing became unmanageable. Inflation soared. World Bank measures led inevitably to cuts in subsidies to basic commodities. Nature intervened as the world became aware of the 'biblical' famine in Ethiopia in 1984, but less was made internationally of the drought in Sudan, especially Darfur. Tens of thousands of starving westerners descended on the three towns to live in shanty towns, in defiance of the army trucking back desperate people to Darfur. By 1985 tens of thousands of

Darfuris had perished of starvation. Western charities went in to help, but also pointed out that the big mechanized farms along the Nile were harvesting grain, but not sending it to Darfur. Numeiri seemed unmoved by the drought and famine in his own land.

Numeiri had garlanded himself with extra titles from field marshal to Supreme Commander to Imam, and he was both prime minister and president. He had restarted the war in the south and bankrupted the economy, while alienating nearly all his erstwhile political and religious supporters. Only the ever-patient Muslim Brotherhood, burrowing deeply into all strata of society, remained as his ally. In March 1985 he finally turned on them and blamed the Brothers for all the country's woes. Hassan al-Turabi and other prominent Brothers were arrested for religious plotting. Hundreds of rank-and-file Brothers were also incarcerated. Numeiri installed another layer of kangaroo courts that meted out even more public floggings, amputations and executions.

By April 1985 Numeiri seemed unaware of the seething state of the nation. He flew off to Washington to see his doctors and to beg for more loans from the World Bank and the USA. He would not have left the country if he had had the wit to realize how fragile his position was. A general strike on 4 April 1985 paralyzed the capital. The president had just one remaining ally, the army, but many senior officers were sickened by the abasement of Sudanese society. The minister of defence, Major General Abdel Rahman Swar al-Dahab, announced on national radio that the army would respect the people's wishes and depose the president, but they would stay in power for the time being. Numeiri tried to fly back to Khartoum. His plane was diverted to Cairo, however. His military friend, President Hosni Mubarak, provided him with a luxurious villa in a plush suburb where he stayed for the next fourteen years. Sudanese took to the streets to rejoice at the fall of the military dictator, as they had done before in 1964. History was repeating itself again, as farce. Or perhaps they had short memories, for when Numeiri returned to Sudan, in May 1999, he received a rapturous welcome. The next year he ran again for president against the incumbent, Omar al-Bashir, but secured less than ten per cent of the poll. 'The people still love me, but the polls were rigged,' he must have told himself.

The military were in power once more; they had simply changed generals as head of state. They had already tried two rounds of rule by generalissimo and the politicians had essayed two periods of chaotic civilian governance. And the southern war was raging. So what next? Major General al-Dahab did try to bring in civilians. They met at the staff club of the University of

Khartoum to sort out a joint front for the new regime. They called themselves the 'modern forces', but regressed to ancient feuds. The military, traditionally suspicious of indecisive politicians, moved quickly to set up their own Transitional Military Council. It was made up of different factions, as ever, but the council consisted mainly off senior officers in command of elite units that could rapidly control the three towns, if necessary. The Military Council governed by a state of emergency, but the generals did release many political prisoners in Numeiri's jails. They also hollowed out a traditional enemy, the hated state security service. A few prominent cronies of the ousted president were put on trial. One proved embarrassing for important intelligence links: Vice President Omar Muhammad al-Tayib, who had run the state security organization. The details of his televised show trial annoyed the Central Intelligence Agency and Mossad because al-Tayib had been a central player in Operation MOSES. Organized from the US embassy in Khartoum, nearly 8,000 Falasha Jews were airlifted from Sudanese camps, where they had fled persecution and famine in Ethiopia. The Israelis uncharacteristically leaked the semi-covert operation in January 1985.This prompted Arab states to influence Sudan to stop the mercy mission. Later, two other CIA/Mossad operations (JOSHUA and SOLOMON) rescued the thousands of remaining Falasha still trapped in the Horn. Al-Tayib had reputedly been paid a few million US dollars to assist his foreign intelligence friends. That might have covered his massive court fine, but not his sentence of life imprisonment.

The Military Council ruled in conjunction with a toothless provisional council of ministers, which included some southerners, but not John Garang who refused to travel to Khartoum. He correctly assessed the situation as 'Numeirism without Numeiri'. The civilians and military occasionally met together to discuss the possibility of a new constitution, *sharia* law and southern autonomy. Unsurprisingly, no resolution was achieved, not least because the interim leaders knew that a new election was to be held. It was easier for any politician to pass the buck and postpone such troublesome decisions.

Getting the balance right between keeping the men in uniform well paid and well-fed but apolitical has often been tricky in African and Middle Eastern armies. Numeiri had managed to demoralize his entire army and starve them of resources in the last years of his regime. With the onset of the renewed southern offensive by the SPLA, the regular army of around 60,000 had been reduced to a defensive strategy of trying to hold and re-supply garrisons in the main southern towns. The SPLA boasted perhaps as many as 10,000 trained full-time insurgents, with perhaps double that number either in training or in part-time militia roles. The collapse of the hated Numeiri regime had been a big boost to the SPLM. Although some southerners took part in the transitional government in Khartoum, the fact that Garang remained aloof burnished his credentials in the south. It also made him more important for Khartoum to court him, as the shift in the military balance of power in the south suggested that a political deal was required. Secret meetings were held in Ethiopia at the start of 1986. But talk of a government of national unity inevitably foundered on hard-line attitudes among the political parties, especially the Brotherhood. And some senior army officers were not inclined to rescind Numeiri's policy on *sharia* law. The war still had a long time to run before attrition encouraged northern compromise.

Return to civilian rule, once again
One positive sign was a promise kept by Major General al-Dahab, the transitional supremo. He agreed to put the clock back to the electoral system of the 1960s. And the same disunited coalition resulted, although the Brotherhood's front party, the NIF, did unexpectedly well. Their underground planning had paid off, although they were still biding their time before trying to seize power. Despite the security situation in the south, some electioneering took place there, often in the urban areas, but the southern parties had little influence in the revived assembly in Khartoum. The new government was headed by Sadiq al-Mahdi, the long-term leader of the Umma party, which had taken ninety-nine seats.

Al-Mahdi returned as prime minister in May 1986. He faced the same hoary problems – except most of them had got much worse, especially the war. He headed another coalition, but desperate optimists believed that he was the civilian leader who could finally lead Sudan to the promised land. After all, he was a highly educated Oxbridge man who also had spiritual clout as the descendant of the Mahdi, and the religious head of the *Ansar*, as well as boss of the Umma party. Therefore, as a politician and imam, he had the religious authority and intellect to curb the excesses of the Islamic fundamentalists, led by Hassan al-Turabi, who did not join al-Mahdi's coalition. Moreover, since al-Turabi was his brother-in-law, perhaps the family connection might ease relations with the Brotherhood. Yet much of the political infighting in Sudan's elite had long been within family relationships, so kinship was probably the least persuasive element in the optimism. Al-Madhi's previous tenure as premier, twenty years before, had been brief. Now, matured by exile, a death sentence (in absentia) and numerous political battles, he had the chance to prove his worth. He started well with visionary speeches about ending the hated September Laws that would be a precursor to a southern peace deal. He would be a peacemaker, but as reinsurance he promised also to reform and re-equip an army that was taking a real pasting from the SPLA. Of the economic collapse, he said little, though many hoped that peace would bring its own financial dividends.

Except for refurbishing al-Mahdi family properties and lands seized under Numeiri, the premier showed little energy after his first bout of speechifying. He seemed incapable of acting on his declared vision. His three years in power were marked above all by indecision. As the war worsened, northerners became embroiled in the everlasting crisis of Arab identity versus pan-Sudan unity. The influx of foreign Islamists added to this renewed sense of Arabism, as did increased support from Iraq, Saudi Arabia and Jordan, and even Libya; Gaddafi was always keen to promote his version of Pan-Arabism, especially now that his former protégé, al-Mahdi, was in power.

The kaleidoscope of changing political alliances – most of them based on pettiness not principles – defies concise description. Perhaps the most perplexing was al-Madhi's decision to appoint his brother-in-law as attorney general once more, to reform the September Laws that al-Turabi had originally devised for Numeiri. Since the Brothers had made it clear that there could be 'no replacement for Allah's laws', little reform could be expected. More promising were the sporadic talks in Addis with the SPLM and, in November 1988, a temporary ceasefire was agreed – one of many in the north-south saga. Divisions over a deal with the SPLM helped to split the al-Mahdi-led coalition. In February 1989 al-Mahdi managed to patch together another coalition, this time with his brother-in-law, finally bringing in the National Islamic Front. Senior officers in the army, including the minister of defence, resigned, partly because the NIF was hostile to a peace deal. Al-Turabi was promoted to deputy prime minister and minister of foreign affairs. Other Brothers in the NIF took over key security portfolios such as the ministry of the interior. Behind the scenes they also built up their financial interests in the Islamic banking system. In 1983 the Al-Shamal Islamic bank had been set up in Khartoum; this had close links with the Saudi investments in the Faisal Islamic Bank of Sudan. The Brotherhood was inching towards supreme power. The work was not yet complete, however, not least in the number and strength of Muslim Brotherhood cells in the army. The commander of the army and 150 senior officers sent a written ultimatum to the prime minister that he should form a national government to deal with the SPLM and reverse the plummeting economic decline. Nearly all the political parties (except the NIF) and many professional bodies and unions signed a 'National Declaration of Peace'. They wanted a national unity government, but – as ever – unity was *the* elusive Sudanese ingredient.

Sadiq's war

Sadiq al-Mahdi was failing on all fronts. Since the start of his administration he had been committed to resolving the southern crisis. He spent a whole day talking to John Garang at the OAU summit in Addis in July 1986, although their long discussion was not fruitful. Nevertheless, a bigger north-south dialogue took place in the following month, based on the Koka Dam Agreement of the previous March. This seemed to be producing results, but then in August 1986 a Shilluk SPLA unit deployed a shoulder-launched SAM-7 to shoot down a Sudan Airways Fokker Friendship on a scheduled domestic flight from Khartoum to Malakal, killing all the sixty passengers and crew on board. Al-Madhi was given intercepted SPLA signals information that the Shilluk commander had gloated about the shooting. The prime minister publicly decried the SPLA as terrorists and sent militias in the pay of the north to destroy a wide swathe of Shilluk villages. This was almost a replay of what happened in Rhodesia in 1978. A SAM-7 was fired at a civilian Viscount aircraft flying on a scheduled flight from the holiday resort of Kariba to the capital, Salisbury. The leader of the insurgents responsible, Joshua Nkomo, was perceived to have laughed in a radio interview about the incident. The Rhodesian prime minister, Ian Smith, broke off promising secret peace talks with Nkomo, calling him a terrorist. Instead Smith ordered a series of reprisal raids on Nkomo's bases around Lusaka, Zambia. In both cases a shoulder-launched Russian Strela missile ended possible peace talks in the two African states.

When al-Mahdi came to power his influence in the professional army was weak. The rival *Khatmiyya* sect was stronger among the officer corps and the Muslim Brotherhood had already made many inroads; hence his tendency to rely on surrogate forces, especially the pro-*Ansar* militias. The militia strategy was not new, though it was accelerated under al-Mahdi. Over three years the alternative strategy not only failed, but caused numerous human rights' abuses and it alienated the regular army.

More immediately, Garang's advance was partially thwarted by Khartoum's use of southern tribal militias and Anya-Nya 2 holdouts who had been fighting the SPLA, partially because of lingering feuds or intrinsic ethnic differences. A new guerrilla 'hearts and mind' campaign began to have some success, especially as the SPLA's more disciplined units looted from the villages far less. More and more peasants could see that the insurgents were confining the northern army to the towns and thus the peasantry were less harassed by the army. And, then in a virtuous cycle, the army's reprisal raids on villages accused of supporting guerrillas played into SPLA hands. Meanwhile, Khartoum had to try to administer the south. A Council of the South failed to organize aid for the mass of refugees, often sick and starving, in the garrison towns held by the army.

Although Khartoum's propaganda described the SPLA as mere pawns of their Ethiopian hosts and Cuban instructors, a new patriotism began to infuse the southern rebellion. More and more volunteers poured into the insurgent training camps, including youngsters. The 'child-soldiers', who were plentiful, played into northern propaganda, while disturbing genteel supporters in the liberal salons in Europe and America. Training, weaponry and discipline improved as did morale as the guerrillas scored more and more victories against a zombie-like administration in Khartoum.   In November 1987 the guerrillas captured the small town of Kurmuk, near the Ethiopian border. It was over 450 miles from the capital, but the nearby dam provided most of Khartoum's electricity. For its own short-term ends the government encouraged a panic in the three towns and urged the citizenry to arm themselves against a barbarian invasion. The army soon recaptured Kurmuk, but Sadiq al-Mahdi had shot himself in the foot in propaganda terms. Khartoum was not threatened by a minor temporary tactical guerrilla success on the Ethiopian border, adjacent to their sanctuaries, but the panic had brought home to northerners how nervous the government was about containing the southern advance.

Khartoum faced more serious reverses when the SPLA captured and held towns such as Pibor and Jokau. Assaults were also made against crucial economic targets, such as Bentiu's oil installations, and then the oil depot at Malakal airport was blown up. The northern army was on its knees and the prime minster resorted to a large-scale deployment of the *murahiliin*, for example the deployment of Arab militias in the Bahr al-Ghazal region. The breakdown of civilian administration and the spread of famine and drought had created a restless, and reckless, army of young unemployed and leaderless men. For generations, the Baqqara coalition of Arab tribes (including the Rezeigat and the Missiriya) had fought the southern Dinka tribes, including the Twic, Malwal and Ngok, over grazing rights and water.

The contest was often vicious and usually equally balanced; periods of 'blooding' of tribal youths were often interrupted by agreements between headmen and chiefs. Sometimes the central government had interceded via the army and police. The ancient disputes had often been settled by elders who knew the customary law and rights. Then the economic collapse of the Numeiri years was accompanied by the spread of drought from Darfur and Kordofan down into the Bahr al-Ghazal by the mid-1980s. With the traditional cattle wealth often devastated by drought, the government now handed out automatic weapons to angry and desperate Baqqara militias. Many Dinka had been driven north by the southern war and famine. It was not just a case of pushing south over the unmarked border, militias started to drive out settled Dinka communities in the north. In March 1987 thousands of Dinka were massacred in Darfur after Rezeigat militia attacked a Dinka church at Ed Daein, in east Darfur, where the militia had wrongly been informed that solar panels on the church were 'secret SPLA communication devices'. Hundreds of Dinka were then put by police on a train bound for Nyala, but it was intercepted and burned by Arab militiamen. Khartoum denied any such massacres had taken place, the first of many such denials about tragedies in Darfur.

Massive cattle rustling raids then ensued in Bahr al-Ghazal. Thousands of Dinka sought SPLA protection, as guerrilla units moved north into Kordofan to retrieve some of the cattle and punish joint army and militia units. Khartoum's answer was to release bigger arsenals of weapons to the Baqqara to repel SPLA advances in early 1987. The SPLA pushed deeper into the north, nonetheless. The so-called Volcano battalion occupied parts of the Nuba Mountains. In Wau, the capital of western Bahr al-Ghazal, the government forces struggled on to hold their besieged garrison. Some of the government-supplied militia units came over to the SPLA. Khartoum rushed in extra money, supplies and weapons to keep them loyal. The Bul Nuer militia's loyalty was crucial, for example, in the defence of the Bentiu oilfields.

The SPLA's successes were partly the result of disciplined command and control, which came at a price. Garang was criticized for a Stalinist style of leadership. Even his old comrade, now a major general, Kerubino Kuanyin Bol, with whom Garang had plotted the Bor mutiny which began the second war, was arrested and imprisoned. The SPLA did not have it all its own way. It was caught off-balance by an unusually successful spring 1988 offensive by the army. Several large SPLA units were destroyed in the Upper Nile and, then farther south, the army recaptured the symbolic town of Torit. To augment its unexpectedly successful counter-offensive in the deep south, Sadiq al-Mahdi decided to again unleash his Arab militias in the border areas against the Dinka. No quarter was given – the men were killed and women raped and sometimes the children were enslaved as servants or labourers for the Missiriya nomadic Arab tribes. Schools and clinics were put to the torch and wells polluted with the dead bodies. This form of tribal blitzkrieg set the pattern for the future so-called *Janjaweed* raids in Darfur after 2003. The militias' rapacity of the late 1980s across the southern border was often so shocking that the regular army on occasion took action against them, to protect the Dinka and in the Nuba Mountains, even though the militias were acting under the (very loose) direction of Khartoum.

War, famine, drought and now rinderpest were laying waste the south. Tens of thousands starved, even in the besieged army garrison towns; the SPLA mined roads and blew up bridges to use food as a weapon of war. Two million southerners took refuge in the north, many around Khartoum. Apologists for Khartoum tried to argue that the government did not practise 'genocide' against the southerners (although that definition might have applied to militia raids on the Dinka) because southerners fled *towards* the capital, unlike the German Jews who ran away *from* the Nazi capital of Berlin. It was not an entirely convincing argument, not least for the tens of thousands who sought refuge in Ethiopia or in the camps in Uganda and Kenya. In late 1988 the drought was broken by unusually heavy rains. Around the three towns, over 100,000 homes were inundated and that meant that the insufficient aid for the south was redirected for reconstruction in the north. November 1988 also brought another, temporary, ceasefire.

In the beginning of 1989 a fresh SPLA offensive took the important Upper Nile town of Nasir, after heavy fighting. In February the politically significant town of Torit was recaptured by the rebels. More and more southern towns fell in March and April. Over the border in the Nuba Mountains, the SPLA overwhelmed combined army and militia units. The SPLA now controlled large swathes of the south, waiting for the remaining government garrisons to fall like ripe plums. Juba was under siege, relieved only by air. But the carcasses of cargo planes that littered the end of the runway suggested that the capital too could fall. The northern militia raids dwindled as they now were more inclined to hug army bases for protection. By the summer of 1989 the Sudanese army was on its knees. The SPLA, under the tyrannical but highly effective leadership of John Garang, was clearly in the ascendancy. Garang now toured Washington and London as a conquering hero, while Sadiq al-Mahdi appeared to be cowering in

Khartoum. He was clearly losing on the battlefield. Would his Arab allies come to his rescue?

At the start of his period in power, al-Mahdi had to pay back his IOUs to Gaddafi. Libyan dissidents in Khartoum were rounded up and sent to Tripoli to an unpleasant welcome home. Gaddafi had the oil money and manic propensity of backing nearly every horse in every race — he financed, for example, nearly all the different sides in Chad's endless civil war, often at same time. At one stage, under Numeiri's rule, Gaddafi had been sending money and arms to John Garang. That stopped, but in return Gaddafi wanted a free hand in Darfur, which he planned to absorb into his domain. Sadiq al-Mahdi could never publicly agree to that and also remain in power, so typically he prevaricated and turned a blind eye to Libyan meddling in Darfur. The Islamic Legion and Baqqara militias, armed and funded by Gaddafi, swaggered around Darfur's few urban areas. Gaddafi was more concerned with operations across the border into Chad. When some of Gaddafi's proxy forces were defeated in Chad, they flooded into Darfur. In the Kufra oasis, Gaddafi trained his legion and various bands of pan-Arabic mercenaries. The indigenous Fur peoples formed their own army to fight back against the Arab nomadic militias and their Libyan allies. The Fur across the border in Chad supplied their tribal brethren with arms to defend themselves. The Rezeigat militias soon entered the fray in what became known as 'the war of tribes'. Sadiq al-Mahdi supported his old tribal allies from the days of the Mahdi; in fact some of the tribal conflicts went back as far as a century *before* the Mahdi. The Fur insurgents were crushed. Khartoum was too distracted to think about another region that was embroiled in internal war, stirred up by Libya and Chad. The chaos was to cause an even bigger war – internationalized by the media and US film stars – after 2003.

Relations were as fraught in the east as they were in the west, although Sudanese politicians, north and south, used to meet in Addis Ababa; often under the umbrella of the OAU. The Mengistu regime regarded al-Mahdi's government as weak as well as hostile. Al-Mahdi often castigated the Ethiopians for arming and hosting the SPLA, in their ambition to spread a communist government to the south, and even to the whole of Sudan. When southern forces crossed from Ethiopia to capture Kurmuk, all-out war between the two states loomed. Khartoum was aiding its allies, the Eritreans and Tigrayans, in their war with Mengistu's regime, while Mengistu's sinister Derg apparatus succoured its ally, the SPLM. The secessionist wars in Ethiopia were reaching a peak, which complicated calculations in the whole region. The SPLM was officially committed to Sudanese unity at this stage and opposed Eritrean war aims. Khartoum provided political support and asylum for the exiles of the anti-Mengistu wars, but they could not match the supply of weapons and instructors that the SPLA received from Addis. The SPLA had other sources of supply and many of their operations were far removed from their Ethiopian sanctuaries, but the Mengistu connection was still very valuable.

So where was al-Mahdi to turn? Saudi Arabia had been open-handed with oil credits and loans. The Gulf states were generous too after the fall of Numeiri. The Americans were lukewarm. Washington had been annoyed by Khartoum's disclosures of CIA entanglements in Operation MOSES during the long-running al-Tayib trial. Moreover, US embassy officials in Khartoum had recently been attacked by Palestinian radicals; in 1973 the US ambassador had been assassinated in Khartoum by Yasser Arafat's men. The American embassy was drastically reduced in size and, although al-Mahdi visited Washington during his premiership, the US remained distant. The Saudis were still helpful, but Khartoum needed US and World Bank money to save the economy. Adnan Khashoggi's dodgy deals had been cancelled and Khartoum also backtracked on a West German industrialist who was going to pay to dump nuclear waste in the northern desert. The war in the south was costing perhaps as much as $2 million per day and the debts on massive new loans from the Saudis and the Gulf, as well as longstanding loans to Moscow for weapons, could not be serviced. Soap and bread were often in short supply as was electricity. Inflation was around 80 per cent per annum. Strikes and protests were almost daily crises. Food shortages were becoming critical especially in the south. In April 1989 Operation LIFELINE SUDAN was set up. This was an agreement between Khartoum, the SPLA, UN and NGOs to co-ordinate (sometimes) to supply food and medical aid to the separate areas controlled by the government and rebels. This was possibly the world's first humanitarian programme to assist civilians on both sides of a civil war in a sovereign state. It caused a shift from the tactic of using starvation for military purposes, although most of the southern aid was purloined by the SPLA. The OLS saved many tens of thousands of lives, but such extensive foreign feeding programmes for north as well as the south also indicated the extent of the administrative collapse of the country.

What of the oldest ally, Egypt? Cairo adamantly refused to extradite Numeiri when the new government requested it in 1986. Field Marshal Hosni Mubarak would not consider giving up Field Marshal Numeiri, least of all to a man who was the living embodiment of the old Mahdist threat to Egypt. Then al-Mahdi compounded Sudan-Egyptian tensions by promoting al-Turabi to be deputy prime minister and, worse, foreign minister to deal with Cairo. Mubarak hated the Brotherhood and al-Turabi was its leading light in Khartoum. The government also had poor relations with the Gulf states, where al-Mahdi's rival sect, the *Khatmiyya,* had entrenched religious ties. Except for the Saudis and Iraq, Sadiq al-Mahdi had managed to fall out with all his neighbours and to antagonize nearly all domestic power-brokers in the north, while waging a full-scale, and losing, war in the south. Some record, not least for a man who entered power as a purported peacemaker to inspire national salvation. The disaster was partly of his own making, but he had a devil on his shoulder, his own brother-in-law. It was al-Turabi's plan to reap the revolutionary whirlwind and to use it to blow away what he perceived as the chaff in Khartoum.

Egypt would not save Sadiq. On the contrary, it was rumoured in spring 1989 that the Egyptian army would restore Numeiri. The head of Egyptian military intelligence confessed: 'One day we will have to go back and re-conquer that country because these people are such a mess and they are incapable of governing themselves.'[3]

Things were so bad that the parliamentarians in the Constituent Assembly finally took notice. They demanded the prime minister's resignation; before he did resign he should end the state of emergency and freeze the September Laws he had promised to repeal right at the start of his premiership, but somehow never got around to doing. In June al-Mahdi called for a permanent ceasefire in the south and he initialled the suspension of the September Laws, to be endorsed by the assembly later. Desperate for a political breakthrough, al-Mahdi had reluctantly agreed, some months before, to a peace conference with the southern rebels. It was due to take place at the end of June 1989. It didn't happen. In some interpretations, the army and the NIF decided on a bold pre-emptive move to prevent what they saw as a possible surrender to the south.

History repeated itself once more. On the night of 30 June 1989, the army — led by Brigadier Omar al-Bashir — swept away the house of cards that Sadiq al-Mahdi had erected. The Brotherhood and the National Islamic Front were hovering in the wings. How was the latest round of the military versus the now-dominant Islamists going to play out? Would it be a repeat of the Egyptian experience? It all depended on the new military leader, the one who had led the revolt. He seemed to have come from nowhere.

Chapter 4

The Makings of a President

Who was this man who suddenly burst on to the national and international stage in the 1989 coup? Where did he come from? What made him tick?

Omar Hassan Ahmed al-Bashir was born on 1 January 1944 into humble farming stock in Hosh Bannaga, 100 miles north of Khartoum. The village is located on the outskirts of Shendi, on the east bank of the Nile, in the River Nile state. Shendi was once the main marketplace of the country before Khartoum existed, and it was also the centre of the slave trade. The town is about thirty miles south-west of Meroë, the capital of the ancient Kushite kingdom. Here you can walk alone, untroubled by Sudan's rare foreign tourists, and feel you are discovering, almost for the first time, the ancient pyramids. The hundred pyramids may be much smaller than their Egyptian counterparts and many of the summits were lopped off by a nineteenth-century Italian tomb robber, but it is still today an atmospheric and compelling location.

In 1944 Hosh Bannaga was a quiet backwater. Omar's father was a smalltime dairy farmer. Omar belonged to the Al-Bedairyya al-Dahmashyaa Bedouin group, part of the larger Ja'yyalin coalition of tribes which dominated the middle northern section of Sudan. Many of the future politicians of Sudan would come from this tribal coalition, based in the town of Shendi.

Omar's birth appeared then as an inauspicious event. True, on the same day, another future Muslim politician was born: Zafarullah Khan Jamali, later to become the thirteenth prime minister of Pakistan. Yet, in 1944, neither Sudan nor Pakistan existed as independent states. Of perhaps more relevance to Islamic historians is that, on 1 January in AD 630, the Prophet Mohammed set out towards Mecca, which he would seize without bloodshed. The boy, 'Omeira' as he was nicknamed – Little Omar, would seize the Sudanese capital, also without bloodshed, forty-five years later.

If January 1944 was insignificant in local Sudanese affairs, it was a pivotal month in the world war outside Omar al-Bashir's village. In Europe, the Red Army was massing to smash its way into Nazi-occupied Poland and to occupy the Baltic states. The Americans were fighting hard in southern Italy; on 1 January General Mark Clark replaced the famous General George Patton as commander of the Seventh Army. Patton had been sidelined because of his infamous slapping and berating of two of his men suffering from what is now called post-traumatic stress disorder, though Patton was also deployed in a deception operation, FORTITUDE, to mislead Hitler as to the location of the D-Day landings in France. The British on that day were planning experiments with the first use of helicopters in naval warfare. From the broader imperial perspective, the Sudanese Defence Force, founded in 1925, had recruited members of the al-Bashir family. Four of the future president's uncles had fought alongside British forces in the North African and Abyssinian campaigns, including one who had distinguished himself at El Alamein. The Sudanese volunteers were initially assured by the British, 'The Italians are bad – they are going to rape your wives.'[1]

Omar went to the local primary school, but had to move in 1953 when his father Hassan took his whole family of four boys and four girls to a new village, Sarasir, 100 miles south of Khartoum, to seek work in the booming cotton industry. Decades before, the British had set up an extensive, well-organized and well-irrigated scheme. Despite his pronounced northern accent, Hassan settled in well in the village of about 2,000 souls. The houses were made of mud bricks. The residents were not indulged with electricity or running water. The only radios were to be found playing loudly in the shops. Some of the mud-brick houses had survived when I visited the village to talk to the president's cousins who still live there, albeit now in modest, but brick and breeze-block, houses with outside loos.

Treated with great hospitality I listened to endless stories of the country's ruler as a young boy. Some elderly relatives started jumping around on one leg, like demented Long John Silvers, because I struggled with the Arabic translation of the game of hopscotch. As youngsters they also played *tiwa*, a ball game, and marbles. Of course, the young Omar was described as a paragon. 'Very obedient to his father,' one cousin said proudly. Well, he would say that to a writer accompanied by the president's men, wouldn't he? Eventually, I got to a bit of minor sinning. Omar was described as feisty and pugnacious, active in organizing the local boys to take on the next village's youths with catapults and sticks. Some evenings they would swim in the irrigation canals built by the British, even though they were not supposed to.

The young Omar was a keen footballer. 'Always in defence,' a cousin said. 'That's why he went into the army.' The pun seemed to work in both English and Arabic. A love of football stayed with Omar al-Bashir. When he later moved to Khartoum North, he was an avid supporter of Al-Hilal, one of Sudan's most successful clubs, though in his later political life he had to be seen to support the national team.

President al-Bashir's stepson, Mohamed, told me an instructive story when I visited the compact but very well-tended presidential farm in North Khartoum in early 2014. A few years before, when the president was more agile, the national team had finished playing, and the president went on to the pitch and took a penalty shot against the professional goalkeeper, who saved the ball from the net. The referee gave the goalie a yellow card. The president took another penalty. The goalkeeper rather obviously jumped the wrong way, and the ball went in. The whole stadium erupted with applause and laughter.

The president has a reputation, in the West, for being very authoritarian and very anti-Western. Normally, his advisers encourage him to do interviews in Arabic only, though Omar al-Bashir speaks good English. I was interested in his attitude to his early British colonial roots. On a number of occasions he spoke very fondly of one of the three British teachers, a Mr Collier, a Scot who taught maths at the boys-only school in Sarasir. Despite the large classes of forty boys, they received a sound education. Omar's ebullient brother, Mohamed Hassan, two years junior, also spoke with warmth of the same Mr Collier. Indeed, Hassan kept singing a rather tuneless version of *Auld Lang Syne* to entertain me.

Another brother, Sidiq, has lived quietly in England for over thirty years, working as a medical practitioner. Many of the president's relatives and political cronies lived, studied and worked in the UK. When I was arrested for the first time in Sudan, in 1996, coincidentally by the Minister of Justice himself, the first question that came to my mind was not 'Why am I being arrested?' but what Oxbridge college the pukka minister had attended. I often scratched under the apparently rabidly Islamist and xenophobic exterior and soon discovered a genuine anglophilia. And it was more than mere politeness to a British guest (or arrested journalist). The English (language) colonial heritage ran deep, in the ruling party, and in their children, who rushed to study in the UK or USA.

* * * *

The president's mother, Hadiya, frail in her eighty-eighth year when I visited her in the presidential compound, was more frank about British influence. She recalled how the district commissioners used to speak harshly sometimes to workers in the cotton estate. 'They used to boss the local farmers about,' she said. She added that the British provided no medical care. 'We used traditional ways and herbs.'

In his teens, she said, her son's ambition was to be a 'military fighter pilot'. 'But I didn't want him to fight. I used to lose sleep when he was fighting in the south. I begged him not to serve in the south.' She added: 'I didn't want him to be president. I was scared for his life.' She confessed that she now wanted her son to retire. 'He has done enough for the country.' And she complained about living in a goldfish bowl; she dearly wanted to return to the traditional family home in Khartoum North. 'He is tired, but the people won't let him retire. They believe if he goes, it will be a big mess. But I think he has done enough.'

Hadiya obviously preferred to talk about her son when he was very young. Clearly, he was a right little tearaway. 'He was quick – as a child he was hard to catch. And he used to quarrel with his older brother, Ahmed. Ahmed used to bully him or at least try to.' She told me that she used to get Omar to learn poetry nearly every day, and then quoted one of her favourite poems. She also recalled that when Omar was six or seven, he refused to accept a beating from his mother. He grabbed the stick she was using, and starting hitting his mother instead. Infuriated, Hadiya retrieved the stick and resumed the beating, only to be physically restrained by her own mother, who berated her loudly for punishing young Omar.

She returned to her theme that she wanted her son to give up the presidency. 'Then I can go back and live in the family home [in Khartoum North]. Here in the presidential compound we live like strangers.' Though she did concede that her son visited her nearly every day, when he was in the country. 'That is his best quality,' she said. 'He is very kind to me and the whole family.'

There is no doubt that the tough military and political leader has a real soft spot: his family. He married his cousin, Fatima Khalid, but — like Numeiri — produced no children. The president's PR people tend to spin this with clichés about his being married to the whole country. 'I am content with my destiny given by God,' the president would say to friends. But the desire for children may have been a partial motivation, in 2003, when the president took a younger second wife, a widow called Widad Babiker Omer. She had four children, one boy and three girls. The youngest girl, Amna, was obviously doted on by the president. He clearly loved her and indulged her, even embarrassing her by attending her parent-teacher events. Widad was the widow of one of al-Bashir's closest military friends, Ibrahim Shams al-Din, a fellow plotter in 1989, who had been killed in an aircraft crash while on duty. Marrying some of the many military widows was made fashionable by the president's choice. I spent some time, alone, with the stepchildren and, although they disliked the isolation of being in the first family, they clearly adored their stepfather whom they had called 'Dad' from the start. The president would often reminisce about his friend to the children so that they could get a full understanding of their birth father.

I spoke to Madame Widad, as the president's second wife is addressed, on a number of occasions. She was bright and charming. Our official interview was in Arabic, but she spoke good English when we chatted informally together. I could not help but ask the obvious Western question about competition with the first wife. And she said, honestly. 'Yes there is competition, it's quite natural.'

She confided that she and her husband talked politics.

'Does he listen to you?'

'Sometimes,' she said. 'He can be a good listener.'

Working habits?

'He often works late, but doesn't bring work home. He wants to come home with a "clear soul".'

And she lauded the president's humour. Some of it would be a situational quip, sometimes a formal joke. 'He tells a joke every day.'

I was too polite to ask the wife whether her husband managed a *new* joke every day.

I have never met the president's older first wife. I did ask for a meeting, but I was told she was unwell. She officially runs a major NGO, as does Madame Widad – although of course it is a very different NGO.

Omar al-Bashir also raised the children of his older brother Ahmed, after he died. Then he brought up the three daughters of his younger brother, Mohamed Hassan, who is almost the spitting image of the president, 'albeit much better looking', Hassan would tell me – regularly. Mohamed Hassan was working in the UAE, and his daughters were studying in Khartoum. I interviewed or spent considerable time with the three very attractive nieces; all were highly independent, modern young women. They complained about their uncle's strictness, but said that 'Umo' – Uncle Omar – was very loving and supportive.

I asked one highly-educated niece whether she thought her uncle should not stand again. No, she said. 'He should have got out at the top – after Naivasha [after the signing of the successful peace talks with the south in January 2005].'

Returning to domestic matters, the nieces said he is 'really a morning person'. They would cook his breakfast personally, a sort of porridge called *foul*. This Sudanese speciality looks but does not taste foul. They did not like the pressure of being in the first family. Nor did they ask for favours in school and college; rather they felt they had to do even better to overcompensate for any allegations of favouritism. One niece confessed that when she travelled she tended to avoid using the surname 'al-Bashir' so she could behave as a normal citizen.

It is deeply ironic, not to say hypocritical, that all the president's younger family members, the stepchildren, the nephews and nieces and their spouses, all speak excellent if American-accented English. All have had first-class private-school and university education in Sudan, the Gulf and the UK. This point is significant: they were well educated, usually in English. Yet the first thing the Islamic revolutionaries did after 1989 was to Arabize and Islamize the schools and universities. Although universities multiplied, standards dropped. A whole generation of Sudanese high achievers lost out on a good education, not least in the international language of English. The president's brother, Mohamed Hassan, did admit to me that it was the president's biggest mistake: 'The changes in the educational system – he should have kept English.'

The president is undoubtedly a dedicated family man who insisted that his greatest influence was his father. Omar's father, Hassan – although illiterate – encouraged his sons' education. Initially he could not write, but taught himself to read by endlessly scanning newspapers. Later the autodidact collected a small library of books in his home. Hassan continued to be the dominant influence on his son Omar, right up until his death in 1986. He cautioned his son in 1983 and 1984 not to engage in politics while in the army. He was so concerned about the dangers that he urged his son to resign his commission. Had he not died when he did, perhaps the son may not have led the 1989 coup. Al-Bashir senior seemed a formidable sort of fellow. I watched a long family video of him recorded in the early 1980s. Despite his somewhat uneducated northern accent, he spoke very fluently, confidently and directly to the camera; at length in a strong voice. Obviously the son, the future president, learned rhetorical gifts from his father.

Sarasir was and is a very political village. During my visit to the school, mosque and family homes, the locals and al-Bashir's extended family engaged in heated debate about current affairs. As in much of Sudan, everyone is an amateur politician.

I recalled a recent conversation with a senior intelligence officer in a narrow dusty lane in central Khartoum. A poorly dressed elderly woman was selling glasses of tea from a small tray. 'There are twenty million politicians in this country. See that tea lady there,' the officer said, pointing. 'She would have strong political opinions and she would share them.'

I thought: True, they are quite free to chat on the streets or in cafes, but far less free in the newspapers.

* * * *

Omar al-Bashir's family moved to Khartoum North, to a small pink-painted house opposite a hostel for mentally ill people. It was at this home that I had arranged to meet some of the leader's secondary schoolmates and a handful of his teachers, now long in the tooth, but alert. Omar attended a government-run school in Khartoum North.

I was inundated with polite platitudes:

'He was a quiet boy, very disciplined.'

'Very religious, or perhaps I should say traditionalist.'

'Always knew he would become something.'

'If you wanted a prefect, you would choose Omar.'

'He was especially good at maths and English.'

I persisted, especially with a teacher who spoke excellent English and who had lived in my home town, Cardiff. He was disappointed that Omar did not go to university – something that perhaps continuously played on the president's mind when he had to deal later with much better-educated people in his own party and urbane foreign politicians.

One of Omar's classmates confessed that 'when we were fourteen occasionally we would bunk off school and go to the cinema'. So, thankfully, young Omar was not a saint. More interestingly, I discovered from his teachers that around about age 15-16, Omar was kicked out of the Muslim Brotherhood for smoking. That fact has been left out of his official CV. But Omar had relatives in the movement and he was later allowed back in.

Al-Bashir was not lazy. He played a lot of sport, volleyball and squash as well as football. Although keen on sport, he did not possess an athletic or imposing build. Relatively short, at about five feet nine inches, he had to work on his fitness. He was also usually short of money. He worked in school holidays helping his father in his farm-work as well as with a local mechanic in his garage.

It was partly financial pressures that prompted his move into the army rather than university. Young Omar wanted to be a doctor (a career taken up by one of his brothers). His second choice was a soldier and his third a teacher. He completed his Cambridge Certificate and he joined the armed forces, initially – he hoped — to train as a pilot.

Recalling his uncles' service in the imperial forces, the young Omar had also hoped to train in Britain. 'I was going to study in the UK, but the UDI crisis stopped me,' the president told me when we were reminiscing about his early life choices. He was referring to Rhodesia's illegal declaration of independence in November 1965. Britain's half-hearted reaction to the white rebels caused outrage in many African states.

He studied for two years at the Sudan Military Academy, and was commissioned as an officer in December 1966. The imperial connection was cemented by British Army instructors (who were later replaced by Russians). The cadet officers at the military academy were divided into three platoons, each with about 100 cadets. Omar al-Bashir was in the 3rd Platoon. I spoke to some of the president's fellow cadets, who admitted that the 'British had left many good principles'. Cadet al-Bashir responded well to the British-style discipline system, according to his fellow cadets. After commissioning, he was sent to Darfur, where he spent two years in all. For the young lieutenant it was a tough posting; first at Abokarinka, west of Nyala, as a rookie officer in charge of thirty-two men. In the desert and savannah terrain, his job was to contain the traditional tribal disputes.

A fellow cadet in the same cohort, later to become a general, told me, 'He had the charisma of a commander from the start, and he was a decision-maker, although he was a simple man, from a simple family. I have never seen him drink alcohol or smoke. He is a very religious man, but full of jokes.' Privately, the general told me *sotto voce* that his old friend had been a great soldier, but the ruling party had 'poisoned his mind'.

A number of senior officers, some retired, commented on Omar al-Bashir's personal physical fitness, leadership from the front in combat and popularity with his men. One general said 'He showed good moral as well as military leadership.' Another very senior officer told me, 'The President still stands up when he meets his former military superiors – he is a real army man.' Again – in private – some of his army comrades, still loyal to him, blame the ruling party for 'capturing' him. Some of his most loyal military and intelligence leaders supported an aborted palace coup in 2012, against the party, but not him, some would say. Nevertheless, the army remained a major part of his natural constituency throughout his long career, partly because of his inter-personal skills. He was seen as a natural leader, but who would consult carefully with his colleagues. Professor Ibrahim A.

Ghandour, a big beast in the ruling National Congress Party, put it best, in his immaculate BBC English: 'Nobody pushes the President around, but he is a man of *Shura*.'[2]

After his Darfur posting, Lieutenant al-Bashir underwent six months' intensive paratrooper training to secure the coveted red beret. Then, for nine months, he studied at the Egyptian Military Academy in Cairo where he specialized in further paratrooper training. He was taught by Russian instructors and became a fully fledged paratroop officer in 1969. During his career, he completed sixteen jumps, though none were operational. He was promoted to captain in 1971.

In 1973 he returned to Egypt. 'We were sent as an act of solidarity during the 1973 war. We were proud to go,' said the president. He was part of a joint Sudanese-Egyptian special forces group, which was based forty miles from the Israeli front line, as a shield against the possibility of General Ariel Sharon's advance formations pushing on into Cairo. Omar al-Bashir experienced intermittent shelling, but was not part of the SF units which crossed over the Suez Canal in hit-and-run ambushes on Israeli troops.

The young officer showed promise in liaising with foreign forces, because he was sent in 1975 to be a military attaché in the United Arab Emirates. It wasn't all diplomacy: he did a tour of duty in 1976 with the Arab League peacekeeping force in Lebanon. He was promoted to major while serving there. He also spent time at the infantry school in Abu Dhabi. From 1979 to 1981 he was a garrison commander in Khartoum; in 1980 he had been made a lieutenant colonel. Next, he was promoted to be a commander of an armoured parachute brigade, a post he held until 1987. In 1981 he had been promoted to full colonel. During this period, he obtained, in 1981, a master's degree in military science from the Sudanese Command and Staff College. In 1983 he achieved a second master's in military science in Malaysia. He wrote his dissertation, in English, on counter-insurgency. (In 2011, he secured another master's via part-time study at Al-Jazeera University in Medeni.)

Extensive combat experience was gained in the south of his own country. During his home postings, he spent a total of three years conducting counter-insurgency operations against the SPLA. Some of it was conducted from his role as garrison commander at Mayum, in the oil-rich southern Unity state. While there he became an expert in working with the pro-Khartoum Nuer militias, especially the 'army' formed around Paulino Matip Nhial. The future field marshal described the conditions as very tough, especially during the rainy season. Although privately he admitted that leading an armoured brigade was a career highpoint, he said, 'During the war, there were no happy times.'

'The people were suffering in the south. But we were also suffering from very bad conditions – we suffered from shortages of food, equipment and medicine. The SPLA would often attack when we were sleeping at night.' Typically, al-Bashir would lead from the front, even on foot patrols of four or five days' duration.

I asked the president whether he had been wounded in combat.

'I had a lot of close calls, but, no, I was never wounded.'

Most presidents and military men with lots of combat experience tend not to underplay their pasts; al-Bashir seemed to be genuinely modest about his career achievements. He played it straight.

* * * *

A number of his toughest critics, including American envoys, accepted that, although Khartoum politicians had a reputation for deviousness, the president always played a straight bat, to use a cricketing analogy. I spoke to a number of senior journalists in Khartoum who knew the president well. One said that he had travelled a lot with al-Bashir abroad. 'There is no pomp and circumstance – you feel you are travelling with a normal person. We share meals with him. Whenever he meets journalists he will ask about their families.' Another commented on how the president would visit ordinary people's homes and weddings, and always without guards.

If a journalist travels a lot with a president and goes to the same weddings, he is obviously an insider. So I spoke to another senior hack who had been on the inside of the government's prisons a number of times. I asked the opposition writer about the alleged corruption in the al-Bashir family. He said that he 'was sure the president was not personally corrupt', but some of the people around him probably were.

So why doesn't he stop them?

'Fighting corruption is like fighting an octopus,' said the independent journalist. 'But a number of politicians have been prosecuted – two of the president's relatives have been put in jail for bouncing a cheque.'

The anti-government journalist left a final thought with me as I shook hands to leave: 'Without Bashir, there would have been three or four countries, not two.'

* * * *

Omar al-Bashir developed an impressive military pedigree, but how did he become a political soldier? From schooldays he had been involved with the Islamic movement. His temporary postings with the Egyptian army must have influenced him with some of the Nasserist ethos which pervaded many Arab armies. But only so far in al-Bashir's case, because Islamic tendencies would have precluded the modernizing, *secular* approach of military revolutions in neighbouring states. After 1977, and with Numeiri's regime reconciling its differences with the Brotherhood, the Islamist movement began a conscious policy of infiltration of the armed forces. Despite attracting the attention of Numeiri's *Mukhabarat*, al-Bashir managed to quietly work away at securing the influence of the Islamist movement in the army.

The British tradition of an apolitical army had been lost in Sudan. As Omar al-Bashir admitted to me, 'The armed forces were involved in politics. There were various political movements *within* the army – Ba'athists, communists, Islamists ... Remember that the communists in the army tried to stage a coup against Numeiri in 1971.'

After Numeiri was toppled in 1985, there were rumours that al-Bashir was involved in a possible coup attempt to bring into power the National Islamic Front, led by the charismatic and erudite preacher Hassan al-Turabi. To keep him away from the limelight in Khartoum, and safe from the immediate attentions of the secret police, sympathetic senior generals posted al-Bashir to active combat duties in the south. He performed well and was promoted to brigadier in 1988. He was on active duty until just before the coup of June 1989. The Islamist movement had chosen him as potential leader of their military wing.

Al-Bashir was a chosen one, but not initially *the* chosen military supremo. Partly because of chance, some of the plotters were removed. One was posted to Egypt, another was sent to an isolated southern posting. As Omar al-Bashir confided to me, 'We thought we had a 50-50 chance of succeeding. Originally about 300 officers were involved, but many were moved.' Some of the others were divided on the timing.

The core conspiracy was reduced to thirty officers, ranging from lieutenant to general. Al-Bashir did much of the careful preparation. As a commander of mobile armoured units he was in a key position. 'I was the leader. It was one of the crucial points of my career. We had strong armoured backing, but it proved unnecessary and we did it from the *inside*. It was a success, and without any fighting or bloodshed.'

After the coup, al-Bashir became minister of defence. In 1993 he became

President of Sudan and later in his presidency was promoted to field marshal. Not bad for a farm boy. But he was an army man through and through. How would he sublimate his loyalty to the army to the demands of party politics? He had proved himself as a military leader, and had exhibited skills in underground politics, but how would he rate as a player on the national and international political stage?

Chapter 5

The Duopoly

On the night of 30 June 1989 Brigadier Omar al-Bashir led the coup with a small core officer component of just thirty. 'The people were fed up with Sadiq al-Mahdi,' al-Bashir told me straightforwardly. 'We did it from the *inside*.' His years in the paratrooper units around Khartoum meant that they followed his orders in efficiently capturing the strategic sites in the three towns. It was rapid and bloodless like the 1969 Numeiri military takeover. And for a while many Sudanese assumed that it was a coup like any other. It was not: al Bashir would still be in power more than twenty-five years later.

The military trappings were initially similar. The officers set up a Revolutionary Command Council, which echoed the Nasserite tradition. But this was by no means a secular putsch. It had been carefully planned with the National Islamic Front party. Its head in the constituent assembly, Ali Othman Muhammed Taha, had spent months joint-planning with al-Bashir as to precisely what the coup was intended to achieve. Al-Bashir's radio and later TV address talked about al-Mahdi's 'failures of democratic government'. Few Sudanese expected an Islamist revolution to replace the very flawed democracy; a revolution fashioned by a visionary who had planned for this day for decades: Hassan al-Turabi. Al-Bashir worked behind the scenes to stabilize the army and concentrate on trying to claw back the military defeats of the previous government. Al-Turabi, however, was soon to hog the spotlight at home and abroad, via his incessant travelling. The military leader behind the coup kept a low public profile. This was not to be a cult-led revolution based on the Nasser model.

Although al-Bashir's underground political work in the army had roused the interest of the state security organs and military intelligence, especially under the paranoid Numeiri, the new military supremo was not known to the general public. When he made his first broadcast to the nation immediately after the coup, al-Bashir's mother was travelling from Medeni to Khartoum on a public bus which stopped because of a street crowd, roused by the putsch. In her astonishment at finding out the new leader's name, she told some of those around her that it was her son who had led the coup. Few believed her at the time. Except for one brother, informed a few hours before, al-Bashir had not risked his family's safety by confiding in them; just in case it all went wrong. He had reckoned that his chance of success was 50-50, despite the years of planning.

The leading northern politicians, including Sadiq al-Mahdi, were locked up. Al-Bashir also cleaned out potential opponents in the army by also accommodating over 100 officers in Khartoum's Kobar prison. More military purges soon followed, amid rumours of a counter coup. So far, so obvious. Then a very unusual component of the coup occurred: al-Bashir sent his spiritual patron to Kobar as well. Al-Turabi was given time to pack a suitable case, not least containing the Imam's beloved books. He was given a very comfortable minimum-security cell, although al-Bashir made the point that the other political leaders were also well-treated. 'It was the Sudanese way,' he insisted. The junta apparently wanted to show its even-handedness to all political leaders. Perhaps the designers of the coup wanted it to look like a normal nationalist military coup to save the country from inevitably incompetent politicians. And perhaps they wanted to smuggle in an Islamist revolution without upsetting the Egyptians or the West. A born teacher, al-Turabi spent his few months in comfortable confinement lecturing fellow inmates on the new Islamic state he would soon create. This was not fantasy for, when he was released, all the new military leaders, led by al-Bashir, took the *bayaa* oath of allegiance to him, a practice inaugurated by the Prophet himself. At the time al-Bashir said he was proud to follow al-Turabi's instructions – 'without hesitation'.

Not only the new military boss and his fellow-travelling officers, but a section of a whole generation of intellectuals was prepared to venerate the temporary jailbird as the architect and imam of the Islamist revolution. The (brief) jail term was oddly prophetic, for al-Turabi was to spend a lot of time in prison or under house arrest in the next twenty-five years, and not of his own volition. Al-Turabi created the revolution that was later captured by his co-plotter, al-Bashir. The spiritual leader then spent years undermining the military president, and working with the many enemies of the regime abroad and in the south. In many other countries he would have been executed for treason, but somehow the spell that al-Turabi cast over a generation of students, military officers and politicians was still potent, despite their subsequent disillusionment with him. Over the years I have asked hundreds of former acolytes of al-Turabi, some in power in Sudan and others in exile in the West, about this paradox. Very few would directly castigate him, not out of fear but out of lingering respect. The most they would say was, in essence: 'He was/is a great imam, but a bad politician.'

If Sudanese history is a tragedy, then Shakespeare's *Macbeth* is perhaps an analogy. From 1990 to 1996 al-Turabi fashioned and led the revolution; from 1996 to the coup within a coup in 1999 his star waned. Thereafter, even when in prison or under house arrest, al-Turabi hovered like Banquo's ghost over the Sudanese polity. His power was sometimes exaggerated and he later became a convenient straw man for the regime, but much of his influence was real, formidable and malevolent, for example his intercession with Khartoum's enemies, especially in Darfur and the SPLA. It was fitting for a man committed to a universal faith that he appeared to be everywhere, lurking just beyond the horizon, if not behind the curtain, when peace deals were suddenly derailed. The story of northern Sudan's recent political life cannot be understood without appreciating the initial duopoly of power: the Hassan-Omar double act. In the beginning it was clear who was pulling the strings, but after a year or two, the power shifted to a more balanced diarchy, then in a few years the military took back the reins, and al-Bashir became the undisputed leader. How this happened and how it affected the civil war dominated the first decade of the al-Bashir presidency.

Within weeks of the June revolution, it became clear that this was not just a bunch of disgruntled middle-ranking officers, unhappy with Sadiq al-Mahdi's floundering war strategy. A core of officers inhabited a defined Islamist programme, devised by al-Turabi. The remnants of secular influence, especially unions and other political parties, were banned. Nearly all senior army and police officers not sympathetic to the Islamists were ousted. Most newspapers were closed and the state radio and television closely supervised. The surviving media made it clear that the RCC government was committed to orthodox Islam, Islamic law, and also Islamic dress for men and, especially, women.

The RCC was technically the state's supreme body. Behind this façade stood a *shura* called portentously the 'Council of the Defenders of the Revolution' which met in secret after curfew. It comprised some zealous army officers, but it was dominated by NIF civilians. The Council, dubbed the 'Committee of Forty', was chaired by the energetic head of the NIF, Ali Othman Muhammed Taha. One close observer said his 'low-key style, his child-like features and his apparent quiet demeanour' encouraged many people to overlook his much tougher side. Taha had been at the same Khartoum North school as al-Bashir, although the future president was two years older. He had been al-Turabi's personal assistant as well, and was for long a true believer. After disillusionment set in, Taha's star rose alongside al-Bashir's and he became a vice president, and later a chief fixer of the 'final' peace deal with the south in 2005.

In January 2014, Taha was shifted sideways from real power and went into semi-retirement. He felt able to talk more frankly when I visited his plush government-owned house in Khartoum. I asked him when the Bashir-Turabi breakdown began. History usually suggests 1996 or sometimes even as late as 1999. Looking back, Taha said:

> The split started early in the nineteen-nineties – as early as ninety-one or ninety-two. Turabi wanted to be the kingmaker. We accepted that. The way he did it was the problem ... It was all about political power, not religious ideology.

The tough-minded Taha was clearly emotional when he described the events of two decades before. And he was still conflicted about al-Turabi, even though he said, 'He has done so much damage to the president, the people and the country itself.'

This was in the future. At the beginning of the revolution al-Turabi was seen by Islamists as the saviour of the country. But the new government had little popular support in the rural areas or in the towns among the more secular intelligentsia and commercial middle class. Not surprisingly, internal security became the RCC's priority. The intelligence system had ossified under Mubarak al-Mahdi, the former prime minister's cousin. The professional formal structure, later called the National Intelligence and Security Service (NISS), was revised along traditional lines. It was divided into an internal branch, similar to MI5 in the UK, and an external branch, not least to spy on exiled Sudanese, in the West and Middle East. The parallel here was Britain's MI6. A third unit was set up to deal with military intelligence; that was not just to collate useful military data, at home and abroad, (cf the Defence Intelligence Staff in the UK), but also to monitor the constant rumblings inside the army. Alongside the full-time professional structure a new more informal Islamic system comprised a much bigger part-time army of students and young Islamists called the *Amn al-Jabha.* After the 1989 revolution that was the common term used when Sudanese whispered about security matters, although foreign experts still used the generic Arabic term of *Mukhabarat* or NISS. The *Amn al-Jabha* also co-operated closely with the numerous members of the Popular Defence Force that was originally set up at the end of the previous government, but was fully developed as an Islamist military and intelligence organization, under the influence of al-Turabi. Much of the money to fund these Islamist organizations came from the Faisal Islamic Bank. Major General Bakri Hassan Saleh, a revolutionary zealot, was put in charge of the whole system. The secret services were to play a dominant role in ensuring the stability of the government for decades. Ironically, it usually managed to defang the coup potential of the army, but – reviving the age-old question, *quis custodiet ipsos custodes* – it proved to be the only state organ which could later seriously threaten the system erected by al-Bashir

The internal branches of the *Mukhabarat* set about removing all potential opposition in the three towns and other urban centres. They also enforced Islamist standards. Female state employees were encouraged to go home and look after their families; those who were deemed absolutely necessary had to dress in conservative Islamic style. Many professionals, particularly doctors, lawyers and, by definition, journalists were imprisoned, usually without trial. The judiciary was also purged. Detention camps were set up. Foreign media reports listed the 'disappearances' and the torture meted out in the 'Ghost Houses' (so called because people were picked up at night, when the ghosts were about). Khartoum disputed these accounts, but the public floggings for manufacturing, owning or even drinking alcohol were publicized. Drug dealers were also executed publicly. Illegal dealing in foreign currency was punished, though with sanctions later and a purely cash economy it became almost a patriotic duty to deal in foreign currencies, especially US dollars, without which the economy would seize up. The draconian imposition of *sharia* law prompted an exodus of professionals, especially doctors and engineers, whose skills were valued throughout the Middle East.

A part of the sudden growth of the Sudanese diaspora consisted of politicians who had been released from confinement or who had fled to avoid jail. The displaced political parties, unions and professional organizations, all hostile to the 1989 coup, formed the National Democratic Alliance (NDA) based in Asmara, the capital of the soon-to-be independent Eritrea, which had fallen out with Khartoum. The SPLM joined the NDA in 1990. The northern politicians still debated the tired questions about *sharia* law in the south and secession versus unity, but since the SPLM was the only NDA party with an army that could defeat the hated NIF government, the exiled northerners tried to fudge a compromise. Along with other dissident groups such as the Beja Congress, they agreed on the Asmara

Accords (June 1995) to keep fighting until the NIF regime was overthrown. All the plans of frustrated exiles and guerrilla fighters were predicated on what they all assumed would be a *temporary* revolutionary regime in Khartoum. Nearly all the Western experts on Sudan also regularly predicted the imminent collapse of the al-Bashir government – for decades.

Meanwhile in Khartoum the RCC and NIF rapidly took control of the military, the executive and also the judiciary. They wanted a total revolution. As Mussolini put it: 'All within the state, nothing outside the state, nothing against the state.' Al-Turabi wanted to create a theocracy where enlightened Islamic scholars meeting in a *shura* would reach a consensus on interpreting the divine will. The tough September Laws initiated by Numeiri were replaced by another harsh version of *sharia* throughout the country, thus obviating any hope of a deal in the south. NIF apologists argued that the absence of beheading, for example, ensured the new code was less harsh than Numeiri's version. Sudan was becoming the first Sunni theocracy, Khartoum suggested. The West, especially the Americans, argued that Sudan was copying Iran, its *bête noire*. Khartoum's defenders explained that Iran could never be a model. For example, they, as Sunnis, had no system of direct rule by the clergy, the Ayatollahs, as in the Shia approach, and insisted that they were applying a form of Islamic democracy.

Nevertheless, if Iran was not a religious model, Khartoum sought security advice from its new friends in Tehran. In December 1991 the Iranian President, Ali Rafsanjani, visited Sudan for four days, along with 150 advisers, mainly security and military experts. This led to the permanent stationing in Khartoum of Hassan Azada, head in Lebanon of the *Pasdaran,* the Iranian Revolutionary Guards. Later, *Pasdaran* specialists in artillery and logistics followed. The Iranian connection initially focused on assistance with the Popular Defence Force (for details, see Appendix). The PDF was intended to galvanize the whole of society, as well as bolster the overstretched army. Planned to number over 100,000 volunteers, the PDF's elite would take a combat role in the south, and a counter-coup role in the three towns. Media and mosque campaigns emphasized the jihadist duty and the glories of martyrdom. Some middle-class youths, especially students, were not entirely convinced of the advantages of swapping their degrees for an early entry into paradise. Eager volunteers there were, however, especially as a PDF recommendation was often required for a job, continued study or even an overseas trip. (A certificate proving service in the army was also required for some state employment, including doctors.) Others were press-ganged into the PDF. Some PDF units – comprising genuine volunteers for combat – did perform well, although the initial training was just three months. Occasionally, the Iranian influence inspired futile human-wave attacks against astounded SPLA machine gunners in entrenched positions. The army was often opposed to fighting alongside the PDF volunteers because of their inexperience, and because so much money was being diverted to this ideological rather than military mission. The PDF worked better in the countryside, especially in the west, where residents were often well acquainted with small arms. Sometimes the PDF merged into tribal militias, with dangerous results later in Darfur. Nevertheless, even among the faithful in the three towns, the often coercive recruitment methods of the PDF proved unpopular. After al-Turabi's star waned, the PDF was often seen as a political, not a religious or military, endeavour.

Nevertheless, the Iranian influence and the style of PDF recruitment did contribute to the growing Islamist nature of the regime. Southerners and Christians were confirmed as second-class citizens. So were women. True, Sudan did not go in for the Afghan burkhas, or the princess-head-chopping and driving bans of the misogynistic Saudis. And part of the intended 'clean up' was genuinely trying to protect the honour (and property rights) of women. Prostitution, pornography and the use of the female form for commercial purposes were forbidden. The *tobe*, traditional flowing robes and head covering, though not necessarily the veil, were promoted. Al-Turabi preferred the more modern *ibaya* dress, more like a kaftan, and opposed the more restrictive *tobe*. He had liberal views on the role of women compared with most Islamic clerics. His wife, Wisal al-Mahdi, Sadiq's sister, was a well-known (and charming) women's leader, and a 'feminist' in the Sudanese context. I was a guest at the al-Turabi home, in the upmarket Riyadh suburb of Khartoum, for a small dinner, where she presided in her husband's absence, unusually for a conservative society. Also, on another occasion, I interviewed her on the flat roof of her home, to discuss the issue of female genital mutilation about which she was vociferously liberal. Al-Turabi was influenced by his wife on the question of women's rights, as Wisal confirmed to me. That might have explained why women, although second- or third-class citizens in Western terms, still had some of their rights protected, not least in (separate) education. The government continued to exhibit a fetish about women not wearing trousers, and was still threatening to flog those guilty of such sartorial infelicities decades after the al-Bashir regime was entrenched. The leitmotif of 'immodest dress', and the moral campaigns waged by the PDF in the urban areas, seemed odd to Westerners, especially in the face of a war which was being lost in the south.

Al-Turabi was a man of many contradictions. In 1996, for example, I interviewed him in his office of parliamentary speaker. We talked about the topic *du jour* – slavery. He argued that the Americans were using the slavery and terrorism issues to undermine Islam and the Khartoum government. 'The Americans know that the African-Americans are very sympathetic to Sudan,' he claimed. 'They want to persuade the African-Americans that US policy towards Sudan is alright because Sudan is involved in slavery. There is *absolutely* no slavery in Sudan.' We also talked about Osama bin Laden, who had lived almost next door to him in the Riyadh suburb. He stressed that the Saudi had been engaged purely in business matters, especially construction. Then the Imam talked about his studies in the US and France. One of the dicta that al-Turabi regularly trotted out to his acolytes about Islam versus the West was: 'We know them better than they know us.' Which was probably true. The Sorbonne-educated Imam was very clever and closely followed Western politics. Like many Islamists, he exhibited in private conversation a brooding belief in the appalling corruption of Western society and, like Lenin, an assurance of its inevitably self-destructive tendencies. On the other hand, al-Turabi rejoiced in his mastery of foreign languages and cultures. We did not discuss Sudan's most famous novelist, Tayeb Saleh, but Saleh's most famous work, *Season of Migration to the North* (1969) captured some of al-Turabi's ambivalence towards the West, and especially its women. Saleh, who sought exile in London, and work with the BBC, saw his novel banned in Sudan, even though it has been described as 'the most important Arabic novel of the twentieth century'. He was, however, rehabilitated in Khartoum and, when he died in 2009, a major literary award was named after him.

Al-Bashir was less fixated with the cultural and social issues, and even with the installation of a theocracy. He left those matters to his better-educated Imam. After the coup, the general was utterly focused on reforming the army and winning the war in the south. As a soldier's soldier, al-Bashir was determined to increase the size and efficiency of the armed forces. The Sudanese economy was still weak, however. The inherited annual defence budget was guesstimated at around $500 million, not including the enhanced internal security systems. Before the oil bonanza, the size of the army was increased by only ten per cent to around 65,000, although al-Bashir wanted to raise it to 78,000. It was still a volunteer force, and the unemployment levels were high enough to offer lots of recruits. As oil revenues came in, the army was pushed up to 100,000 and in 1998 conscription for the army was fully introduced from those aged 18 to 30. This was the first time conscription had been used for the forces. The size of the air force was doubled, although the combat strength improved only slightly because of poor maintenance, and the lack of foreign currency to purchase spares. The PDF, which drafted in tens of thousands, was a stop gap. A small professional army and a large militia force disturbed the army top brass, but the militia experience in the west and along the border had worked to an extent, so the army sought to improve the training and integration of the *murahiliin,* in their various guises, until funds arrived to train a large professional army that could defeat, not just contain, the southern rebels. The PDF never became as effective as their occasional mentors, the Iranian Revolutionary Guards. In the south they sometimes performed well, as in operations in Equatoria and Blue Nile, but they also ended up occasionally as cannon fodder. In the west, they reverted to banditry on occasions. And, for all the martyrs' sacrifice, the PDF was not as potent as the Islamist revolutionaries had hoped. They were more successful in urban areas as a militia for the NIF in public order roles.

World Revolution

As with the Bolshevik revolution, al-Turabi's variant split those who advocated revolution in one country and those who believed in the world revolutionary mission. Once out of prison and officially under house arrest in the first months of the coup, al-Turabi worked with his wife on founding the International Organization of Muslim Women, which was set up in late 1989. The occasion for the acceleration of his world mission was the perceived humiliation of Arab states in the First Gulf War, and above all the positioning of US infidel troops in the same country as the holy places of Mecca and Medina. Khartoum's clunky diplomats incensed the Americans by appearing to back Saddam Hussein, though they later glossed their gross faux-pas by saying that they opposed the Western intervention to remove the Iraqis from Kuwait, while not endorsing the original occupation by Baghdad. Their explanation was usually lost in translation.

Partly for economic reasons, but also ideological ones, Sudan now allowed all Muslim brothers to visit the country without a visa. This enveloped brothers of all stripes, including battle-hardened Afghans. Al-Turabi started to travel extensively, including a return trip to the US for a Palestinian conference in Chicago. (He had first visited the USA for six months on a US government student scholarship in the 1960s.) In spring 1991 al-Turabi set up the Popular Arab and Islamic Congress (PAIC) as a sort of alternative but more radical Arab League. The first meeting in April

1991 was dubbed the 'most significant event since the collapse of the Caliphate'[1] by the subservient Khartoum media. Islamists from the Middle East were there in strength, but small groups also came from the USA and Britain. They secretly agreed to form the 'Armed Islamist International', an umbrella group for radical Sunnis. Al-Turabi toured and lectured in Islamist hotspots such as Afghanistan and Pakistan. Although he disagreed with much of what the Ayatollah Khomeini said and did, for example the *fatwa* on Salman Rushdie, the Sudanese visionary emulated some of the Ayatollah's techniques of circulating CDs and videos of his lectures, which were popular in many parts of the Islamic world. Al-Turabi's world mission soon led to a wide variety of radicals coming from Kashmir, Afghanistan, Pakistan and North Africa. Provocatively, Khartoum also welcomed *mujahedeen* from Egypt. The most controversial guest by far, however, was Osama bin Laden, who moved to a large house in a plush suburb of the capital in late 1991. His personal executive jet had its own secluded and well-guarded area at Khartoum airport. The presence of bin Laden was a major factor in the later US imposition of sanctions on Sudan.

Al-Turabi concentrated on his international objectives, confirming his relationship with bin Laden by allowing the Saudi millionaire to marry his niece, as bin Laden's third wife. Just coincidently, bin Laden also invested $50 million in al-Turabi's favoured Al-Shamal Islamic Bank in Khartoum. Meanwhile, al-Bashir quietly consolidated his own position domestically, especially in the military. In October 1993 the RCC was dissolved and al-Bashir became president of the republic. The new low-key president did not air his views in public about al-Turabi's comments on world Islamic renaissance, or the increasing American concern at the influx of jihadists into Sudan. Al-Turabi did not involve himself with any formal government role, appearing to believe that his internationalist mission was far more important.

While on a lecture tour of Canada, on 26 May 1992, al-Turabi, now 60, was attacked by an exiled Sudanese karate champion. Apparently, the disgruntled Sudanese, Hashim Mohammed, had not planned the assault. He said he just saw red when he happened to spot al-Turabi at Ottowa airport and hit the Imam twice with two hard jabs of the edge of his hand. Al-Turabi was severely hurt and spent weeks in hospital, recovering from a coma. He suffered for a long time with slurred speech and had difficulty in walking, but gradually recovered. Thereafter, whenever al-Turabi did or said something controversial, many Sudanese would give a knowing look and mutter something about 'that bump to the head, you know'. When I interviewed al-Turabi in August 1996 he seemed extremely articulate and incisive. I saw no evidence of brain damage in his speech or walking. The urbane intellectual still continued to be at home, whether in a tie or turban, and to charm his many visitors and lecture audiences. The army and al-Bashir, however, grew less enamoured of their formal patron.

The US State Department was increasingly agitated about alleged terrorist camps in Sudan, for the foreign legion of *mujahedeen* who had been invited or sought exile in Sudan. Khartoum consistently denied the charges of terrorist enterprises. The Sudanese were also accused of supporting attacks on US troops who took part in the UN RESTORE HOPE operation in Somalia in 1992. On 26 February 1993 a bomb exploded in the World Trade Center in New York. Six Americans were killed. Although blamed mainly on an Egyptian Islamic group, Washington accused Khartoum of complicity. The US government listed in detail the foreign Islamic groups in Sudan, noting especially the Palestinian Liberation Organization and the Palestinian Hamas as well as Lebanon's Hezbollah, prime enemies of Washington's ally, Israel. Sudan was officially placed on the US list of states sponsoring terrorism. One writer described the Sudanese in-gathering 'as a Davos in the desert for terrorists'.[2]

Al-Turabi seemed oblivious of the decline of Sudan's position in the diplomatic world, especially in the West. Revelling in his new fame in the Islamic world, perhaps he didn't care. He appeared convinced that the collapse of the USSR heralded a new Islamic dawn. In December 1993 he held another bigger congress of prominent Islamists from around the world, including those from the Caucasus fighting the Russian army. Former senior intelligence chiefs from supportive countries such as Pakistan's Inter-Service Intelligence agency (ISI) were also there. The poor treatment of Muslim minorities in the West and Russia were highlighted and al-Turabi predicted that a united Islamic nation was on the horizon.

Southern Jihad
Khartoum's military had their focus on a much more proximate jihad: in the south. After a failed peace initiative by the former US president, Jimmy Carter, John Garang worked on securing the active support of African states, especially the more radical southern African countries that had secured victory in Zimbabwe and were now pushing to topple the apartheid regime in South Africa. The Namibian insurgents also helped in practical terms, by donating surplus arms to the SPLA. Garang worked hard to assuage suspicions that his unified democratic Sudan policy could still work, despite

the new hard-line government in Khartoum. Garang had to mend fences because his main support base in Ethiopia collapsed with the fall of the Mengistu administration in 1991. Garang had helped Mengistu fight the separatists in Ethiopia that had been backed by Khartoum, especially the Oromo Liberation Front. When the Khartoum-allied insurgencies in Eritrea and Tigray provinces merged into the Ethiopian People's Revolutionary Democratic Front (EPRDF) and conquered Addis, the new regime paid back its dues to Khartoum. The EPRDF ejected the SPLA from its camps inside the Ethiopian border and closed its offices and radio station in the capital. Hundreds of thousands of southern Sudanese refugees were also kicked out. Uganda took up the slack in military support for the SPLA, one reason why Khartoum later aided Ugandan rebels such as the Lord's Resistance Army. If Uganda became the military pillar for the SPLA, then Kenya grew into the main base for diplomatic and humanitarian succour for the southern rebellion. The SPLA had forged a coherent fighting machine, but it lacked a coherent political sensitivity to the social conditions in the south, exacerbated by the new refugee influx. Garang was regularly criticized for his domineering authoritarianism, not least for killing or imprisoning rival commanders, most famously his former close ally, Kerubino Kuanyin Bol. The Dinka commander was held in harsh confinement for six years in one of the archipelago of prison camps run by Garang. He managed to escape in 1993.

The big SPLA schism

Coming on top of ejection from the Ethiopian sanctuaries, the big split in the SPLA in 1991 was to undermine the military resistance for years and leave a political legacy that festered for decades. A number of commanders, including the usual suspects, Lam Akol and Riek Machar, planned to displace Garang. Khartoum assiduously courted these dissident commanders, but the majority of the SPLA top brass supported Garang, not least because unity was paramount at a time of weakness following the crucial loss of Ethiopia. Many Nuer, however, were prepared to follow their traditional general, Machar, and the Nuer units around Nasir openly backed him. Instead of toppling the SPLA, Machar and Akol, a Shilluk, responded by founding a rival organization, SPLA-Nasir. This hardened the ethnic divisions that plagued the southern resistance movement and also helped prompt the civil war after independence.

Nasir was a war-ruined shell of a town, but it had an airstrip that was used for relief flights by NGOs. It was also the venue for an unusual and tragic story. Riek Machar and Emma McClune, a tall, beautiful and idealistic English aid worker, met and fell in love. They married (although Machar had a wife by a traditional marriage). After making love, Emma said, she would get up and help her warlord to write his manifestoes. Highly irritated by the young Englishwoman's intervention in southern politics, Garang once sarcastically described the schism as 'Emma's War'. The name stuck, and it became the title of a powerful and lyrical book by Deborah Scroggins.

Even more irritating for Garang, Khartoum sent weapons and cash support to the SPLA-Nasir. Re-armed, Machar pushed into traditionally Dinka areas and eventually the mainly Dinka command of the SPLA felt forced to retaliate. Machar's armed push was intended to show his strength and prise other commanders away from Garang, although attacks on the Dinka were much more likely to confirm Dinka solidarity around Garang, another classic Machar miscalculation. Machar's Nuer troops and militias, known as the 'White Army', captured much territory belonging to their rivals. The White Army was largely made up of Luo Nuer, from the Upper Nile and Jonglei, who would traditionally smother their faces with white ash. Their main preoccupation had been cattle-raiding, especially against their age-old enemy, the Murle people. On 15 November 1991 Machar's motley array of fighters captured Bor and killed over 2,000 Dinka, according to Amnesty International figures; other estimates were much higher. Although Machar dubbed the 'Bor massacre' a 'myth and propaganda' at the time, he apologized for the atrocity in 2012. The massacre was never forgotten in the south, and it became a brutal symbol of the Nuer-Dinka rift. Garang soon led the SPLA to inflict a major retaliation against the SPLA-Nasir, after the news of the massacre reached his HQ in Torit.

Despite the Machar-Akol trouncing by the 'official' SPLA, Khartoum continued to treat both commanders seriously. Al-Bashir, who had experience of divide and rule in the south, appointed a top-ranking military team to deal with Machar's militia. Senior military intelligence officers met Akol in Kenya and Germany to make vague promises of a federal south. Machar might well have thought that the new arsenal from Khartoum was more important, not least tactically, to fend off the SPLA advance. Khartoum had other ideas: using its new alliance, the regular northern army was allowed a free passage through Nuer territory to reach the core SPLA positions as far south as their HQ in Torit, displacing Garang. The SPLA general sought a new refuge in the deep forests of the Didinga Hills, beautiful and often shrouded in clouds.

Garang ordered a diversionary attack on the southern capital, Juba, in July 1992. The rebels temporarily captured much of the town, aided by southern troops in the garrison. Eventually, the attack was repelled with heavy SPLA losses, especially in equipment, which it could ill afford to lose. A number of Equatorian troops and civilians were summarily killed in Juba by government forces. Having held Juba, just, Khartoum did not go on the offensive, partly because of an intelligence assessment that suggested that the recent arrival of US peacekeeping troops in Somalia might presage an American no-fly zone in southern Sudan. This was wide of the mark, because the Americans proved incapable of controlling the air space even around Mogadishu where its helicopters were downed by local fighters.

Senior Equatorian commanders, not consulted about the Juba attack, now defected to the SPLA-Nasir. To further thicken the alphabet soup, SPLA-Nasir renamed itself SPLA/M-United and the SPLA was now sometimes referred to by outsiders as SPLA-Mainstream. Both SPLAs – whatever their titles – fought each other vigorously. (A little like in Afghanistan when the roughly forty m*ujahedeen* groups spent more time fighting each other rather than the Russian occupiers in the 1980s.) The northern army inevitably took advantage by deploying heavily armed convoys to try to retake towns such as Rumbek, which stayed in rebel hands, however. The army made more progress in the Nuba Mountains; the last town held by the SPLA, Um Durain, fell in August 1993. President al-Bashir then publicly announced that the whole of Nuba would be conquered by the next dry season.

Garang managed to keep his official SPLA from falling apart through iron discipline and increased foreign support. The Machar-led schism could never resolve the central contradiction: he advocated southern secession – in opposition to Garang's holistic view – yet Machar and Co had to rely on a tough Islamist Arab regime that was unlikely to grant that secession. The OAU, and especially the Nigerians, made several attempts to reconcile the Machar-Garang divisions and to unify the southern rebellion. The Americans, now much more involved in the Sudan conflict, suggested that the local organisation, IGAD (Intergovernmental Agency for Development), the main regional diplomatic grouping, replace the Nigerian peace efforts. Garang and Machar were brought together in Washington in late October 1993. Nothing much came of the meeting, but it was an important symbol of Congressional interest in the civil war, which would be soon manipulated by powerful US lobbies, especially the Christian right and African-American groups. Various IGAD-backed meetings in the region failed either to reconcile the southerners or entice Khartoum.

The fratricidal chaos of the civil war within the civil war allowed Kerubino to escape his hole in the ground. He was one of the most colourful SPLA commanders. A Catholic, born in 1948, he had grown up in the same Twic Dinka clan as Garang. Considered trigger-happy and impulsive by other commanders, he had represented the movement as 'deputy commander in chief' at the 1986 peace conference in one of the Emperor's old palaces near Ethiopia's Koka dam. With his omnipresent shooting stick, he used to give occasional press interviews in Nairobi, where his various wives and some of his twenty children were safely ensconced. He obviously harboured aspirations for the top job. So Garang's pre-emptive strike against his friend was probably not just Stalinist paranoia. As with so many other dissident southern leaders, Khartoum offered him the chance to form a pro-government Dinka militia, but Kerubino could not match Garang's popularity among his own tribe. He ditched the government side and resumed independent command in the south, managing in January 1998 to seize Wau briefly. On the strength of this achievement – he was an able field commander – he asked Garang to take him back into the main SPLA. Garang was not a forgiving man, but took back his old clan friend, though he kept him in HQ as a staff officer, not entrusting him with another field command. Angered by this, Kerubino once again defected north, where he allied with another renegade commander, Paulino Matip Nhial. Matip went on to lead the most powerful pro-government militia in south Sudan; he also set up a commercial empire among his Bol Nuer people. A competent field commander, Matip swapped back and forth between the SPLA and Khartoum (but with more strategic effect than Kerubino) and he also became a rival of another prominent Nuer commander, Riek Machar. It is not clear whether Khartoum's effective military intelligence had a hand in another plot to kill Garang in Nairobi at a meeting of IGAD, but it may have been involved in Kerubino's demise at the same time. Kerubino fell out with Matip and murky rumours surfaced of a shoot-out in which the old Dinka warrior met his martial fate. Few apart from himself ranked Kerubino as a national leader, but his chequered career did indicate the Byzantine world of southern leadership and the frequent successes of the north's intelligence agencies in manipulating it.

Pro-government northern militias sometimes used an old and highly offensive phrase to describe the divide-and-rule strategy: *Aktul al-abid bil abid* – kill the slave through the slave. More diplomatically, the technique was called the 'peace from within' strategy – doing deals with rebels who would work with Khartoum, unlike the official SPLA. This was soon

1. Sudan's pyramids at Meroë are much smaller than their Egyptian counterparts, but their lonely and largely unvisited location is very atmospheric.

2. General Charles Gordon was a religious crank who disobeyed explicit orders to evacuate British and Egyptian officials and troops from Khartoum in 1884.

The London News

FALL OF KHARTOUM

MURDER OF GENERAL GORDON

3. Gordon's death made him a Victorian icon. There were no reliable Western eye-witnesses to his death, but that did not stop the British media reporting lurid accounts of his 'martyrdom' to the imperial cause.

4. General Horatio Herbert Kitchener defeated the Mahdists at the Battle of Omdurman in 1898. Sudan remained under British control until independence in 1956.

5. The leader of the Mahdists was Muhammad Ahmad ibn Abdullah. He proclaimed a jihad not only in Sudan, but also throughout the Middle East. His tomb in Omdurman. (Author.)

6. Contemporary picture of the governor's palace where Gordon was killed. After independence it became the presidential palace. (Author.)

7. The command vehicle used by General Omar al-Bashir in the 1989 coup. (Author.)

8. Al-Bashir greets Sadiq al-Mahdi, the former premier, in early 2014. (Sudan government archives.)

9. The Sudanese President greets his old rival, Dr Hassan al-Turabi, during a reconciliation process in early 2014. (Government archives.)

10. Dr Hassan al-Turabi was more interested in international jihad rather than the details of domestic governance, but he was a highly gifted intellectual and spiritual leader. He was equally at home in tie or turban, and in English and French as much as Arabic.

11. For the first years after the revolution of 1989, al-Bashir concentrated on military matters, but eventually he removed al-Turabi from power and became politically dominant by 1999.

12. Bigwigs in the ruling National Congress Party, Dr Ibrahim A. Ghandour (left) and Ali Othman Taha, who led Khartoum's team during the peace talks with the south (2002-2005). (Tony Denton.)

13. The charismatic but authoritarian leader of the Sudan People's Liberation Army, Dr John Garang. He died shortly after the signing of the Comprehensive Peace Agreement.

14. Garang's successor was Salva Kiir, who became the first president of independent South Sudan. (Irwin Armstrong.)

15. Riek Machar became Kiir's deputy in the new republic, but rebelled against him in December 2013.

16. In 1998 US President Clinton sent cruise missiles to destroy the Al-Shifa facility in Khartoum. It was not producing WMD precursors, but instead anti-malaria and veterinary medicines. (Author.)

17. In 1996 Riek Machar joined Khartoum as part of the 'Peace from Within' policy. In June 1996 government troops march as a part of a peace rally in Juba, the southern capital. (Author.)

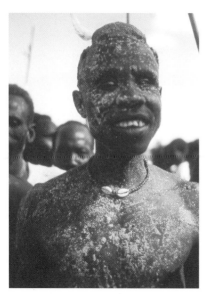

18. Tribal dancer taking part in a peace rally in Torit, June 1996. (Author.)

19. Sudan Liberation Army (SLA) insurgents, near El Fasher, Darfur, 2004. (Author.)

20. SLA insurgents, Darfur, 2004. (Author.)

21. Cameraman Irwin Armstrong with SLA troops, 2004. (Author.)

22. Government counter-insurgency forces, Darfur, 2005. (Author.)

23. US aid for IDP camp near El Fasher, 2004. (Author.)

24. Mosque in Sarasir, the village where al-Bashir grew up. (Tony Denton.)

25. Diplomatic duties: al-Bashir at the 12th AU summit. (Government archives.)

26. Unlike most heads of state in Africa, al-Bashir is a patient and ready listener, even to Western journalists. (Tony Denton.)

27. Al-Bashir's second wife, Widad Babiker Omer. She is the widow of a fellow conspirator in the 1989 coup. The President's second marriage made it fashionable in northern Sudan to marry widows of 'martyred' soldiers. (Tony Denton.)

28. Mohammed Hassan, the President's younger brother and look-alike. (Tony Denton.)

29. Hadiya, the President's mother. She was 88 when interviewed for this book. (Tony Denton.)

30. Al-Bashir is very much a family man, seen here with his second wife and stepdaughter, at his farm near Khartoum. (Tony Denton.)

31. The President doted on his youngest stepchild, Amna, pictured here in conversation with the author, at the presidential farm. All the stepchildren, nephews and nieces speak English fluently, albeit with an American accent. (Tony Denton.)

32. Al-Bashir accommodated his three nieces (the children of his brother, Mohammed Hassan)

33. Salva Kiir voting, in Juba, during the 2010 election. He had trouble finding his name on the voting lists at the correct election centre. (Irwin Armstrong.)

34. SPLA policeman guarding a voting centre in Bentiu, April 2010. Police and party workers were often accused of 'helping people to vote', although the majority of the population, especially females, were illiterate. (Tony Denton.)

35. Author interviewing an election official near Juba during 2011 referendum. Irwin Armstrong was the cameraman. (Marty Stalker.)

36. In private, al-Bashir was usually a quiet considered man, but he took on another persona in front of crowds. A fluent orator, not to say rabble-rouser, his rhetoric sometimes got the better of him and he would launch into sweeping over-statements and colourful threats to his opponents. But this is very much in the style of Arab political speeches. (Government archives.)

37. The President at his farm in January 2014. He insisted he wanted to retire to take up farming full-time. (Tony Denton.)

38. Breakfast with Bashir. The Sudanese are famously hospitable to foreigners. On the author's first visit to the country, however, he was arrested by the Minister of Justice himself. On the last visit, nearly 20 years later, he enjoyed a late breakfast with the President at his farm, January 2014. (Tony Denton.)

developed into a Peace Charter, formalized in 1997. It was redolent of the so-called 'internal settlements' adopted by the white regimes in Rhodesia and later South West Africa. The apartheid government also tried to do the same with its homelands policy, while cutting out the African National Congress. In the end, the whites had to deal with the real leaders of the liberation movements, just as Khartoum was to discover.

The SPLA-United continued to seriously hamper the rival official movement, but soon failed to live up to its own name of 'United'. Inter-Nuer tribal clashes as well as traditional non-political disputes with neighbouring tribes caused many casualties, especially now government arms were plentiful. The SPLA-United held its first major congress at Akobo in September 1994 to re-organize itself. In the traditional southern manner, a new name, it was thought, would work wonders. Some of the commanders who had been considered too close to Khartoum, such as Akol and Kerubino, were ousted. Machar, the great survivor, took command of the newly minted South Sudan Independence Movement/Army (SSIM/A). The strategy failed and Machar retreated to a government outpost at Kodok on the White Nile. Many of his Nuer troops and commanders rejoined the official SPLA. Desperate, Machar travelled to Addis to join up with the exiled opposition to Khartoum, the National Democratic alliance, in which Garang was already a prominent, if ill-fitting, member. Machar, however, was kicked out of the country by the new government. He tried reviving his local support in Nuerland, but he was, for the time being, a busted flush.

He had nowhere else to go but Khartoum. With Kerubino at his side and other tribal leaders, he signed a separate peace, more an unconditional surrender, with President al-Bashir in April 1997. It was based on the Peace Charter signed a year before. The charter made clear that Sudan would remain unified, but at some unspecified date southerners could have a referendum on a federal system. This was a great propaganda tool for the government. In the summer of 1996 I travelled around the south on the so-called peace train. The tall imposing Machar, charismatic despite his lazy eye and gap-toothed smile, could charm foreigners with his educated manner (he was awarded a PhD at Bradford University in the UK) but – except for his ever-loyal core of Nuer — he seemed to have trouble persuading the smallish crowds in government-held towns such as Wau that he could replace his arch-rival, Garang, or that Khartoum would grant meaningful southern autonomy. A sad brass band, dressed in a strange uniform apparently from the French revolutionary period, greeted Machar when he arrived at the main government garrison inside Wau; it was the most tuneless music that I had ever heard in my life. It was symbolic of the pointless charade.

According to one acute observer, 'The Peace Charter had not only not brought peace, but it had failed to halt the SPLA's political and military resurgence. Neither Riek nor the government had much to show for their collaboration.'[3] It also accelerated the civil war within the Nuer. Machar had helped to weaken – temporarily – the SPLA and also effectively handed over the control of the oilfields to Khartoum.

Paulino Matip, who had been made a major general in the Sudan army, was incensed that Machar had been chosen by Khartoum to lead the Nuer and refused to serve under him, though the government continued to pay Matip to deploy his Nuer militia to protect the oil installations at Bentiu. Machar had disgraced himself in the eyes of many southerners. The SPLA had been battered by infighting and heavy government offensives in 1993-94. In April 1994 Garang had convened a large congress at Chukudum. Roughly half the 500 delegates were civilians, the rest were commanders from across the south and the Nuba Mountains and the southern Blue Nile regions. Garang wanted to demonstrate his support from both civilians and military, and that he was concerned about the peasantry, despite numerous allegations of human rights abuses. The SPLM was poorly organized abroad, but a handful from the diaspora also attended. The question of independence versus the unified 'New Sudan' was not resolved, but the appearance and some of the substance of the SPLA's claim to represent all the southern peoples were attempted.

The resurgence of the SPLA, along with the effective collapse of Machar's army, meant that the bulk of the fighting was now done not by pro-government southern militias, but the regular army and the PDF. Khartoum endured heavy casualties, including the death of one of President al-Bashir's brothers, Ahmed, who had been a volunteer in the PDF. Government forces started to pull back as the SPLA won a series of victories in Equatoria in late 1994 and in Bahr al-Ghazal in early 1995. In these reverses the PDF especially, as well as the regular army, suffered thousands of dead and wounded in the first months of 1995. Despite strict censorship, Khartoum was always a leaky place for secrets, and soon reasonably accurate reports spread on the rumour mill. Volunteers for the PDF dried up. At the beginning of 1996 morale was so low in the government forces that occasionally garrisons in the south would refuse to leave their fortifications. Al-Bashir conducted another purge of officers to remove the defeatists. Except for a number of major towns, the SPLA now took control of almost the whole south; militias which had been long-term Khartoum allies turned their weapons in favour of the SPLA. Even tough Arab militias in the Nuba Mountains made deals with the SPLA. A whole battalion of the Sudanese army surrendered at Yirrol, south-east of Rumbek. By spring 1996 the SPLA looked unstoppable. The military-led northern revolution seemed to be stuttering; al-Turabi's emphasis on forging a new jihad by moral conversion could not work against the guns of the SPLA. Society might have been changed, but the battlefield had not.

The Egyptian assassination attempt
Al-Turabi did travel to the south on occasions to rally the faithful in their regional jihad, but he was still obsessed with the international mission. His third Popular Arab and Islamic Congress was held in Khartoum in March 1995. All the main Islamist groups attended, including those on the frontier of the *Umma*, the *mujahedeen* from the Philippines, for example. A major sticking point for some attendees was the use of 'Arab' in the Congress title. Many African delegates were unhappy, as was Louis Farrakhan's delegation from America. Farrakhan, a calypso singer-turned imam, led the Nation of Islam. Amid the fractiousness, al-Turabi did manage to broker an agreement between rival banned jihadist groups from Egypt. This seriously discomfited the Egyptian government of Hosni Mubarak, who had a strong personal distaste for al-Turabi's Islamist ventures. Cairo had on occasions used the ancient territorial disputes between Sudan and Egypt to crank up pressures on Khartoum. He also cracked down again on the Muslim Brotherhood and its affiliates at home.

The March summit of Islamists was used by Egyptian radicals to finesse a plot to kill Mubarak, according to Egyptian intelligence. It had been planned for over a year. Dr Ayman al-Zawahiri, later to lead al-Qaeda after its founder's death, was allegedly the ringleader (though bin Laden was a resident of Khartoum at the time). Two months later, on 26 June 1995, President Mubarak flew in to the airport at Addis Ababa to attend the annual OAU summit. Egyptian intelligence had prudently provided their president with an armoured limousine to drive him from the airport into central Addis. A blue van pulled in front of the limo and two men came out firing machine guns, while snipers on nearby rooftops joined in. Mubarak was saved by his bullet-proof glass and his bodyguards, who killed five of the would-be assassins. The president ordered his limo to return to the airport from where he promptly flew home and gave an impromptu press conference at which he blamed Sudan for the attempted assassination (the third of six serious attempts during his career). It was lucky that Mubarak turned around to go back to the airport, because a second ambush awaited his cavalcade. Later, the assassins were identified as coming from Egypt's *Jamiat al-Islamiyya*, aligned with the Islamic Jihad. Cairo, however, immediately denounced al-Turabi as the mastermind of the plot. Khartoum issued a bland denial and condolences, though al-Turabi rather undermined the government's attempt at fence-mending by calling the assassins 'messengers of the Islamic faith'. Adding insult to injury, the narcissistic al-Turabi also said that he found Mubarak 'to be very far below my level of thinking and my view, and too stupid to understand my pronouncements'. This was not an ideal way to treat the leading Arab nation and a sensitive neighbour with a powerful military. Khartoum was often its own worse enemy in the diplomatic game. At his comfortable but rather ordinary home in Khartoum North, al-Turabi gave interviews to journalists denying his involvement in the Mubarak plot, but nonetheless praising the attempt to get rid of the 'Egyptian Pharoah'.

A UN report later revealed that the weapons used had been flown into Addis by Sudan Airways; a bit of a giveaway, that. And stupid because Ethiopia was awash with weapons and it would have been much easier, and more deniable, to smuggle the guns across the porous border. Some of the assassins had been issued with Sudanese passports and had sojourned in Sudan. Khartoum had been caught redhanded.

There was no evidence to directly implicate President al-Bashir who was still keeping a low profile, but Mubarak also lashed out at him calling him a 'pygmy despot' (though he was of average height). Soon Mubarak found out that the house in Addis used by the assassins had been rented by a Sudanese agent acting on behalf of Sudanese intelligence. He became incensed and called Khartoum a 'fountain of terrorism' and run by 'thugs, criminals and crackpots'. He even threatened to invade Sudan and attack the alleged terrorist training camps. Anti-Sudan protests were organized in the streets of Cairo. Troops from both sides faced off along the border of the disputed Halayeb Triangle. This territory along the Red Sea, 7,950 square miles, was created in 1902 by the British colonial passion for drawing borders with straight lines, cutting through tribal allegiances. In addition, some oil was found there. The Egyptian army ejected Sudanese police and officials and took possession, although to this day Khartoum claims the territory – practically the one thing on which the government and the rebel Beja Congress (which claims its tribal possession) can agree on. The fact that Khartoum almost fought a full-scale border war with Egypt in 1995, while waging, in the Sudanese context, an almost total war in the south, demonstrates the high-wire act that the government was attempting to pull off. Somebody would soon fall off. In the military in Khartoum, al-Turabi was blamed for the crisis with Egypt, as well as many other problems. The man couldn't keep his mouth shut, was the opinion of some senior officers.

The Islamist jamborees, the influx of *mujahedeen* (although the visa requirement for the brothers was quietly reinstated in 1995) and finally the assassination attempt on Mubarak had alienated the country's neighbour. Egypt was literally up in arms. Libya was hostile and still trying to encroach in Darfur. Ethiopia was truculent, not least because of the assassination attempt on its own soil, and Khartoum's on-off support for Islamists in Somalia. Kenya and Uganda were staunchly supportive of their black brethren in the south. Zaire, the Central African Republic and Chad were unstable and sometimes hostile. Eritrea had changed sides and was now supporting the Beja Congress attacks in eastern Sudan. Some Arab states, notably Syria, were concerned about Khartoum's appetite for radical Islamists. And the West was generally hostile to the north and increasingly supportive of the southern rebellion. Would the military regime in Khartoum collapse again? African experts predicted that outcome almost daily.

It got worse. The UN Security Council ordered Khartoum to extradite three surviving gunmen from the Addis attack on Mubarak who had sought refuge in Sudan. Khartoum dragged its feet, not least in the UN. It takes a lot to unite the Security Council, but Khartoum managed it: in January 1966 Resolution 1044 imposed UN sanctions on Sudan. In addition, the US accused Khartoum of providing a safe haven for terrorists. A few months later, more sanctions were imposed on the country, for example restricting travel for its diplomats. Sudan had become a pariah state, surrounded by enemies on all sides. One way out was to offer Osama bin Laden as a sacrificial lamb.

Osama bin Laden and the intelligence conundrum
I had long taken an interest in bin Laden since I had worked in Afghanistan in 1984 and his base was next to where I was temporarily located. The Afghan *mujahedeen* I was accompanying were rigorously kept away from 'the Arabs', so I didn't get to meet him. I followed his career from then on, however. In summer 1996 I flew out to Khartoum hoping to interview him, but he had flown the coop shortly before I could get there. After he had left Sudan, Khartoum launched a PR campaign to say that the Americans, British and Saudis had refused intelligence contacts that suggested Khartoum would have done a deal over Osama. The Sudanese emphasized that they had

handed over Carlos the Jackal to the French in 1994. Was the bin Laden offer genuine? If it were, then the whole of world history might have been different. The story is still shrouded in mystery, however. The Sudanese *Mukhabarat* was good at 'grey ops': mixing some facts with clever disinformation. Nevertheless, President Clinton admitted in his memoirs that turning down the bin Laden offer was the 'greatest mistake' of his presidency. This was hindsight, however, five years before the abominations of 9/11.

Washington regarded the ejection of bin Laden from Sudan as a victory. Grabbing him was not apparently on the radar. On 18 May 1996 a chartered C-130 plane took bin Laden, his wives, children and over 100 of his followers to Jalalabad in eastern Afghanistan. En route the plane refuelled at the Gulf state of Qatar – which had close ties with Washington – but was allowed to proceed unhindered.

If the handover offer were serious why didn't the CIA respond, or at the very least react to a fax allegedly sent by the *Mukhabarat* detailing the exit plans of the Saudi Islamist? It would have been straightforward to intercept the plane, not least in Qatar. The deal was supposed to be that the US would drop sanctions against Sudan. And, moreover, Khartoum offered close intelligence liaison – this offer was taken up tepidly in 2000 and intensely after 9/11.

The CIA had initially fingered bin Laden for the 1993 World Center attack, assumed he had a hand in the assassination attempt on Mubarak, and certainly, the Americans said, he had organized terror training bases in Sudan. After US sanctions were imposed in 1996, the US embassy was closed in Khartoum and this reduced the quality of American intelligence, which had to rely on well-paid but unreliable if imaginative local sources. The Sudanese insisted that bin Laden was engaged only in engineering projects and charity work. Nevertheless, Washington leaned heavily on Khartoum to kick out the Saudi, saying that he could go anywhere, except Somalia. Washington was still smarting from its military debacle in Mogadishu. According to a senior Sudanese minister who knew bin Laden well, the Saudi was 'very angry' at his ouster. Bin Laden told the Minister, 'The Saudis and the US didn't even pay you; you are throwing me out for nothing.' Nor was bin Laden paid the large amount of money he was owed by Khartoum for his extensive construction projects, especially road building. Bin Laden had become the largest private landowner in the country, with vast interests in the east. It was also estimated that he had left $50 million in equipment and other assets. The Saudi's parting shot was to call the Khartoum government 'a mix of religion and organized crime'.

During this international intelligence debate, I interviewed Lieutenant General Gutbi al-Mahdi, who had just (officially) retired as head of the *Mukhabarat*. He denied that bin Laden had been energetically setting up the embryonic al-Qaeda while in Sudan. The spymaster said:

> When he was here, he was under close surveillance. We were watching him. He was busy. He was preoccupied by his business … Kicking him out was a big mistake … In Afghanistan no one could watch him, not even the Americans.

He said that he offered the CIA the bin Laden files in mid-1997. The *Mukhabarat* had watched his every move, literally. Equally important were the details of the many Islamists who had travelled to meet the Saudi.

Could the information in those files have prevented 9/11?

'Definitely,' al-Mahdi said. 'The Americans didn't want to look at those files.'

Why on earth not?

'Because their preoccupation was demonizing the government of Sudan rather than tracking down terrorists.'

A key question remains: if bin Laden was not up to anything in Sudan, why were the files intelligence gold?

Once bin Laden had gone, Sudanese intelligence conveniently played up their alleged offer of the Saudi warlord's head on a platter. The many opponents of Khartoum argued that Khartoum was too implicated to hand the Islamist over to the CIA. Inside the Washington intelligence community there was intense debate, mostly after the Saudi had moved to Afghanistan. Most intelligence experts said to me, in essence: 'If the offer was really there, we would have taken it. Why not?' A good question. With hindsight, the State Department worried that no hard evidence was available to convict bin Laden in an open court in the US. Others considered the Khartoum offer a bluff. Even if it were not, intelligence dialogue would weaken the sanctions pressure on a 'rogue' state the US was trying to isolate.

The Sudanese line at the time was the American campaign to kick out bin Laden and Khartoum's compliance angered the Saudi so much that this turned him on to his international jihad. Prevented from plying his trade as an engineer, war was the obvious alternative. This is not an entirely satisfactory psychological explanation for bin Laden's behaviour, especially as he had trodden the warlord path in the 1980s in Afghanistan.

In 1998 bin Laden was held responsible by Washington for the US embassy bombings in Tanzania and Kenya, with heavy loss of life. Partly in response to these bombings, the Pentagon launched a wave of cruise missiles against Sudan (and Afghanistan). Unfortunately, the main target in Sudan turned out to be not a chemical weapon precursor site, but the al-Shifa medical facility, which produced anti-malaria and veterinary products. Embarrassingly, the British ambassador had recently attended the opening of the facility. I carefully checked through the site, after the bombing, and saw only destroyed medicines. Scientists in British intelligence confirmed this to be true and the Americans, much later, admitted the factory had no proven connection to bin Laden or chemical weapons, although they did not rush to compensate the innocent owner of the facility. Moreover, the film cameraman I worked with had been given total licence to film inside al-Shifa just before the missiles completely destroyed the factory. There were no guards there at all, my colleague said.

The fashionable Khartoum line at this time – and it had some resonance in Washington – was that President Clinton, who had form in the trouser department, had used the raids to distract the media from the Monica Lewinsky scandal which threatened his impeachment.

Nevertheless, the terrorist attack in 2000 on the USS *Cole* was blamed on an increasingly active al-Qaeda network. After 11 September 2001 the worldwide manhunt for bin Laden re-awakened interest in the Sudanese connection. The bin Laden question was part and parcel of a larger diplomatic row. Khartoum argued that Washington was demonizing Sudan because it wanted to topple the Islamist government. This was the era of the US doctrine of regime change. The Americans were the real terrorists, said al-Bashir in various speeches, because Washington had, at different times, encouraged Uganda, Eritrea and Ethiopia to support guerrilla and conventional incursions against Sudan. Because of lobbying by the US black Congressional caucus and by the religious right, Washington had consistently supported with diplomacy and money (almost $30 million per annum of overt, non-lethal aid) the southern rebels. Such dangerous meddling, said Khartoum, along a Christian Muslim fault-line, could plummet Sudan into anarchy, a second Somalia, and create further breeding grounds for international terrorism. Khartoum also emphasized that it had handed over Carlos the Jackal and claimed, repeatedly, to have discreetly offered to extradite bin Laden to the US. And at the very least they had clearly told bin Laden to leave, because of US *demarches*. After the 1998 cruise missile attacks, Khartoum offered to allow US inspectors to examine al-Shifa and other alleged WMD sites in

Sudan. As one Sudanese diplomat explained later to an American audience: 'You guys bombed Iraq because it blocked UN weapons inspectors. We're begging for a UN inspection and you're blocking it.'

Washington finally took up the intelligence liaison invitation in May 2000: a joint FBI-CIA team arrived in Sudan to investigate the alleged terror connections. The visiting team was given carte blanche, said Khartoum, to search for any terror infrastructure – camps and banking networks. According to Sudanese intelligence sources, after a year the joint FBI-CIA team was prepared to 'sign off' – dismiss – the main terrorist allegations. Even after 9/11 US intelligence showed little immediate interest in the 400 major files on al-Qaeda affiliates that were held in Sudan's intelligence HQ in Khartoum. The files were very detailed and had full CVs on key al-Qaeda operatives, with photos in most cases. (I examined some of them myself.) This perhaps paralleled the Western failure to collect valuable Taliban data when the Northern Alliance and US special forces captured Kabul in late 2001. The Russians moved in quickly and took much of it away. British and American agencies had to resort to trying to debrief Western journalists and securing photographs from them. A CIA team did arrive in Khartoum in late 2001 (with a large photocopier in a transport aircraft) to make copies of the extensive Sudanese files. Sudanese intelligence also claimed that they offered access to their former colonial masters. They said, however, that MI6 showed little interest in the al-Qaeda files, but were more prepared to look at Sudanese data on Hamas and Hezbollah. An intelligence team from London was scheduled to visit, but was cancelled by London at the last minute. This is all from Khartoum sources. The British and Americans said that the Sudanese were never as helpful as they pretended to be. As one senior Foreign Office official told me: 'They have a lot of skeletons in their cupboard. They do not want us to get too close. And you should not take their offers at face value.' Caution noted.

The Sudanese intelligence top brass were definitely rattled and feared another dose of cruise missiles. In January 2002 I gained access to the shiny new Sudanese intelligence headquarters to meet Yahia Hussein Babiker, whose role was roughly equivalent to the deputy head of MI6. Sitting in his deep grey-green swivelling leather chair, he conceded that the possibility of another US missile strike was 'low', but 'suitable preparations' had been made. He did not expand on how Sudan could counter cruise missiles. As the intelligence boss conducted his one-on-one briefing, a TV screen by his side showed an American NBC programme with a prominent map of the USA's potential counter-terror targets. It included Sudan.

Khartoum's nervousness about an attack was palpable – despite the official line that they were not a target. This was highlighted by an unsolicited offer to interview the head of state. In January 2002 I was shown into the presidential palace for my first face-to-face meeting. I asked President al-Bashir what specific steps his government was taking to help Washington in the war on terror.

Speaking in formal Arabic, he said, 'What we can offer the US government in the fight on terror is that we can exchange information and also we have given our commitment to not allow a haven or transit for terrorists.'

I pressed him on whether his *Mukhabarat,* perhaps one of the best intelligence agencies in Africa, was certain no terrorists were operating in the vast country.

'I can assure you that there are no terrorists in Sudan because no Sudanese has been accused of being a terrorist.' I did not interrupt this rather sweeping statement. The president continued, 'All of those who have been accused of terrorism are not Sudanese. We have good control of all those non-Sudanese who are living here. We know that we do not have cells nor individual terrorists.'

At the end of the interview, the president added one of his favourite debating points: 'John Garang's group is not listed as a terrorist organization by the US. This is the important question we are asking of the Americans who compiled this list [of states sponsoring terrorism].'

The Sudanese explanation for the CIA's foot-dragging on intelligence co-operation was not entirely convincing. The agency was spending billions on tracking al-Qaeda so why didn't they jump at the Khartoum offers? The Sudanese counter was that 'US intelligence was too politicized'. A presidential adviser, Dr Ghazi Salahahudin Atabani, told me that 'US policy has been ideological not pragmatic. There was no way to break the barrier.' The UK-educated physician may have had a point, because British and American intelligence processes had been distorted by politicization in the run-up to the war against Iraq. But it was deeply ironic because Khartoum too had indulged in intensely ideological politics.

Eventually the CIA piled into the *Mukhabarat* treasure trove of al-Qaeda files. And even MI6 and MI5 became less reserved about Khartoum's offers as the British beefed up their previously lacklustre or ill-resourced monitoring of Islamist extremists in the UK. (This was the period when French intelligence nicknamed the British capital 'Londonistan'.) Perhaps the unofficial Sudanese jibe to the Americans – 'If you want to bomb a country with Islamist terrorist cells you should try hitting London or Saudi Arabia' – had found its mark.

One of Khartoum's many critics, the London-based deputy editor of *Africa Confidential*, Gill Lusk, warned that the whole intelligence lure was just spin.

> The National Islamic Front government is trying to delay as long as possible any US military reprisals because Sudan is perceived as a poor third-world African country by Western and Arab governments and the longer the government is seen to be appeasing Washington, the worse the international backlash will be against an American attack.

She summed up their policy as 'diplomatic deterrence by a very manipulative government' in Khartoum.

After bin Laden was driven out of Afghanistan by Afghan and American troops, it was often rumoured that the Houdini of international terror had returned to his old haunts in Sudan. One Canadian diplomat in Khartoum said mischievously, 'There have been lots of sightings of Osama – about the same number as the sightings of Elvis in fact.' (The CIA, however, generally believed that bin Laden was comfortably ensconced in Pakistan, though it was awkward to accuse Islamabad, its purported ally in the war on terror.) Over the years I spoke to many people in Sudan who knew bin Laden well. In elite government and business circles all described him as gentle, intense and courteous. He always asked people about their children and enjoyed talking in fine detail about construction equipment. Apparently he was most happy discussing JCBs, not jihad. His Khartoum travel agent fondly reminisced about the warlord giving him lots of business and paying with his American Express gold card.

In 2014 I asked a confidant of the president whether history could have been different if the Americans had let bin Laden remain in Sudan with his engineering projects, perhaps 9/11 might not have happened.

'And at least the road to Port Sudan would have been a lot better,' I said.

'Actually,' the Sudanese said, smiling, 'the main road bin Laden built soon fell apart.'

In retrospect, the offer to hand bin Laden over was probably just spin. In 2014 I spoke to many senior politicians who admitted that it would have been 'un-Islamic' to hand over a Muslim guest. The powerful former vice president, Ali Othman Taha, said, 'The maximum we could do was to tell him to go away.' In a frank admission Taha added:

I tried to persuade the Americans to talk to him, not to kick him out. He hadn't   dropped the jihadist issues, but his main concentration was on engineering ... I told visiting US diplomats to engage him. [As they had done when they were effective allies over the Russian occupation of Afghanistan.] But they always fobbed me off with an excuse about it not being part of their mission in Sudan. Then Osama bin Laden's concentration was genuinely with commerce. Those Americans made the mistake of their lives.

The what-ifs of history aside, bin Laden's five years in Sudan cast a long shadow on the Khartoum government, and particularly his main host, Hassan al-Turabi. The spiritual architect of the 1989 revolution and its very public showman was becoming an anathema to many at home, not only in the army, but even in the ruling party. He was called all sorts of Arabic variants of 'he is a Machiavellian windbag'. The joint ruler, al-Bashir, emerged slowly from the background, but still bided his time. Discontent had started in 1991, but al-Turabi's nemesis took years to evolve; finally the president's patience was exhausted and his religious patron was overthrown in a constitutional coup. Meanwhile, the tempo of international pressure mounted, as did the endless war in the south.

Chapter 6

The General Takes the Reins

The fall of al-Turabi.
President al-Bashir had always seen himself as a soldier first and a politician second. That is one reason why he left the religious and political manoeuvrings to al-Turabi, who had avoided formal political office. Al-Turabi was committed to what he regarded as far more important, his world Islamic renaissance. Petty local politics and administration were beneath him. As the frictions within the regime began to intensify, al-Turabi decided to seek political power. This was a mistake. Al-Turabi's soaring rhetoric and calls to jihad did not directly challenge the diarchy; moving into formal politics did.

   Al-Bashir had studiously concentrated on his power base: the military and security services. The man who held it together was Major General Bakri Hassan Saleh. Born in Dongola in 1949, at around six feet four inches and thick set, he was physically imposing. For an officer in charge of the intelligence services and later defence minister, this proved a useful attribute especially when, as a colonel, he helped al-Bashir first seize power in 1989. Tough, big and smart, he was said to terrify even his superiors. He certainly terrified me. In January 2002 he gave his first ever interview to a foreign journalist. The towering officer wore dark sunglasses inside, which added to his sinister image. I asked him about the recent controversial defence expenditure, using the new petro-dollars to buy expensive foreign kit, including, it was rumoured at the time, Russian MiG-29s.

   He said:

Oil does allow us extra revenues which permit some modernization, but if we modernize we are accused of militarism. This is a dilemma for us. But we have to be concerned with modernization because there are nine countries around us and we need helicopters, for example, to guard the pipelines.

In purely military terms, the Sudanese army had performed relatively well by African standards. Their equipment was often poorly maintained, but their generals managed to conduct, simultaneously, regular, semi-conventional and counter-insurgency wars over many years. Their battle-hardened neighbours had on occasion provided brigade-level fully armoured forces to support the SPLA. Despite the mismanaged economy and the manic zeal of the al-Turabi project, the army had done well to survive the SPLA advances, and the regular predictions of Western military experts that the army would collapse. True, the PDF took many of the casualties and the militias often did much of the fighting. The main reason for the survival of the army, and the ability to sustain the southern war, was partly due to the increasing oil income, but also the determined military leadership of al-Bashir, while General Bakri kept a lid on dissidents within the army and without. Major civilian demonstrations had broken out, for example in September 1994 when Khartoum University students led thousands of people to protest about food price inflation. Other riots about the cost of living spread throughout the north. More anti-government disturbances protesting about electricity and water shortages followed. The Islamist militias, as well as the army and police, had to work hard to contain the protests. Bakri purged the security services and quietly displaced civilian National Islamic Front influence. This, in effect, removed the al-Tuirabi factor from the security and armed services.

The army had had enough of al-Turabi. Despite its increase in personnel, the secret services were run ragged monitoring all the foreign Islamists whom al-Turabi had invited in. Some of them displayed good tradecraft in counter-surveillance, such as Hezbollah, for example. A rule of thumb in surveillance work in the West is, if a priority subject is being observed, that three shifts comprising, ideally, a total of fifty people are required, especially if the target is streetwise. And the time taken to monitor equipment, audio and video, as well as street and car squads, can be enormous. It is almost possible to feel sorry for the Sudanese *Mukhabarat* as they tried to keep tabs on thousands of trained radicals, some of whom were not communicating in Arabic.

One of them had been egregiously removed: Carlos the Jackal, aka Illich Ramirez Sanchez, who was not an obvious part of the Islamic renaissance. He was a hard-drinking and womanizing Venezuelan Marxist, who had led a very exotic life of revolutionary (often pro-Palestinian) violence, sometimes funded by the KGB and the East German Stasi. In a deal which involved financial inducements, and possibly an arms deal, the French secret service was allowed to abduct him from Khartoum on the night of 13 August

1994. He was recuperating in a villa after a minor testicular operation. The principle of the 'sale' of Carlos – especially the obvious implications for the demands to remove Osama – split the army/security matrix and the NIF led by al-Turabi. The botched assassination attempt on Mubarak and the local and international blowback tore at the frayed sinews of the NIF/security nexus.

Al-Bashir determined to remove Osama bin Laden. He could not simply hand over the Saudi to the Americans – that would create a storm in the Arab world. The Saudi government was asked to 'invite' bin Laden to come home. If the Saudis chose to hand him over to the Americans, that was their business. Claiming that bin Laden was no longer a Saudi citizen, the Saudis refused to play ball. Realizing that his own reputation was on the line if his guest ended up in American hands, al-Turabi used his connections to arrange a safe haven in Afghanistan.

The removal of bin Laden, while appeasing the Americans, did not improve the pariah status of Sudan. The UN Human Rights Commission, as well as individual NGO reports, condemned Sudan for extensive human rights abuses. Khartoum decided that the domestic base of the regime needed to be shored up. Al-Turabi's elaborate and dysfunctional system of local and regional *shuras* was transformed into a partly elected new national assembly in early 1996. Al-Turabi contrived to be elected for the assembly – after two impressive rival candidates mysteriously withdrew – and then organized his further election as speaker of the national assembly. The traditional party leaders were mostly in exile, but Sadiq al-Mahdi, in Khartoum, called the new assembly a farce. By making himself just another (senior) politician, al-Turabi had extricated himself from the secure Islamic carapace of revered theologian. Now the 'Islamic Pope', as detractors dubbed him, could be attacked by other politicians without the risk of being seen as anti-Islamic.

Sadiq al-Mahdi was hosting a wedding party in his own home's luxuriant garden, and his brother in law, al-Turabi, was a guest. The Umma leader, assuming that his *Muhhabarat* tail was relaxing, slipped away from the garden and country to join the National Democratic Alliance, the opposition coalition in Asmara. Al-Mahdi also met with President Mubarak, still an implacable enemy of the Khartoum regime. General Bakri's recent reforms of the security services could have led to some self-flagellation about al-Mahdi's flight. It was strongly rumoured, however, that Khartoum had wanted to get rid of al-Mahdi, who would inevitably sow confusion and disarray in the NDA, which he obligingly did.

Khartoum lost a number of senior NIF officials and ministers, as well as top military officers, in a (genuine) air crash when an Antonov-26 went down in the Sobat River after overrunning the airport in February 1998. Al-Bashir used this opportunity to set up a new cabinet more to his own liking, although it still contained NIF supporters, as well as some from a breakaway faction of al-Mahdi's Umma party. It also boasted a token southerner or two, including the persistent Lam Akol, head of the rump (of a rump) SPLA-United, as minister of transport. In May 1998 al-Bashir won a referendum to change the constitution which in effect legalized the 1989 revolution. This boosted the power of the presidency and finally accepted *sharia* as the sole source of law. Having secured his own base, and sidelined al-Turabi, the new government tried to improve its very tarnished image in the world, by allowing the old political parties to re-emerge after a decade of enforced hibernation.

Not to be outdone, al-Turabi reorganized the NIF into the National Congress Party. He also set about campaigning to boost the authority and influence of the position of speaker of the assembly. The plan was to use parliament and his party to limit the new powers of the presidency. Al-Bashir would become merely a titular head of state; real power would be back in the hands of the versatile and ambitious Imam. Al-Bashir moved to expand his domestic base by seeking reconciliation with the NDA, especially the man he had displaced, al-Mahdi. All the seized assets of the Umma party were returned. Al-Turabi upped the stakes by offering to meet al-Mahdi in Mecca. The schism between the two main Khartoum leaders could no longer be hidden – acerbic exchanges between them became public knowledge. Al-Turabi pushed hard to influence the election of the powerful state governors, as well as further trying to restrict presidential powers. The national assembly was due to vote on al-Turabi's proposals on 14 December 1999. Two days before, about forty of al-Bashir's closest allies, both in the old NIF and the army, met at the presidential palace at 5.00 pm. They debated until 4.00 am the next morning. A leading participant was Ali Othman Taha, whose legal skills were used to draft the decree to change the constitution and close the parliament.

Reminiscing years later, al-Bashir used a striking word to describe his action that morning. He told me he wanted to 'freeze' al-Turabi.

Al-Bashir sent his trusted armoured brigade to surround the assembly – a two-storey building that is reminiscent, ironically, of the Israeli Knesset. The president dissolved the assembly and sacked al-Turabi. In one of his regular radio talks, al-Bashir warned al-Turabi's followers: 'We are calling for freedom in Sudan, but those who think that freedom is a call to anarchy and abuse to the martyrs are under an illusion.' A state of emergency was declared, but elections were promised for the following year. Al-Bashir had finally broken the umbilical ties with his patron. From now on Omar al-Bashir was flying solo as the leader of Sudan.

The army welcomed the moves, not least because it resented the rival and erratic influence of the PDF and the NIF militias. Many of the more conservative Arab neighbouring states welcomed the fall of al-Turabi, especially Egypt. Al-Bashir assured President Mubarak that al-Turabi and his Islamist renaissance movement would not make a comeback. The political Imam was out of power, but was still capable of full-throated roars. In May 2000, on the al-Jazeera TV network, he urged the Sudanese to take to the streets and depose the military dictatorship. Thereupon he was banned from all political activity and removed as secretary general of the National Congress Party. So he organized a new party, the Popular National Congress (PNC) and used the party's newspaper to attack al-Bashir.

On 20 Feb 2001, on behalf of his fledgling party, al-Turabi signed an agreement with the SPLA which promised the right of self-determination in the south in exchange for a joint opposition to al-Bashir. Why the famed Islamist should make a deal with his lifelong enemies, the unbelievers in the south, was hard to fathom, except for personal vengeance against his former ally, the president. This was more than a political mistake; it would be interpreted as treason by many in Khartoum, even outside the al-Bashir circle. Al-Turabi was incarcerated the next day. He was back in Kobar prison, and not in quite as capacious a cell as the last time. He faced charges of communicating with the enemy, some of his senior associates were arrested and al-Turabi's PNC party was proscribed. Nevertheless, the Imam still had a lot of support The *Mukhabarat* worried about a 'third force' emerging from the militias, and the PDF. The PDF did not rise up, partly because the army had integrated them more closely. University students did protest on behalf of al-Turabi; this was a minor disturbance, but the army still feared an armed pro-al-Turabi insurrection. Al-Bashir gave a pep talk to a large gathering of the PDF personnel:

> Sudanese youth are fighting in the war zone while other youths in the world are busy with discos and parties. We thank Allah we have prepared these youths as the future of Sudan. *Allah Akbar.*

The government needed to maintain some sort of unity in the face of the war in the south.

As a sop to avoid any further Islamist disturbances, al-Turabi was moved from Kobar prison to house arrest. His immediate power base had been disrupted but, despite regular bouts of house arrest and imprisonment, al-Turabi was to remain a thorn in the side of the president for the next decade. Al-Turabi was jailed for dealing with the SPLA/M, a necessary prerequisite to end the civil war, a step which al-Bashir took himself a year or so later. Al-Turabi, typically and perhaps prematurely, had acted as a lone wolf. He seemed unable to learn from his mistakes. He repeated the manoeuvre by making a deal with the main rebels in the western war, in Darfur. He went further than parleying with them: he was accused of arming and funding them. Al-Turabi was also accused of helping to organize a major incursion from Darfur of an armoured column which attacked Omdurman in May 2008. Presumably, the president had the self-restraint not to repeat, in Arabic, the famous line: 'Who will rid me of this turbulent priest?'

Consolidation of power.

Freed from the 'meddlesome priest', Al-Bashir consolidated his position. In June 2000 the president had added ten senior military officers to the cabinet. State security and the direction of the south war was his priority. Now the new oil bonanza could pay for it.

In May 1999 the president had officially opened the new oil terminal just south of Port Sudan. This connected the 1,000-mile pipeline from the main Heglig installations and southern oilfields in Unity state. The system had been built by a consortium from China, Canada and Malaysia. The oil exports quickly pulled Sudan out of its hopeless debt situation (it had the world's largest debts to the World Bank and IMF) and created a growth spurt for the next decade of 6 to 8 per cent of GDP. True, the wealth accumulated around the three towns, but some inevitably trickled down. Before the oil, car traffic was sparse in the capital, but soon the skyline changed and traffic jams became common.

The tale of oil was a complex one and, as with most similar African states, the black gold was a curse and a blessing. The original Chevron concessions had been sold because of the war, and the Chinese became the main players. They had been involved with Sudan since the 1970s; the symbolically large Friendship Hall, built in central Khartoum in that period, was used for all sorts of prominent government functions. Khartoum was always eager to court Beijing, not least as a counter to the hostile USA in the UN Security Council. Militarily, China became the chief arms supplier, so the oil deals were a natural accompaniment.

The president's personal diplomacy had been central to oil development. The largest American exploration, via Chevron, had stopped development in 1984 after rebel attacks in the south. But Chevron did not give up completely until 1992. Despite the Chinese military ties, al-Bashir was drawn first to Malaysia. He paid a three-day state visit to Kuala Lumpur in June 1991 as the guest of Prime Minister Dr Mahathir Mohamad. The priority was an oil deal, though Petronas, the largest Malaysian oil company, was very wary, even though the two countries shared considerable political, religious and social links. One of the senior oil experts accompanying al-Bashir put it frankly: 'We feel very close to Petronas, probably because of the skin colour and same names. My people feel at home with Malaysians.'[1] But not sufficiently at home: Petronas dragged its feet for some years. Khartoum actively tried to play off China against Malaysia and later India.

Al-Bashir paid a successful state visit to China in September 1995 and he felt he had been very warmly received. President Jiang talked of pushing Sino-Sudanese relations to 'greater heights'. But the security, financial and technical difficulties had already caused some delays. The Gulf states also took an interest in Sudan's oil exploration. Political pressure eventually forced the Canadian oil company, Talisman, to quit Sudan, but the China National Petroleum Corporation (CNPC) took up much of the slack, as later did India's Oil and Natural Gas Corporation, Videsh (OVL).

The oil developments in the south brought desperately needed money to the Khartoum treasury, but it also excited international criticism because of actions by the army and militias, including the southern Bul Nuer militia of Paulino Matip. They were accused of a scorched-earth policy, driving away local tribespeople to ensure empty and secure oil fields. Organizations such as Amnesty International and Human Rights Watch kept up a barrage of condemnation about human rights abuses in areas adjacent to the fields. The drumbeat of media and NGO pressures deterred nearly all the remaining Western oil companies and left China, Malaysia and India as the dominant players. They seemed less vulnerable to the NGO lobbies.

Before the oil really started to flow in 1999, the economy was on its knees. Sudan's chronic debt problems prompted its expulsion from the World Bank. Severe foreign currency shortages crippled the economy, which was ravaged by inflation. But even before the oil salvation, prices for cotton improved on the world market. Sugar exports boomed too. And one product was always exempt from US sanctions – gum arabic, which was extracted from a certain type of acacia tree which grew in the Sahel. As a prime ingredient of chewing gum and Coca Cola, no American government could be seen to deny these delights to its citizens.

Once oil reached 512,000 barrels per day, some of the Gulf states rushed to invest (Qatar was especially interested in agricultural developments). Money poured in for smart new hotels in Khartoum for visiting businessmen. The most impressive was the oval-shaped five-star Corinthia hotel opened in 2008, which locals dubbed 'Gaddafi's Egg', because it was funded by the Libyans. Arab money helped to build the massive Merowe Dam, which was completed by the Chinese in 2008. Siemens constructed the necessary electricity grids to finally provide a reliable source of energy for the three towns. Sudan started building its own cars under licence. Coca Cola and Pepsi plants arrived. The government privatized its telecommunications giant, Sudatel, and its cell-phone partner, Mobitel, that soon transformed urban Sudanese into mobile-phone addicts. In 2004 Turkey erected the country's first shopping mall in Khartoum, with glitzy shops and a supermarket, food hall and cinema complex. Sudanese planners were trying to turn Khartoum into a second Dubai.

Under al-Turabi, the country was accused of returning to the time of the Prophet (actually this was unfair, as he wanted to adjust Islam to the modern era and was hostile to the anti-modernism of Wahhabism). But al-Bashir and the ruling NCP party regarded modernization as a prime benefit of the revolution. Khartoum wags used to joke that al-Turabi wanted to lead the people to the mosque, but under al-Bashir they all went to the souk. The president and his advisers loved to list the new roads and universities, not mosques and *madrassas*. The changes of the more pragmatic al-Bashir's attitude led to accusations that the theological superstructure of the regime was a mere façade. The president could not win. He was condemned for being a religious fanatic or damned for being irreligious. Yet the president wanted his legacy to be as a modernizer who built up Sudan's infrastructure and created economic stability.

No matter how much money came into state coffers, it could not compensate for the true costs of war. The annual defence budget increased by a third from $424 million in 19995 to $580 million in 2000-01, according to the International Institute of Strategic Studies. That was almost certainly an under-estimate as the regular defence budget did not include the costs of the PDF and security services. Moreover, even the tough-minded Indian investors and Beijing's Central Committee were not totally immune to foreign political pressures, and certainly not the security concerns about the oilfields. Al-Bashir had to end the war in the south. Enough was enough.

But could a fighting general be a peacemaker? Could an Islamist revolutionary achieve lasting peace with the unbelievers in the south? Perhaps, like Oliver Cromwell, the president had seen off his Levellers in the form of al-Turabi and his followers. There were other historical parallels for what al-Bashir was about to do. Only an impeccable right-wing and patriotic general such as Charles de Gaulle could have had the courage and kudos to give up on the long savage war in Algeria and grant independence. That was a close parallel. Politically, only Richard Nixon, an ardent cold war warrior, could have done the deal with the Communists in Beijing, and got away with it. Everything the army and religious conservatives had fought for since 1956 – *sharia,* unity of the state and victory over the 'terrorism/mutiny/rebellion' in the south – might be imperilled by a genuine peace process. Could President al-Bashir become a successful peacemaker?

Chapter 7

The Road to Peace in the South

A more pragmatic foreign policy

Chinese diplomatic and military relations were excellent. The oil deals were sweet for both sides, although Sudan was swapping over-reliance on one commodity, cotton, for another, more valuable, one – oil. The Chinese had also largely built the country's biggest construction project, the Merowe dam. Chinese businessmen and workers continued to pour into Khartoum, many of them paying a ceremonial visit to the Mahdi's tomb in Omdurman. After all, a Sudanese hero had killed General Chinese Gordon, a hate figure for many contemporary Chinese.

The fences with Egypt had been partially mended after al-Turabi's ousting. Khartoum continued to improve its relations with Cairo – over twenty properties owned by Egypt in Sudan had been returned. And the Khartoum branch of Cairo University was re-opened after its closure over the disputes about the Halayeb Triangle. Cairo, though, was more concerned about the security of the Nile headwaters. Mubarak wanted a peace deal in the south which could ensure this; he did not want a separate state run by the SPLM that could complicate the control of the Nile. In May 2000 John Garang personally assured the Egyptian president that he wanted a single democratic Sudan. Egypt worked with the IGAD group to ensure stability in the headwaters. Cairo also assisted Khartoum's efforts to restore good relations in the Arab League with countries such as Syria and Saudi Arabia, which had been inimical to al-Turabi's calls for international jihad.

President al-Bashir was determined to improve relations with the south, and one crucial ingredient was the American support for the SPLM. Some American diplomats (usually Democrats, it has to be said) compared al-Bashir with Ronald Reagan. Both were pragmatic populists and both tended to take non-intellectual broadbrush approaches to policy while leaving the details to subordinates. (Actually, al-Bashir was respected by his colleagues for his attention to detail, unlike Reagan.) The State Department hoped that they could work with Khartoum, now that al-Turabi had been banished from power. There was even some talk of returning relations to the period of engagement with Numeiri during his pro-Western phase; at that time the US donated its largest aid programme in sub-Saharan Africa to Sudan.

Relations had gone badly wrong after the 1989 revolution. Almost a lone Arab voice, Khartoum's apparent support of Saddam Hussein's invasion of Kuwait was a big diplomatic mistake which brought Sudan nothing but opprobrium. That was al-Turabi's doing. He was almost as obsessive as Osama bin Laden about US troops 'defiling' the holy places in Saudi Arabia, even though Americans in uniform did not go near Mecca or Medina. The hosting of bin Laden turned out to be Khartoum's most stupendous error of judgement – that too had been an al-Turabi project. Other egregious pratfalls, such as the assassination attempt on Mubarak, were blamed on the mischief-making imam. Al-Bashir claimed to be ignorant of the plot. That was surprising for someone who prided himself on his grip on the security services, but some intelligence sources have acquitted the president of that charge. Nevertheless, sanctions and isolation had left Sudan a pariah state.

This led to a US policy of 'containment, aggression and regime change', as one senior US State Department official put it. Once, Sudan had been a front-line ally against Marxist Ethiopia. Now US policy was the converse: to co-ordinate a front-line alliance with Ethiopia, Eritrea and Uganda to bring Khartoum down. Covert annual aid of around $30 million was going to the SPLM. It was supposed to be for non-lethal purposes, but the C-130s donated were a vital tool of the insurgency, for example. This was said to be part of the State Department's policy – the Pentagon kept largely aloof. The US military considered State's covert forays amateurish. A small complement of US special forces could have made a big difference, but the 1992 intervention in Somalia, given the Hollywood treatment in *Black Hawk Down*, was seem as a partial reason not to re-engage militarily in Africa, despite the Western hand-wringing over Rwanda in 1994. Washington also nurtured the NDA Sudanese opposition in Asmara, along the lines of the Contra policy once associated with President Reagan. Historically, Sudan's neighbouring states held as much sway – if not more – over the east, west and south as Khartoum did, so an American front-line containment strategy made sense. At least until Eritrea and Ethiopia were sucked into a savage border war against each other in 1998.

The Christian lobbies in the US demanded more muscular intervention. The right-wing evangelical groups had played a very large part in the election of President George W. Bush and they wanted a payback. President Bush often displayed a magisterial ignorance of world affairs, but he did actually know something about Sudan. Not only had his father, as vice president, been closely involved with the country during the 1984-85 famine, but also during the exodus of the Falasha Jews. And with the constant accompaniment of evangelist Franklin Graham, son of Billy, as a presidential candidate, Bush had had to pay polite attention to numerous Christian lobbyists in the Bible belt. One of the *causes celebres* was the so-called 'Lost Boys'. Thousands of southern youngsters had to flee the refugee camps when the fall of the Derg forced them from Ethiopia. Their emotive stories of escaping the Sudanese militias, seeking refuge in Ethiopian camps, and then ejection and their long dangerous odysseys to new camps in Kenya, pulled at many heartstrings when some were resettled in the US.[1] Radical Christian groups were also exercised by allegations of Arab slavery of southerners. American Christians raised money for their redemption, although some of the alleged slavery was a bogus cash-raising scam by unscrupulous nomadic tribesmen. Many terrible human rights abuses were happening on both sides in Sudan, but some of it was unduly exaggerated by American lobbies for their own ends. Secretary of State Colin Powell said that the greatest tragedy on earth was unfolding in Sudan and President Bush specially condemned Sudan for violations of religious freedoms. Partly to placate the Christian lobbies and Congress, in September 2001, Senator John Danforth was appointed as a special envoy to Sudan. In the previous year Washington had re-activated its embassy in Khartoum, albeit with a reduced number and rank of staff.

Behind the diplomatic scenes and the media campaigns of the NGOs, a much tougher intelligence game was being played out. The Islamist assault on the World Trade Center made Khartoum much more attentive to US sensitivities. The 1998 cruise missile attacks were a fresh and unnerving memory. Under al-Bashir's direction the Sudanese government went into overdrive to keep Washington happy, particularly the US intelligence services. The president appointed his close confidant, Major General Saleh Abdullah Gosh, the head of the National Intelligence and Security Service, to focus on intelligence and anti-terrorism liaison with the CIA and State Department. The CIA-*Mukhabarat* courtship had begun warily in the late 1990s; in early 2000 a joint FBI-CIA team arrived in Khartoum. The 9/11 abomination did not derail the blossoming intelligence ties; it accelerated the process. The swift American-led removal of the Taliban put the (extra) fear of God into the Sudanese government. Very shortly after the retribution in Afghanistan, Saleh Gosh and Ali Othman Taha met top CIA officials in a London hotel. It was what diplomats call a very frank meeting. The

Americans listed precisely what targets their cruise missiles would take out in Sudan, for example the Port Sudan oil refinery as well as the Sudanese air force, conveniently congregated on two main airfields. All in one afternoon. The Afghan demonstration effect had worked wonders for US leverage. The initial Sudanese intelligence co-operation had provided interesting but not major information from the vast wealth of material that the *Mukhabarat* had collected on nearly all the Islamist groups that had assembled or lived in Sudan from 1990 to 1996 and especially a cornucopia of data on bin Laden and his thousands of employees and acolytes. Most of his foreign radical followers had been kicked out or left, but those who had remained suddenly seemed to disappear. A few were said to have re-appeared, in manacles, in the USA, but others, allegedly, were rendered to prisons in pro-Western states not over-burdened with intrusive legal systems.

The enhanced demonstration effect of the US-led invasion of Iraq transformed the *Mukhabarat* into one of the CIA's closest 'friends'. So much so that Saleh Gosh spent a week at Langley, the HQ of the CIA, as an honoured guest. He was feted in a fashion usually reserved for senior spooks from major NATO states. In October 2005 I attended an elaborate garden party in the grounds of the new National Security HQ in Khartoum. Saleh Gosh was the host; he was in good spirits, backslapping his peers and even dancing on stage while the band played. Many of the top spooks in Africa – it was a summit for director generals of intelligence agencies – had assembled in the Sudanese capital. It was officially called the 'Fourth Conference of the Committee for Intelligence and Security Systems in Africa', which operated under the AU umbrella. No one could complain about the quality of the food, and big fans kept the guests cool. Spooks rarely let their guards down, but this was a unique occasion to relax among very discreet peers. MI6 and the CIA had sent senior people. They were incognito of course, so they did not expect Major General Gosh to call the senior CIA officer forward, by name, to step up to the well-lit platform and give him a handshake and a hug, a mark of a close male relationship in northern Sudan. The CIA man smiled awkwardly when he was given a spangly carrier bag full of small gifts. Then the MI6 spook was called up and given the same treatment. It was a touching display of rapport in the intelligence world, but a tiny bit awkward as a sprinkling of senior press people had been invited (to advertise that Khartoum was respectable again). I sat next to a distinguished journalist who wrote for the UK *Guardian*, a newspaper not always favoured by the intelligence community.

This process of détente had already started when President Bush's emissary, Senator Danforth, arrived in Khartoum in late 2001. He was met by senior officials determined to please. Danforth was no placeman. He was a high-powered, moderate Republican who was once tipped to be Bush's vice-presidential nominee. A Princeton and Yale graduate, he was a lawyer and an Episcopalian minister. He was also energetic and hardworking – a good choice to try to bring peace to Sudan. Danforth toured the south and then the Nuba Mountains where he helped to negotiate a ceasefire. He then beavered away at formalizing a ceasefire in the south. But President Bush's Sudan Peace Act in October 2002 soured some of the goodwill in Khartoum. This authorized relief money for the south in SPLM-held territory. It also threatened harsh penalties such as sanctions on oil exports used to purchase weapons and even further prohibition of World Bank and IMF credits to Sudan. The US peace initiative would be closed down if Khartoum did not act in good and prompt faith. Al-Bashir had hoped that Washington would drop existing sanctions, not threaten to increase them. Although the peace treaty was finally signed in January 2005, the outbreak of a major conflict in Darfur in 2003 was to derail Khartoum's hopes of a full rapprochement with the USA. Al-Bashir felt personally betrayed by Washington, but the US lobbies were soon to focus on an altogether new onslaught because of alleged genocide in Darfur. The al-Bashir government was caught out by the Darfur crisis, because almost its entire intelligence effort was concentrated on bringing peace to the south, not the west.

The old imperial power, Britain, was courted too, not least in closer intelligence ties, though the British were initially more reserved than their cousins in Washington. In a highly symbolic visit in January 2002, Prime Minister Tony Blair sent his independently minded Minister for International Development, Clare Short, to Khartoum. Always a straight hitter, the minister seemed pleased by what she had found. During a conversation in Khartoum, she told me:

> Any objective observer in the world can see that the government of Sudan has moved. Turabi has been removed from power. They have co-operated since 11 September. Sanctions have been lifted by the UN. There's been progress.

Despite the love-in between Gosh and Langley, the affair was not unconditional. The *Muhakbarat* yearned for the respect of, and co-operation with, MI6. Force majeure and a deep suspicion that regime change was still Washington policy encouraged Khartoum to ask MI6 to do more of the heavy lifting in the ongoing talks with the south. The British had (eventually) sought specific data on al-Qaeda, as well as other Middle Eastern radicals. Above all, the British FCO was not trying to finesse a change of regime. Also, most of the talks were taking place in Kenya, a British sphere of influence in US-UK intelligence terms. The Kenyan general, Lazarus Sumbeiywo, who co-ordinated the north-south talks, had been 'spotted' early while he was a cadet at Sandhurst in the early 1970s. Eventually, under President Arap Moi, General Sumbeiywo became head of Kenya's revived intelligence service. When he was re-jigging the service, he was ably assisted by his old mentors in MI6. Because of the post-colonial ties and nifty MI6 footwork, London was to play an unusually large secret role in the final settlement of Africa's longest war.

The lobbies
The improvement in diplomatic relations with both former enemies and old friends could perhaps provide the right international context for real progress in the south. Yet public diplomacy and covert intelligence networking did not tell the whole story. What was equally significant was the activity of influential lobby groups, mainly in the USA, but also in Europe. A so-called 'constituency of conscience' emerged in the US. A few older lobbyists, mostly Democrats, had worked on succouring dissidents in the Soviet system, but the collapse of the USSR allowed some to pivot their consciences to Africa. Younger Christian activists in the Republican Party also took up what they termed the 'Wilberforce Agenda', especially in south Sudan. A good example was Andrew Natsios, who later became President Bush's envoy to Darfur in 2006. The allegations of slavery obviously resonated emotionally with African-Americans and politically, especially in Congress, while the persecution of Christians in south Sudan energized the Bible belt, both black and white. America's most famous evangelist, Billy Graham, was a frequent visitor to south Sudan. His son, Franklin, was even more committed – he raised millions of dollars to set up hospitals in the region. The movement to help south Sudan became bi-partisan – Sudan was often the only thing the two rival parties could agree on. This cross-party alliance later morphed into the Save Darfur lobby. Millions, if not billions, were raised for humanitarian aid, often via Operation LIFELINE SUDAN. Technically, Khartoum had to give permission for aid flights into the south, but often the aid and visiting lobbyists entered the country illegally from Uganda or Kenya. Some aid reached starving civilians, but much of it went directly to the better-fed SPLA troops.

The issue of slavery had a special and much more current resonance in the US compared with the UK. The USA was also a much more fervent Christian society, especially compared with secular Europe. In addition, in the 1990s, Europeans tended to be more distracted by massive human rights abuses and religious war on their doorstep, in the Balkans. Further, pro-south Sudanese lobbyists in the UK were convinced that the FCO was still staffed by too many romantic Arabists.

One of the most important lobbies in the UK was the Swiss-based Christian Solidarity International, a sort of Amnesty International at prayer. It was led in Britain by John Eibner, an upstate New Yorker who had settled in London. The most well-known (and formidable) British member was Baroness Caroline Cox, who prided herself on working for the Lord in the Lords. Ennobled by Margaret Thatcher – with whom her toughness was compared – the former nurse and always devout Christian took her first trip to Sudan in 1992. She later castigated slavery as a counter-insurgency tool of the Sudanese army. Eibner activated his 'buy-back' scheme where slaves were redeemed for as little as $20. The CSI claimed to have emancipated over 80,000 slaves. Black churchmen and Congressmen took up this cause, although critics argued that this cash flow could incentivize, not curtail, slavery.

These lobbies made a lot of noise in the media, but – as ever – more was being done quietly in the shadows, or specifically in the gloom of the Otello Italian restaurant in Washington. This is where the 'gang of four' met to plot the destiny of south Sudan. They were influential, very, on US policy, but the policy wonks were not as all-powerful or sinister as Khartoum came to believe. In particular, President al-Bashir was adamant in his conversations with me that the gang had done much harm to US-Sudan relations and contributed to the disasters in the south. So who were these 'gangsters' and what did they do?

The gang comprised more than four people, but the members of the inner core – never more than seven – dubbed themselves the 'Council' and gave themselves playful titles such as 'emperor'. From the 1980s they plotted in support of John Garang. A prime member was Roger Winter, a former State Department envoy to Sudan and well-known as a younger diplomat for his pony tail. Another was Eric Reeves, a university English professor. John Prendergast, who set up the Enough NGO, was a co-founder, as was Ted Dagne, an Ethiopian-American who worked in the congressional research service. Susan Rice, later a US ambassador to the UN, was an occasional lunch member. All exerted extensive influence in Washington. They smoothed the path of visiting south Sudanese as well as helping to shape US legislation. 'We never controlled anything, but we did try to influence things in the way we thought most benefitted the people of south Sudan,' Roger Winter said. Winter was dubbed the 'spear carrier' in the Council.[2] Francis Deng, a southerner who was later to climb the ladder at the UN, was also a member. Deng used his southern connections to get the lobbyists into the liberated zones: Winter first met Garang there in 1986.

Because the SPLA had originally received so much support from the austere Marxist government in Addis, the lobby worked hard to persuade Washington that the movement was not caught on the wrong side of history. The gang of four arranged for US congressmen to visit the south to see that Garang headed a modern democratic organisation, not a throwback to old-style communism. Dagne, in particular, formed a close bond with the garrulous Garang; they spoke on the phone almost daily, according to Dagne. He addressed Garang as 'Uncle' and the general reciprocated by affectionately calling Degne 'Nephew'. The council was united in its respect for Garang, even though the Americans wanted independence for the south, whereas the general still proclaimed unity.

Until 1993 and the World Trade Center bombing, the State Department clung to the official line that they could not deal with the SPLM and instead had to work with the legal government in Khartoum. All the terrorist issues from bin Laden's sojourn in the country to the assassination attempt on Mubarak swung the balance in favour of the gang of four's activism. Winter persuaded many Africanists in the State Department that the Khartoum government was 'too deformed to be reformed'. By the late 1990s millions of dollars of surplus US military equipment was going to the SPLA via Uganda, Eritrea and Ethiopia. And some military training was provided. Reeves joined the gang in 2001. He had no direct experience of Sudan, but he became a prolific propagandist, writing thousands of articles brimming with moral outrage. When George W. Bush became president, Susan Rice and Prendergast, as Clinton people, left government to join think tanks. That left only Dagne, plus USAID adviser, Brian D'Silva, on the inside track. Bush, however, had his own views on Sudan. Ending the war in the south became official Washington policy.

The SPLA's endgame strategy
Would John Garang, an excellent strategist, push for a battlefield advantage before moving into the international peace arena? The long years of intermittent peace negotiations and broken ceasefires matched the

complexity of the impasse. The ethnic, religious and cultural roots of the north-south conflict were clear enough, but the mosaic of conventional and irregular military forces, militias, warlords and plain bandits in the south was of Byzantine intricacy. While both Khartoum and the SPLA adopted the North Vietnamese model of fighting and talking, perhaps the best Asian comparison is with the military patchwork in China in the warlord period (1916-1928), where regional armies and militias loyal to ethnic groups and charismatic commanders flourished. It required leaders of a national status such as Mao Zedong or Chiang Kai-shek to absorb or defeat them, while simultaneously facing an invading Japanese army. The analogy is not precise, but it gives a flavour of the kaleidoscopic texture.

Before al-Bashir took full charge in late 1999, the year the oil started flowing, and before he could fully reform the army and afford new equipment, the government forces in the south were essentially a garrison army. The officer corps had been thinned by purges and promotion had sometimes depended on ideological zeal rather than military merit. The fighting tradition of the Sudanese army since the 1920s had relied on warlike volunteer other ranks from the west and south; now they had been partly replaced by more loyal but less hardy and more urbanized northern riverine Arabs. The introduction of conscription and the use of the PDF militia further de-professionalized the army that was often stuck in isolated outposts, unable to use the mined 'roads', and dependent upon air supply. Air power did give the north a major advantage, but the other key asset, armour, was often useless in the bush, especially during the rains. The Soviet-era tanks, mainly T-55s, were often forced to deploy in dug-in static defence. The array of armoured fighting vehicles from venerable Russian, Chinese and even British stock were often difficult to maintain, with spares in short supply. Technical support was weak. The same applied to the air force. So, under-strength and under-resourced, troops had to wait for air supply in the rains, but the aircraft were then vulnerable to shoulder-launched surface-to-air missiles let alone technical faults. And, in the dry season, the complete lack of tarmac roads (except around oil installations) and the often heavy bush offered endless opportunities for guerrilla ambush.

Richard Dowden, the director of the Royal African Society, aptly summarized the conflict:

In the rainy season the SPLA would spread out from its bases, surround small towns and garrisons and sometimes capture them. In the dry season the Sudan army would counter-attack, retake lost towns and restock its garrisons. Militarily the war went nowhere.[3]

Because South Sudan had almost no all-weather roads, campaigning often related to the seasons. And there were few airstrips in such a massive theatre of war, so the fighting was rather like a boxing match on a football field. So this was a struggle of minor sieges, regular skirmishes and rarely major pitched battles in the Western sense, although frequent massacres occurred, usually inter-tribal.

The SPLA often debated the need to capture the capital, Juba, as a symbol of their success. They almost managed it in 1992. For years Juba was under more or less close siege. In June 1996 I flew to the besieged capital in a government Antonov cargo plane. Two large Russian transports had been abandoned on the edge of the runway. A sense of despair and dereliction hung over the town like a cloud. Gutted petrol stations and fleets of vehicles mounted on bricks littered the lush equatorial landscape. I stayed at the Salaam Hotel, Hotel of Peace. Certainly, I was not disturbed by any service or amenities. Nobody was shooting at me or the film cameraman, Irwin Armstrong, because we were told that the SPLA had been pushed sixty miles from the capital. We were minded by four large military policemen, one of whom I discovered was a Catholic. Somehow I persuaded him to take me in the dead of night, in a tropical rainstorm, to visit Paulino Loro, the Roman Catholic Archbishop of Juba, who was under house arrest. The archbishop bravely opened up to me and said the guerrillas were all around the town and indeed *inside* it. The priest lashed out at the forced Arabization of the south and the many attempts to undermine the Christian faith. His frankness, despite many death threats, was impressive. The next day I flew in a Puma to Torit, the on-off HQ of the SPLA. It was under temporary government control, but the small town was in ruins.

By 1996 the SPLA had recovered from most of the effects of the schism of 1991 and ejection from Ethiopian sanctuaries. In January 1997 the SPLA's 13th Division launched Operation BLACK FOX as part of its dry-season offensive. (The wet season varies according to latitude and is generally no more than eight to nine months a year, beginning as early as April and continuing usually to October but sometimes as late as December.) The operation captured Kurmuk again as well as other southern Blue Nile towns, once more panicking Khartoum because of the seizure of northern territory. The government mobilized a large armoured column that retook the towns. The SPLA counter-attacked the overextended government force and almost wiped out a complete Sudanese brigade. The SPLA also repelled another government attempted offensive north of the Blue Nile fight. Having contained the northern dry-season offensive, the SPLA cleared out many government outposts in central Equatoria. Thousands of government troops were killed or captured. Garang also started to eliminate pro-government militias. When the Juba garrison troops finally risked leaving their fortifications to try to secure the Wei-Juba road they were severely thumped by the SPLA and retreated back to the capital. The SPLA then mopped up nearly all the remaining outposts in central Equatoria. Then they retook Rumbek on the road to Wau. En route they gave a beating to another pro-government militia, Kerubino's SPLA-Bahr al-Ghazal. Other towns, such as Warrap, fell to the guerrillas before the onset of the rains.

John Garang's strategy of taking on the SPLA splinters and outright government militias forced Khartoum to rationalize its militia strategy, which had been ad hoc before. In April 1997 al-Bashir had tried to forge some kind of unity from the chaotic ethnic and personal rivalries in the southern militias. They mainly consisted of:

Riek Machar's South Sudan Independence Movement/Army (SSIM/A)
Kerubino Kuanyin Bol's SPLA-Bahr al-Ghazal
Theophilus Ochang Lotti's Equatoria Defence Force
Arok Thon Arok's Independence of the Bor Group
Muhammad Harun Kafi's SPLA-Nuba
Kawac Makuei Imayar's Independence Movement for Southern Sudan

Khartoum had dubbed this alliance a peace agreement, but it was obviously a temporary stratagem to divide and rule and weaken the successful SPLA offensives. The cliché of herding cats applied to nearly all attempts to unify southern factions, especially in alliance with Khartoum, against whom they were supposed to be fighting to achieve southern independence. The militias were aggregated for military containment, but al-Bashir also realized that it needed a political front. In August 1997 Riek Machar was made president of a 'Council of the South'. This had little effect. Al-Bashir tried to further integrate the militias into the army by giving their commanders the rank of brigadier. The ever-touchy Kerubino was made a major general, but he was angered by the promotion of Machar as titular political council president. In a fit of petulance, Kerubino defected back to the official SPLA a few months later, though this damage was partially balanced by the affable and ambitious Lam Akol's re-alignment with Khartoum. His SPLA-United controlled a large area around the strategic town of Malakal. Akol was a leader of the Shilluk people, but his vacillation lost him support even among his own tribal following.

As recounted earlier, in January 1998 to regain credibility with Garang, his kinsman and former captor, Kerubino attacked and captured Wau, the capital of Bahr al-Ghazal. It was a stunning if brief victory. The army concentrated its forces and its superiority in artillery and air strikes and soon regained the state capital with much loss of civilian lives. Exhausted, both sides declared a three-month ceasefire during the rainy season in Bahr al-Ghazal.

Meanwhile, a more sensible and (and slightly more) effective herding of cats was the National Democratic Alliance's formation of a Joint Command in July 1997.[4] Garang was made commander in chief, but his deputy was a senior defector from the Sudanese army, Lieutenant General Abdel Rahman Said. It made little immediate difference militarily for the eastern front, however.

Al-Bashir had to deal with (sometimes) pro-government militias in the east and west of his own country, as well as clandestine military allies in Chad, for example. One of the most bizarre proxies came from Uganda, although Western critics might say it materialized from a horror movie: the Lord's Resistance Army (LRA). As if the Sudanese imbroglio was not sufficiently fragmented and militarized and not enough religious fanatics were running around with guns, the Lord's Resistance Army further stirred the hell brew. Still not resolved at the time of writing, the LRA, captained by Joseph Kony, ravaged the borderlands of South Sudan, northern Uganda, and later the Central African Republic and the Democratic Republic of Congo. Originally a tribal revolt of the Acholi in northern Uganda, it assumed religious pretensions. It emerged initially from the Holy Spirit Movement led by Alice Lakwena, a self-styled prophetess. Inspired by visions from God, she said, Lakwena formed an 'army' to sweep away tribal enemies in the capital, Kampala. Although usually armed with spears and machetes, she claimed that strict adherence to her rules would permit her followers to be immune to bullets (a not uncommon belief in many primitive insurgencies in Africa). Her acolytes were told to cover their bodies in shea nut oil and they would be invulnerable. Luckily, shea nut oil or butter (known locally as *moo-yahoo*) is very common in Uganda. Unluckily, it didn't work when Alice led her bulletproof army in trying to capture Kampala in August 1987. Perhaps the spiritual army did not follow her other precepts that dictated they never took cover or retreated, or ever kill snakes or bees. Without a Green Party in Uganda, it might have been assumed that her movement would have collapsed when she fled to Kenya, but Joseph Kony, sometimes said to be Alice's cousin or nephew (the spiritual powers were supposed to run in the bloodline), absorbed the remnants of her followers to set up the Lord's Resistance Army. It was based on the Ten Commandments, animist mysticism and Acholi nationalism. Kony's variation was that *moo-yahoo* should be spread on the chest in the shape of a cross. This seemed to work better because his movement lasted for decades, despite being hunted by a variety of modern conventional armies.

For a time in the mid-nineties, Khartoum armed Kony's movement because it raided into South Sudan and distracted the SPLA. This was a riposte to the Ugandan government's support of the southern rebels. A little like RENAMO in Mozambique, Kony's movement took on a life of its own once it had been re-armed. In March 2002, a major offensive by the Ugandan army (Operation IRON FIST) failed to capture the ever-elusive Kony. Khartoum, as part of the peace negotiations with the SPLA, sanctioned the 2002 offensive and a repeat in 2004. Then the International Criminal Court intervened and made it worse, when Kony saw no reason to make peace with Kampala and be sent to The Hague. Even the multi-faceted wiles of Riek Machar failed when he tried to intercede, as the vice president of the autonomous South Sudan in 2006 to 2008. Barack Obama sent in over 100 US special forces in 2011. Though reduced to a rag-tag force of perhaps hundreds, not thousands, Kony kept going in the DRC and CAR, to continue his pillaging and capturing child soldiers. Alice would have been proud of him.

Meanwhile, during the late 1990s, Machar was up to his old shape-shifting tricks. He renamed his SSIM/A the South Sudan Defence Force (SSDF). This coincided with a fall-out with a previous ally, Paulino Matip, who led the South Sudan Unity Army (SSUA). Matip was a military maverick and privateer who was keener on cash than any political ideology. He had become a mercenary to protect the oil facilities in his tribal Nuer areas. The Matip-Machar antagonism extended to shoot-outs in their private homes in Khartoum and at a wedding in Omdurman. Soon the personal animosity between the two men led to serious factional fighting around the main oil facilities in Bentiu. Khartoum had to use force to impose a truce.

Despite his intelligence and charm with Westerners, Machar possessed a genius for spawning vendettas among his own people. During 1998 a number of his units in the Upper Nile broke away to rejoin the official SPLA. In 1999 Machar formed a new political party to fight in a national election announced by al-Bashir. This further antagonized his dwindling band of supporters because any northern-based election would re-enforce *sharia* law, anathema to most southerners. Machar's splinter group splintered again and his latest internal rivals formed the SSDF-2. At least Machar's rivals avoided the common splitters' habit of putting 'unity' in the title. Perhaps they had no sense of irony. Even al-Bashir, a master manipulator of the southern fissures, felt that Machar had outlived his usefulness to Khartoum. As ever, Machar adapted to his changing (and dwindling) fortunes to return to his roots to negotiate in Nairobi to re-align with Garang. Along with Lam Akol and other vacillating militia commanders, they were taken back in to the official fold in early 2002. Garang was tactically generous: he made Machar vice president of the SPLM even though the Nuer commander had lost the support of many of his long-time fighters. This re-integration was at least bloodless, especially compared with Kerubino's second attempt to rejoin Garang. Kenyan security forces had to intervene in a shoot-out between their respective bodyguards in Garang's Nairobi residence. Kerubino then rejoined Matip's pro-government militia and was apparently killed fighting the SPLA in 1998, although it was alleged that Garang had arranged his assassination.

Dealing with on-off allies such as Machar, Akol and Keubino, some of them arguably psychopathic, Garang could have been forgiven for being surprised by the intensity of the government's dry-season offensive in 1999. Northern forces took a number of important SPLA air strips. The offensive in 2000 inflicted serious reverses on the SPLA in the Nuba Mountains. In 2001 the new equipment purchased with the oil money boosted Khartoum's morale and effectiveness and the SPLA started to lose more ground. It was only the arrival of Senator Danforth's peace mission in late 2001 that allowed the SPLA to stabilize its lines, not least in the Nuba Mountains. Danforth's mission included a series of tests of sincerity such as establishing 'zones of tranquillity' which would allow humanitarian relief. But in essence Washington wanted to know whether al-Bashir and Garang could and would make peace. A trial ceasefire in the Nuba Mountains was signed in Geneva in January 2002. Khartoum disrupted World Food Programme missions in the region by an air raid on Bieh, prompting Western criticism in general and, particularly, hawks in Washington to propose sending surface-to-air missiles to the SPLA. Danforth took the standard line of introducing international monitors to audit the goodwill on both sides. An overall Joint Military Mission was set up that included experts for military and civilian protection verification.

The SPLA had been making gains in the east. They had joined forces with a united brigade sponsored by the NDA and they both allied with insurgents from the Beja Congress. The Beja, who are Muslim non-Arabs, consisted of four main clans. One of them was the famously warlike Hadendowa, whom the British had named the 'Fuzzy Wuzzies' because of the distinctive Afro hairstyles, and who were famed for breaking a British square. The Beja people's cattle had suffered severely in the drought years and some of their land had been seized by Khartoum and sold to a new class of mechanized farmers, as well as large tracts to Osama bin Laden. The Beja insurgency had been revived in 1994. In 1999 and 2000 the combined opposition forces overwhelmed a number of army garrisons around the strategic border town of Kassala. The eastern front was now posing a major threat to the government.

Then the forces of the NDA, Beja and SPLA lost their eastern sanctuaries. In January 2000, as part of the post-Turabi diplomatic offensive, Khartoum renewed relations with both Eritrea and Ethiopia. Sudan and Ethiopia had often been hostile neighbours. Eritrea, however, was a new state born in April 1993. It became one of the most repressive regimes in Africa under its war leader, Isaias Afawerki. Once a close ally of the guerrillas who overturned the Derg in Addis, and despite a 'velvet divorce', the former allies fell out over the most pointless piece of desert around Badme. The border area had no oil and hardly any people. Yet Eritrea and Ethiopia fought for two years in a conflict that involved fighter jets, tanks and half a million troops, sometimes in trench warfare akin to the Great War. Both sides admitted that the conflict was 'insane'. It was also one-sided: Ethiopia's population was sixty million compared with Eritrea's four million. Since Eritrea had cut off Ethiopia's access to the sea, it made sense for Addis to cosy up to Khartoum to use Sudanese routes to the Red Sea.

Since independence many of Eritrea's internal tensions had been externalized. Roughly half of the population was Muslim, and Khartoum did at one stage assist a Muslim insurgency, but it also provided massive humanitarian support in border camps inside Sudan, despite limited resources. For a small population the Eritreans were remarkably active in other people's wars – some in the Horn likened Eritrean military enterprise to the Israelis (with whom Asmara had solid ties). The Eritreans had long been engaged with the SPLA, especially in training on armoured warfare. Female Eritreans had fought hard in their own liberation war and were reportedly seen driving SPLA tanks. Asmara also reached out to seize islands belonging to Yemen as well as strips of Djibouti plus fighting in the Congo and Somalia. Its troublemaking drew rebukes from the African Union and its poor domestic human rights record prompted regular condemnation from the UN.

Making peace with troublesome Eritrea made eminent sense for Khartoum, whose forces rolled up the SPLA troops north east of Kassala, inflicting heavy losses. The Sudanese apparently deployed some of their new tanks recently purchased from Poland. The tanks arrived on the very day that Khartoum exported its first oil shipment in May 1999.[5] Military delegations also came from China and the ex-Soviet dealers in Bulgaria, plus Iran. The defence budget now accounted for half of government spending.

Taking a hit in the east, the SPLA tried to regain the initiative by moving for the first time in large numbers into the sparsely populated desert regions of the western Bahr al-Ghazal. Unfriendly locals regarded this as a Dinka invasion and the logistics were difficult. The SPLA withdrew to concentrate on the far more populated and strategic oil areas around Heglig and Bentiu. Matip's pro-government militia had been battling the SPLA commanded by Peter Gadet, who was to develop a colourful military career as a rebel after the peace deal and in the 2013 civil war. The arrival of fresh SPLA forces prompted Khartoum to reinforce quickly, with armour, along the new oil roads. The government also launched an aerial bombing campaign in Equatoria. The fighting was partly an action-reaction cycle and partly an attempt to go into peace talks with a military advantage.

The main Kenyan peace negotiator, General Lazarus Sumbeiywo, had organized a second peace summit in June 2002 at Machakos, in the hill country forty miles south east of Nairobi. The previous IGAD summits had led to endless and fruitless point-scoring. This time, both north and south were utterly war weary. A troika of senior diplomats from the US, UK and Norway were in on the act, as were Eritrea, Ethiopia and Uganda. And the effective ringmaster was Sumbeiywo. The essence of the final deal was agreed in the form of the Machakos Protocol. A comprehensive peace agreement would lead to a six-year transition of joint administration in Khartoum and then a referendum would be held to decide on southern independence or to maintain unity. The north always assumed that if they gave southern politicians a big enough share of the trough they would stay inside one Sudan. After all, Khartoum had rented, if not bought, many senior southern commanders before. And the chief prize was John Garang, who believed in unity anyway. Khartoum had promised self-determination before, but the wording of the new protocol allowed for the north to practise *sharia* law, the main source of southern discontent, while the SPLM renounced its commitment to a secular unified Sudan. This deal seemed the most promising so far and the assembled diplomats had enough clout to bang heads together if either combatant started backsliding too far.

Nevertheless, the ceasefire accompanying the Machakos deal was soon broken over the control of the prized town of Torit. Tribal militias also engaged in their customary cross-border raids. This aside, it was clear that the main combatants would make the real decisions, not arm-twisting foreigners. In July 2003 President al-Bashir and John Garang met for the first time in Kampala. This signified a step change on the steep climb to a final deal. Despite the oil revenues, reformed army and new equipment, the president as general made the military decision that the war was not winnable, at least in the short term. In twenty years of fighting in the second phase of the war, two million southerners had been killed and millions displaced to the north or were anguishing in camps in the south or in Kenya and Uganda. The northern army had suffered tens of thousands of fatalities. Conscription had filled some of the gaps, but volunteering for jihad, either individually or through the PDF, had lost steam since al-Turabi had been ousted. And though southerners were fighting in their own terrain and tribal lands, few understood what the SPLM wanted politically, especially as Garang was in a small minority in not fighting primarily for only southern freedom. Most southern peasants simply wanted the war to end so they could raise their cattle, practise their own religions and, with luck, send their children to school in peace. The southern war was not ideological except for a minority whose nationalism, or perhaps faith, transcended tribal loyalties. Superstition was much more important than any ideology. The spirits of ancestors and recent kin held more sway than any -isms, especially in a land where the dead were many and the living comparatively few.

The peace settlement
Over twenty – if not fifty – years, a solution had not been achieved because, to use a Marxist phrase, a correlation of forces had not been reached. Hardliners on both sides had tipped the apple cart when moderates made some breakthrough in numerous IGAD attempts in the 1990s. Many southern commanders, despite their truces and temporary deals, nursed a visceral hatred of the historical enemy in the north. Some northerners were racist bigots who knew little of the south and wanted the 'mutiny' or 'rebellion' to be crushed by superior force, not least to spread Islam for the infidels' own salvation. Garang and al-Bashir were pragmatic military men who understood that they had fought almost to a stalemate. True, the

northern army was now better equipped and Khartoum was less isolated diplomatically. Garang had also built up his army, largely tempered the tribal divisions, and had the support of the southern neighbours and indeed much of black Africa. Crucially, however, Washington had decided to throw its weight behind the deal and all the IGAD members were lending support, largely directed by the Americans. There was no big external spoiler. China had every reason to be a backroom cheerleader too, because of the increasing oil supplies. In the end, the allure of oil riches, which the war could destroy, was a prime inducement. Both north and south needed to share the oil to prosper as one or two states. They were like two lungs in the same body. The south was desperate for economic development, while the more educated urban society in the north demanded better schools, jobs and pensions. Both Garang and al-Bashir faced a crisis of expectation that only peace could satisfy. Both men had perhaps reached an age when they were concerned with their legacies. What better accolade could there be from their respective audiences than 'the man who ended the longest war in Africa'? It was surely time.

The south was largely behind Garang's peace drive, though some commanders were agitated that disputed areas were not dealt with properly at Machakos, especially Abyei. Contested areas included the Nuba Mountains and southern Blue Nile as well as other irredenta claimed by Juba, including land administered by Ethiopia and Kenya. Critics wondered whether the Dinka ascendancy in the SPLA was betraying other southern tribes and Christians in the north, across the old border. Should the 1956 colonial border be redrawn? The status of the 1,200-mile border problem was to endure, although Garang's vision of unity paid less heed to this problem. In Khartoum, some hardliners in the ruling NCP party and in the officer corps baulked. It was the perennial debate, one that affected contemporary electorates in Britain and America – why pull out of Iraq or, later, Afghanistan with no clear victory? Why betray so many soldiers who had made the ultimate sacrifice? While opposing critics would say simply 'Why reinforce failure?' Of course in Sudan the armies were not expeditionary forces – they were at home, except arguably for SPLA forces over the border. Freedom of religion was a crucial issue in the south, but it did not match the former proselytizing zeal of northern Islam. Would giving up the south be a betrayal of Allah and all his martyrs, the very foundation of the state, and certainly the 1989 revolution? Inevitably, everyone had to give something up for peace, the greater good. That's how negotiated peace deals work.

Sudan's many conflicts were not just north-south, although that was the greatest challenge. The dozen or so political parties in the NDA had been excluded as had southern political rivals of the SPLM. What of the Beja and Darfuris? Doing a one-to-one deal was how the military minds of al-Bashir, Garang and Sumbeiywo managed to coalesce. Perhaps only experienced soldiers, not politicians, really understand how to end wars. That was certainly a mindset in many African circles, especially authoritarian ones.

A hard thirty months of nailing down the fine details of the Machakos deal were still to follow, made more anxious by the outbreak of a full-scale war in Darfur in February 2003. At the same time, government militias – whom peace might leave out in the cold – were involved in renewed fighting around the West Nile oilfields. The scattered foreign monitoring teams were also perplexed by the internecine fighting, especially when Lam Akol quit his rump SPLA-Unity in October 2003 to rejoin Garang, and fighting between the two rump SPLA-Unity militias ensued. The Norwegian-led monitoring team in the Nuba Mountains was very successful, however, and humanitarian aid flowed into the region.

The next round of talks was supervised again by General Sumbeiywo. In October 2002 Ali Othman Taha headed the Khartoum delegation and Garang tended to lead the southerners, or occasionally his number two, Salva Kiir. The crucial issues were power-sharing, wealth-sharing and security, as they had been in the palavering leading up to the 1972 peace agreement. The southerners remembered all the broken promises. In January 2003 the negotiators met again, this time directly face to face. At the next round in April 2003, the Kenyan general wanted to speed up the talks – aware that Darfur could derail the whole process – by offering what he called 'compromise' solutions to bridge the gaps. The next round was scheduled to be at Nakuru. The town was traditionally a hotbed of Kenyan politics, but it was also adjacent to the lake and national park famous for its flamingos. The Kenyans tried to exploit the natural beauty of their country to enhance their diplomacy. Unfortunately, the proposed compromises in the draft for Nakuru were rejected by Khartoum. President al-Bashir was angry at what he saw as IGAD's and, especially, Kenya's favouritism to the south. The power-sharing document diluted the central – his – presidential authority. He was touchy about this, not surprisingly after a ten-year battle with the wily al-Turabi to maintain his position as president. Al-Bashir had a habit of speaking his mind and he could sometimes be impulsive, even in diplomatic circles. He said publicly that IGAD 'could go to hell'. How to share power and all the variations on the federalist theme had always been at the heart of the Sudanese conundrum.

In Khartoum al-Bashir came under pressure from his hardliners, who fretted that a peace deal could ignite support among al-Turabi's supporters for an alleged sell-out. The ruling NCP also worried about yesterday's politicians in the NDA. Al-Bashir did want peace, but not at any price. He did not give in to his hardliners, not least because some of his military allies were worried about the potential scale of the Darfur conflict. Ali Othman Taha told me:

> We were getting the heat on Darfur in the peace negotiations ... We were aware of the qualitative change in the conflict in Darfur. Garang was putting the pressure on. Remember he wanted to unite the whole country – he was treating Darfur as part of his own constituency.

The SPLA was indeed fuelling the rebellion in Darfur to add extra leverage. Also, the popular mood in the three towns was for an end to war. Nor did Egypt and the Arab League want the IGAD-led talks to fail.

The troika of the US, Britain and Norway was also crucial in keeping the peace train on track. I asked Taha who really banged heads together at the talks. 'Sometimes it was the Norwegians,' he said, 'or the Kenyans or the Americans.' Yet in the end the two sides themselves had to agree because external pressure could sometimes be counter-productive. The Ugandan leader, Yoweri Museveni, in a lively breach of political correctness, jokingly asked: 'How can those with turbans on their heads have peace with those who wear ostrich feathers?' The Kenyans were, as ever, more diplomatic: they suggested a one-on-one between the two principal negotiators — Garang and Taha. Both agreed.

The talks took place at the Simba Lodge on the edge of Lake Naivasha in September 2003. Taha was on time. Garang, however, kept Taha waiting for four days before arriving. They were left alone in a room. General Sumbeiywo had positioned one large bottle of mineral water on a small table between them, with two glasses. It was to be a psychological game of who would appear to weaken first and take a drink. They talked awkwardly at first, and then fluently. Both were highly articulate men in English and Arabic. For some hours neither man touched the bottle. As Sunbeiywo put it, 'The fate of the peace talks hung on the water bottle.' Eventually Garang opened the bottle and served Taha a drink. As the Kenyan had hoped, the two Sudanese got on well. As Taha told me later, 'We came to understand each other.' That was fortunate for they talked, sometimes alongside their delegations, for the next eighteen months. Al-Bashir came to visit twice, before the final ceremony, but Taha talked on the phone to his boss almost daily. Taha admitted, 'I felt isolated sometimes. Garang had his family with him. I did not.'

General Sumbeiywo was an attentive MC. He had worked as the Kenyan envoy to Sudan before the talks. Just before the formal negotiations started in 2002, the devout Christian prayed and fasted for three days. He said, 'I really felt that God chose to use me in these negotiations.' Despite all the twists and turns he stuck to it, even though during the talks he was retired as army commander two years early, because of political changes in Nairobi. Sumbeiywo got on well with both sides. On the first day of the Machakos talks the southern delegation asked him whether a specific point was 'OK with Washington'. He answered very firmly, 'I am not answerable to Washington.' The southerners liked that – so did the Brits. Nevertheless, the Americans were constantly supportive of the peace process. In October 2003 Colin Powell, the US Secretary of State, visited the Simba Lodge to encourage Garang and Taha.

President al-Bashir realized by early 2004 that the war in Darfur was not easily containable. The US lobbies were hyperactive in condemning Khartoum. And it was obviously going to get worse. Sudan might soon be stripped of its recently won re-acceptance in the international community. As a pariah it would lose leverage in the Naivasha talks. Al-Bashir would either have to walk away and deepen Khartoum's purdah or delay and secure a less favourable peace deal. On the other side, the SPLM, now actively backing the Darfur rebellion, believed that the northern regime might collapse, given a little more international pressure. Time was working against al-Bashir. The main issues of transitional power-sharing had been agreed at Naivasha as well as agreements for separate referenda on the Nuba Mountains, Abyei and southern Blue Nile, with their mixed north-south populations. Khartoum started to stonewall at Naivasha, but the troika and IGAD helped to persuade the UN Security Council not to impose harsh measures on Khartoum regarding the alleged war crimes in Darfur. More sanctions would have forced al-Bashir to quit the peace talks. His own domestic base would not have permitted any other option.

The stay of execution on Darfur allowed Khartoum to promise to finalize all the deals by the beginning of the new year. The Comprehensive Peace Agreement (CPA) comprised a series of deals and protocols signed during the exhausting negotiations. Designed deliberately with some creative and constructive ambiguity, it ended up as over 200 pages in English. In December 2004 the two sides finalized the details of a permanent ceasefire. As ever, the positioning of forces was a fundamental problem. The 90,000 northern troops in the south had two years and six months to go back to the north. The SPLA had eight months to pull back its smaller numbers (probably 30,000 troops) from the north. During the six-year transitional period of north-south joint administration in Khartoum in a government of national unity, both armies would contribute half of a joint force of 20,000 men. If the two sides stayed inside one country this figure would then be proportionately doubled to establish a national army. Meanwhile, both sides would have their own separate armies to make sure neither side was stitched up.

Oil revenues were supposed to be divided equally. Power-sharing was more complicated. An autonomous Government of South Sudan (GoSS) would run the south until 2011 when an internationally supervised referendum would decide on secession or not. Positions in the central government would be divided 70:30 to north and south, which roughly matched the respective populations. In the disputed border areas this would be a 55:45 ratio. Omar al-Bashir would remain as national president, but John Garang would become first vice president (while Taha was second vice president). *Sharia* was to be applicable in the north, but non-Muslims throughout Sudan would not be subject to Islamic law. With so many southern politicians moving to Khartoum where already millions of southerners, mainly refugees, were settled, it would be impossible to impose *sharia* law without massive frictions that would sink the peace deal. The CPA contained many other annexes, for example on financial matters such as banking. The south would have its own currency, the pound. More importantly, it would fly its own flag and sing its own national anthem.

On 9 January 2005, at a grand international celebration in Nairobi, the CPA was signed by Garang and al-Bashir with international top brass such as Colin Powell as witnesses. Officially the north-south war that began in 1955 was finally over. On 8 July 2005 Vice President John Garang and his wife, Rebecca de Mabior, as well as all the new southern ministers, drove through the streets of Khartoum to be greeted by cheering mass crowds of northerners and southerners. The southern leaders were to be sworn in as members of the new joint government. For Garang, this was to be the start of the New Sudan for which he had fought for decades.

It was not to be. Garang was killed on 30 July in an air crash in the rugged mountains of the deep south of Sudan. He was flying at night in a Ugandan Mi-172 helicopter after visiting his long-time ally, President

Yoweri Museveni. Riots swept through the poorer parts of Omdurman and Khartoum, but a panel of international experts could later find no evidence of foul play. Sudanese intelligence officers were convinced, however, that Garang was deliberately killed and some murmured about a 'French connection'. It remains a mystery, although pilot error still stands at the top of the suspect list.

John Garang was buried in Juba, his soon-to-be independent capital. At the funeral ceremony his wife, Rebecca, promised to continue his work: 'In our culture we say, "If you kill the lion, you see what the lioness will do."' It is rarely accurate to say that someone, especially a political leader, is indispensable, but Garang was the only southerner who could perhaps have made it all work. Instead, his legacy was continued (if much diminished) conflict with the north and bitter civil war in a south he had dedicated his life to set free.

The burden of southern peace now largely rested upon the shoulders of al-Bashir, but he was about to be sucked into an international maelstrom over the war in Darfur. Garang was succeeded by his second in command, Salva Kiir Mayardit, who became the President of GoSS and first vice president of Sudan. He was a military man through and through, which encouraged a meeting of minds with Field Marshal al-Bashir, but he lacked the intellectual political dexterity of his soldier-statesman predecessor. Could both men escape the prison of their pasts?

Chapter 8

War in the West: Darfur

After the success of the Comprehensive Peace Agreement and the ending of Africa's longest civil war, friends in Omar al-Bashir's circle suggested he might be awarded the Nobel Peace Prize. In early 2004 the president was asked if he would attend a reception at the White House. He was regularly phoned directly by President Bush. The CPA was also probably President Bush's biggest (and perhaps only) successful peace deal. Instead, the US visit was cancelled and soon President al-Bashir became the first sitting head of state to be indicted for war crimes by the International Criminal Court. The great peacemaker, Washington's ally and African saviour, was transformed into a hunted war criminal and leader of a rogue state again. How did this happen? The one word answer is simply Darfur.

Journalists are expected to say that Darfur is the same size as Texas or France, depending on whether they are reporting for American or European media. Darfur is certainly big, mainly desert or scrub, and it has a colourful and violent history. The British conquered the Sultanate of Darfur during the First World War. A senior Khartoum minister once told me:

Actually, you British caused the problem – you separated north and south when you ruled Sudan; and you, by accident, sowed the seeds of conflict in Darfur when you didn't give the settled land rights to some of the nomadic herders when you took over in 1916.

Until then Ali Dinar had ruled a largely independent state based in El Fasher. The town had once been the starting point for one of Africa's most famous caravan routes, the 'forty-day road'. Big camel trains, loaded with ivory, ebony and slaves, made the long trip through the desert to Aswan and Asyut in Egypt. There the young male slaves who had survived the journey were usually castrated. It was also the route from West Africa to the Red Sea and maritime access to the culmination of the *Haj* in Arabia. The British had initially supported Ali Dinar, but they soon came to dislike his truculence.

He was probably set up – the word now used is 'entrapped' – by British intelligence using bogus communications with Istanbul. Ali Dinar was accused of dealing with an enemy allied to Germany. The British infantry ambushed and killed the last sultan in November 1916, and promptly made Ali Dinar a martyr. It was also one of the early uses of air power in Africa: two aircraft from the Royal Flying Corps, one flown by a young Lieutenant John Slessor, later to be a head of the Royal Air Force. Technically, the operations in Darfur were designated a local colonial action. This irritated the British officers involved in the Darfur campaign, who could not claim First World War medals for their soldiering. The reason was financial: the bill could be sent to Cairo, not the War Office in London. The introduction of modern weapons, and the arming of local militias, caused endless problems for the French and British imperial authorities long after 1918. There are many comparisons with the influx of new guns to Darfur in the early twenty-first century. It is also ironic that the first use of mounted Arab and African militias in Darfur, armed with modern weapons, was by the British army in its 1916 campaign. Were they perhaps responsible for the genesis of the *Janjaweed?*

The nature of the war
If the Nile provided one source of water power, the alternative was the Chad basin, the biggest inland drainage system in Africa. Lake Chad is in the centre. The basin incorporates parts or all of nine territories, especially Chad, Libya, Niger and west Darfur. In the colonial period it became a French sphere of interest. With the tribal gravitational pull from the west, Darfur often had more in common with Chad rather than the distant Khartoum in the east. For hundreds of years Darfuris fought in wars connected to Chad, more currently in the civil wars beginning in the 1960s, later instigated by the Libyans and sometimes contained by French troops, especially in 2006 and 2008. Even EU troops found themselves involved in Chad after 2007.

Even under distant British rule intermittent fighting had continued after 1916, mainly caused by drought and inter-tribal disputes. But the political background of the latest war can also be traced partly to the so-called *Black Book* published illegally in Khartoum in 2000. It was created largely by the small Darfurian intelligentsia in Khartoum who castigated not only the neglect of their own province, but also the usurpation of power and wealth by the tribal clique of riverine Arabs. Fighting erupted again on a small scale in Darfur in 2000, but the firestorm of the major war did not break out until early 2003 and lasted in a high-intensity form for just over a year.

The full-scale modern warfare disrupted the optimism engendered by the increasingly successful north-south peace talks in Kenya. The complex war in Darfur was distinct, but also related to the war in the south. The first 2,000 Darfur rebels were trained by the SPLA, who clearly wished to see more pressure applied on the Khartoum authorities even as they negotiated with them. The Darfur conflict was tribal and political, but it was not usually racial. It was not Arab versus African, not Omar Sharif versus Kunta Kinte, the hero of *Roots*. Inter-marriage made it often impossible to physically differentiate 'African' from 'Arab' among the thirty-five tribes and ethnic groups which could be roughly divided between nomadic herders and sedentary farming communities.

A critic of Khartoum, and probably the leading Western expert on the region, Alex de Waal, wrote: 'Characterizing the Darfur war as "Arabs" versus "Africans" obscures the reality. Darfur's Arabs are black, indigenous, African Muslims – just like Darfur's non-Arabs.' I travelled in various parts of Darfur and frequently challenged the locals as to whether they could identify a Darfurian stranger as 'Arab' or 'African'. They nearly always got it wrong. Often darker-skinned Darfuris turned out to be Arabs, while the lighter-skinned locals often claimed to be African. The only obvious difference I could discern was that some 'Africans' could speak an African language as well as Arabic. While the historical conflict between Arabs versus Africans has been a recurring theme of wider Sudanese history, it would be wrong to assume that the Arabs were always the victors and the Africans the victims, especially in Darfur.

Ten years after the Rwandan massacres, the US State Department dubbed the tragedy in Darfur a 'genocide'. Figures varied dramatically, but tens of thousands were killed and hundreds of thousands displaced; both sides committed atrocities. Kofi Annan, then UN Secretary General, contradicted US claims when he said, 'I cannot call the killing a genocide even though there have been massive violations of international humanitarian law.'

It is true that Africans – if that term can be used – were in a majority among the displaced, and most of them would say they had fled attacks by the *Janjaweed*, a generic term for bandits, but often also applied to pro-government militias. But there were also displaced 'Arab' communities who were attacked by 'African' groups. Besides inter-'African' ethnic fighting, in parts of South Darfur, however, the World Food Programme could not work because of highly charged traditional conflicts between rival 'Arab' groups. Darfur was an even more complicated war than the southern imbroglio. It was also a much misreported and misrepresented conflict.

In addition, Darfur's catastrophe was caused by factors associated with climate change: the desertification of the Sahel. In this sense, it became perhaps the first environmental war of the twenty-first century. The crisis also had roots in old-fashioned warfare. A government scorched-earth policy had destroyed many 'African' villages, thus draining the Maoist-style sea, to prevent the rebels from operating. Soon after February 2003, following surprise rebel attacks, Sudan's military intelligence initially had free rein to operate in Darfur, and the army and allied militias went in very hard. The military hardliners wanted to crush the revolt before signing an international peace deal in Kenya that might clip their wings.

With their good intelligence ties with America, the *Mukhabarat* believed that Washington would turn a blind eye to a quick surgical suppression of the Darfur revolt, especially as the Bush administration would not want to risk the CPA prize, a foreign policy success useful in a close presidential re-election race. Khartoum also assumed that the Washington elites would be less concerned about the killings of Muslims in Darfur than the murder of Christians in the south. As it happened, the American Christian lobbies were far more exercised about Muslim deaths than many in the three towns. This was despite the massive Western media focus on the war in Iraq.

A war in Darfur was the last thing that al-Bashir wanted after he had expended so much personal, political, military and diplomatic capital over the deal in the south. Khartoum's leaders were desperate to keep the Americans happy because they thought they had cast-iron guarantees that the USA would rescind sanctions as soon as the CPA was done and dusted. Close down the Darfur problem quickly and Khartoum would be welcomed back into the economic and diplomatic community of nations. Al-Bashir's coterie was convinced of that. Washington, utterly distracted by Iraq, chose not to act on Darfur, especially in the first year when fighting was most intense, partly because of the belief in sequencing or compartmentalizing – complete the CPA first, then Darfur could be addressed. Ironic that, to save some lives in the north-south war, the Western diplomats glossed over the slaughter in the west. Some more junior UN diplomats tried to nudge the Security Council to intervene early, but it would not. Two of the five permanent members prioritized the CPA, while Russia was busy selling arms to Khartoum and China was equally busy hoovering up the oil.

In the true Sudanese fashion at least twenty rebel groups emerged, although the Justice and Equality Movement (JEM) and Sudan Liberation Army (SLA) were the most cohesive. They claimed that Khartoum had marginalized the three Darfur states (despite recent improvements in transport, education and physical infrastructure). Factions in Chad, often tribally linked, also meddled across the border; and, equally, Khartoum stirred the pot in Chad. And a fratricidal factor was the intimate civil war within the Islamist revolutionaries in Khartoum. Elements loyal to Hassan al-Turabi had formed and funded JEM. Although US intelligence was rightly concerned about the growth of jihad in the Sahel – a soft underbelly of both pro-western North African states and Europe itself – the alleged al-Qaeda connections with JEM have been overdone. Later in the war, Osama bin Laden did, however, call for a jihad against 'crusader infidels and infidel apostates' in the UN-led force.

In essence the Darfur insurgents had seen what was on offer to the southerners – especially oil money, jobs and autonomy – and they wanted some of the same goodies too. When the emergency feeding programmes had reached a reasonable level of stabilization, the rebels – by attacking aid convoys – sought to use famine as a means of concentrating more international pressure on Khartoum. The African Union initially sent in a small number of peacekeepers, backed by a handful of EU observers, but the rebels wanted to provoke a much larger foreign military intervention. Later the AU size was boosted, then UN peacekeepers joined them.

Historically Sudanese government forces would intervene to settle the tribal and nomad-versus-pastoralist battles. Second Lieutenant Omar al-Bashir's first posting had been to monitor tribal clashes in Darfur in the late 1960s. Formerly Khartoum was seen as a referee, but now the government had become a prime, and sometimes brutal, antagonist. While the rebels called for more African Union and then UN intervention, Khartoum said no, arguing that Western intervention in another oil-rich Islamic state could create chaos, drawing in jihadist crazies from A-Z, Algeria to Zanzibar, to spawn another Somalia.

My first visit to Darfur was in late 2004. After much permit-chasing in Khartoum, I caught an internal flight to El Fasher, capital of North Darfur. If I had moaned about no beer in the Khartoum Hilton, in rundown El Fasher there was no hotel, not much at all in fact – except lots of donkeys, and plastic bags adorning urban scrubland. I was travelling with my friend and cameraman, Irwin Armstrong. We hired a white 4x4 and driver the first day. Luckily, the van was similar to the vehicles used by the African Union peacekeepers. I found out from a friendly South African soldier what time the AU convoy was leaving the next day for the rebel-held areas. On time, it left the AU base, and we tucked in to the end of it. Except for the lack of a big AU sign we looked official. So we sped through the government roadblocks and then through the Sudan Liberation Army (SLA) blockades to enter rebel territory.

After much rough cross-country travel, we reached Debed, the site of a recent air attack by government forces. I managed to find a villager who was a former English teacher; he recounted the details and deaths on camera. Irwin filmed the burnt-out huts. And then I interviewed a loquacious Swedish army major, acting as an EU observer. We also filmed the SLA fighters, with dashing turbans and sunglasses, and all festooned in amulets that they believed made enemy bullets turn to water. Enduring various rough rides, and punctures, we made many forays into the unforgiving desert scrub around El Fasher. We filmed government-held villages, such as Tawila, and later the camps for the IDPs (Internally Displaced Persons) squatting around the dusty capital. Irwin and I recorded detailed life stories about the disruption of traditional ways, of murder and rape. The camps were taking on a dispiritingly permanent air, portents perhaps of Palestinian-style armed anger in the future. The NGOs were doing a noble job, though the Darfurian political activists in the camps sometimes ensured that discipline was maintained by a reign of terror.

We also talked to NGOs. The most illuminating official was Neils Scott, of the UN Office for the Co-ordination of Humanitarian Affairs. At his HQ he told us about the *Janjaweed* – literally the devils on horseback. 'The *Janjaweed* is historical,' he said. 'It's been around for years. What we're seeing now is, to a great extent, criminality ... We're in a bandaging situation. What we need here is a political solution.'

A few months later Irwin and I set out again for Darfur, having secured all our various governmental and military permissions. This time we stayed in the guest quarters of the Wali, or Governor, a kindness sometimes granted to visiting journalists. The most that could be said was that it had a toilet. Still, we were treated with generous Sudanese hospitality. I needed the wali's backing to persuade the army to let us accompany them on patrols against the rebels. The colonel assigned to mind us had no idea at all of what filming involved. He kept putting his hand in front of the camera, even before we left his base. In the end, we managed to secure dramatic pictures of government counter-insurgency, although it was a training exercise, not real 'bang-bang'. Khartoum was often accused of clever PR campaigns to cover up its wrongdoing. In Darfur they totally failed to put their side of the argument, and they did have a case. So, sometimes by default, the Western media castigated the Sudanese forces, who rarely 'put up' a convincing spokesperson or any spokesman at all. Thus, even in the best BBC tradition, it was difficult to 'balance' highly critical stories. Also, it was a very nasty war. Leaving El Fasher was always complicated by lack of planes. Just like the mercenaries in the *Wild Geese* film, we ended up having to run into the back of a lowered cargo flap of a UN plane just as it was about to taxi on to the runway. No health and safety busybodies plagued that airport.

I continued to visit Darfur regularly but enjoyed less freedom to roam around, unlike my early trips. Even in my restricted visits to Darfur, it became abundantly clear that no military solution could be achieved. The African Union-UN hybrid monitoring force could achieve little. It was understaffed, lacking in proper intelligence and kit, especially helicopters. Only a political solution, along the lines of the north-south agreement, could end the war. Despite past brutality, it was clear that the new government of national unity in Khartoum (including Islamists and the SPLA, from 2005-10) was trying to bring peace. The Darfur rebels, ever fractious, were holding out for more and more. What was needed was the kind of Western (and now also Chinese) political investment – banging heads together – that secured the north-south deal.

The various Darfur peace talks had been so close, down to a few million extra US dollars for the hold-outs' personal bank accounts in some cases, to be entirely cynical. By March 2009 the talks between the Justice and Equality Movement and Khartoum were doing well in Doha. Then came the International Criminal Court's decision to issue arrest warrants for the Sudanese president, for his alleged crimes in Darfur. In theory, it was possibly a good idea for monsters such as Mugabe to be dragged off to The Hague. In the case of Sudan it would be a disaster. In the north-south talks, in which President al-Bashir played a paramount role, no mention was made of punishing the many war crimes on both sides. What the ICC decision meant was the Darfur rebels would drag their heels indefinitely, waiting for regime change in Khartoum. They would have had to wait a long time, because the ICC action was taken as an insult to nearly all northern Sudanese, regardless of whether they hated or loved al-Bashir. The ICC entrenched not destabilized him. Moreover, most southern leaders I spoke to were terrified that the CPA deal might collapse and war return.

So the causes of the war were multiple: drought, desertification and rapid over-population had intensified the traditional nomad versus settled famer disputes.

Nor had Darfur been immune to the political changes of the 1980s and 1990s. Arabization and Islamicization had impacted especially on the African tribes. Many of the tribal structures among and between Arabs and

Africans had been eroded, not least by Khartoum's attempts to destroy the old loyalties to the Umma party. Moreover, the southern peace talks were a catalyst to longstanding grievances about Darfur's marginalization, although the west had been considered prosperous in comparison with other far-flung areas. Most of the SLA's demands were local, while JEM's were clearly national or even international. JEM's Islamist leaders had been acolytes of al-Turabi. Some Darfur rebels wanted reforms and more power in Khartoum and provincial improvements, while a few dreamed of secession. JEM, however, wanted al-Turabi-directed regime change. JEM was in some respects a tool of revenge for the ever-meddling Imam. The war's causes were complex, while the consequences were to prove disastrous and long-lasting for Darfur and the rest of Sudan. The army's initial cack-handed COIN turned possibly a short sharp revolt into a very messy and prolonged civil war. It took Sudan's army and military intelligence officers decades to achieve that result in the south; in the west they did it in just over a year.

One savvy critic of Khartoum, Rob Crilly, put it well. There was no intent to wipe out certain groups, he maintained:

> …unlike the cases of Rwanda or Nazi Germany. Darfur was a bungled counter-insurgency that got wildly out of hand and ended up as ethnic cleansing. Furthermore, almost all of the mass killings took place in the first year; by the time the genocide activist campaign got going after 2004, Darfur was much more of a low-intensity guerrilla war than the arena for genocide.[1]

The course of the war
Flint and de Waal, in their seminal work on the war, describe rebel attacks before 2003.[2] On 21 July 2001 a group of Zaghawa and Fur (the latter being the largest African tribe) swore on the Koran that they would unite to fight government onslaughts on their villages. In their view, they would fight an Arab apartheid that was practising ethnic cleansing against non-Arab Muslims. (Nearly all Darfuris are Muslim. Many in Darfur, the source of much military support for the Mahdi, regard themselves as the purest Muslims in Sudan, if not the Middle East.) The rebels started training in their redoubts in the Jebal Marra massif, the greenest mountain range of Sahelian Africa. Various police stations and isolated army garrisons were attacked in 2002. In early March 2003 the rebels seized the garrison town of Tine on the Chadian border, capturing a large quantity of arms and supplies. Al-Bashir furiously responded by saying he would 'unleash' the

army. At that time he had little professional manpower in reserve because of the overstretch fighting in the south and east.

The next rebel attack was dramatic. At 5.30 am on 25 March 2003 a joint JEM and SLA force in a fleet of Toyota Land Cruisers swarmed into the capital of El Fasher in a surprise raid. At the airfield they blew up four Antonov bombers and three helicopter gunships, according to the rebels. They killed over seventy-five soldiers and captured thirty-two, including the base commander, a major general. It was daring, bold and highly successful. Sudan was not used to Israeli-style military efficiency. It literally caught the Sudanese army napping.

Khartoum had to retaliate against such a humiliation. The army formed the core of the COIN, with police units and the PDF as well as militia groups from Arab tribes including the Rezeigat. The insurgents were mainly from the Fur, Zaghawa and Masalit groups. The first year of the war was intense. The greater strength of the government forces could not initially be brought to bear on a highly mobile enemy who used hit-and-run tactics in the desert. The government resorted to very heavy-handed methods. The (surviving) Antonovs were deployed as bombers – simply rolling barrels with 250lbs of explosive out of the back; then gunships would go in, followed by 'technicals' – the open-backed 4x4s plus, sometimes, militia – called *Janjaweed* – on horseback or camels. Although they did hit armed JEM and SLA camps when they could find them, the army's targets were sometimes unarmed villagers. Critics claimed that to remove popular support for the rebels, villages were razed, women were raped as a weapon of war, and all who could not flee were sometimes killed. Wells were poisoned. A donkey or two were used to sample the water. This was scorched earth policy with a vengeance. Many non-Arab peoples fled to the internal refugee camps or across the border to kinsmen in Chad.

Khartoum denied the atrocities and especially the allegedly high number of fatalities among civilians. Al-Bashir was also personally incensed by the accusations of mass rape. 'It is not in the Sudanese culture or people of Darfur to rape. It doesn't exist. We don't have it.' Khartoum also insisted that poisoning water was considered absolutely *haram* in Islamic tradition.

The COIN in the first year was largely organized by military intelligence officers, who were keen to ensure the loyalty of Dafurian other ranks in the armed forces. Critics alleged that sometimes soldiers, Darfuris and others, were forced at gunpoint to kill unarmed villagers and indulge in rapes. Whatever the truth of the allegations, support for the rebels accelerated among the local non-Arab population. Their counter-attacks against the government forces were often highly successful and they were now inclined to take fewer prisoners. The SLA began to shift its area of operations farther east, threatening to extend the war to Kordofan.

The failure of the first attempt at suppression and the shortage of professional soldiers had forced the government to deploy more militia fighters, especially the Baqqara who had generations of tribal warfare throbbing in their veins. They were given money, training, new guns and modern communications. Khartoum supplied the air power and intelligence. This sort of militia strategy had been deployed more or less successfully in the Nuba Mountains and in the south, especially around the oilfields. Within a year of the El Fasher opener, the militias were gaining the upper hand. Hundreds of thousands of refugees created a humanitarian disaster and soon an international crisis, especially after the CPA was signed in January 2005. Another international factor was the increasing involvement of Chad, not least when its army intervened across the border to protect allied tribes against Khartoum's forces.

The Chad government brokered a temporary ceasefire with some of the rebel groups and Khartoum; in August 2004, the African Union sent a small detachment of Rwandan troops to monitor the very shaky ceasefire. The Rwandans were there because they were well-trained, effective and instantly deployable (with US air transports), and they certainly knew a lot about ethnic cleansing. Soon they were joined by 150 Nigerian troops. The UN Security Council now took more interest in what was happening, and the AU boosted the numbers in AMIS (African Union Mission in Sudan) to around 7,000. The fighting continued as did the humanitarian disaster. Sudanese reprisals and hot pursuit raids on rebel camps inside Chad increased the traditional hostility between Khartoum and N'Djamena.

President al-Bashir felt personally betrayed by the Americans after signing the CPA and handing over so much high-grade intelligence. He had done all he had been asked to do and more, he believed. Al-Bashir told me straightforwardly: 'In 2005 at Navaisha the Americans promised to remove sanctions. But they wanted the SPLM to take over from the *inside.*' He had not sought a war in Darfur, partly energized by his intemperate rival, al-Turabi. Ignoring the al-Turabi connection, the President told me that 'Darfur is 100 per cent US made.' A surprising claim, but not in the context of al-Bashir's view of the gang of four's mischief-making in the south. He added: 'There was war for twenty years in the south and there was no involvement with the UN Security Council, but it became involved in the *first* year of the Darfur.' The Security Council, as we saw, was rather reluctant, not eager, to get involved in Darfur, especially as the catastrophic occupation of Iraq was exercising the world body. Washington, however, felt disinclined to remove Khartoum from sanctions and from the list of states supporting terror, not least because of the increasingly high-decibel lobbying about Darfur in the USA.

The Darfur lobbies in America became as active as the anti-apartheid protesters of twenty years before. For all the good intentions, the lobbies often complicated the work of the diplomats actually trying to secure peace. One acute observer commented on the task of diplomats versus celebrity PR: 'The former lived in a world of negotiations, deals, incremental progress and the fine grain of local politics. The latter breathed the purer air of universal principles and moral absolutes.'[3]

The State Department did try to broker peace in Darfur. Under Secretary of State Robert B. Zoellick as well as the AU, Arab League and EU representatives had been busy in May 2006 in Abuja, Nigeria. Abuja was to be first of many rounds of peace talks, but it did produce an agreement between Khartoum and a faction of the SLA led by Minni Minnawi, who was made a senior advisor to the president. JEM and a rival faction of the SLA refused to sign. The agreement had some similarities with the CPA and was indeed called the DPA, Darfur Peace Agreement. It offered power sharing, economic and infrastructure benefits and a referendum on the status of Darfur as well as integration of the rebels into the government forces. If the rebels had gone to war to grab some of the concessions offered to Juba, then this approach made sense. But it would fall on deaf ears with those in JEM who plotted regime change.

The fighting continued, including the rebels killing, assaulting and kidnapping aid workers. Kofi Annan called for a much bigger UN force to replace the AU peacekeepers. Al-Bashir, however, still opposed the introduction of UN troops. The head of the State Department's Bureau of African Affairs, Jendayi Frazer, warned that the tragedy in Darfur would spiral without a beefed-up UN presence. Khartoum initially wanted to find a military solution to Darfur, not suffer the presence of foreign troops. The Sudanese government had tried peace talks, but now that so many troops were being freed from duty in the south, the regular army had enough numbers to do what the militias could not. In September 2006 a major offensive was launched. It was directed by a new intelligence structure. The government of national unity had led to a surprising (if not total) integration of northern and southern intelligence capabilities. The NISS was re-divided into two services, the internal *Amn (al-Jabha)* and the external traditional

Mukhabarat role, which liaised with foreign agencies. The military operations section of *Amn* had responsibility for Darfur. The significance was that now southerners, who controlled the southern operational branch, had a much bigger, and perhaps moderating, influence on COIN in the western war.

At the same time the AU troops were asked to leave, as their mandate was about to expire. They did not have sufficient numbers or mobility to monitor effectively the conflict let alone contain it. Poorly led and sometimes unpaid for months, they were often demoralized. AU troops were sometimes disarmed, and occasionally attacked by the rebels.

Minni Minmawi broke ranks and also called for UN involvement. But al-Bashir said that it would be like a return to colonialism. 'We do not want Sudan to turn into Iraq,' he said. As a compromise, the AU mandate was extended, and 200 UN troops were allowed in to help with the severe logistical and communications problems. The Nigerian government sent their foreign minister to Khartoum to emphasize the need for UN help. In October, President George W. Bush imposed extra sanctions, some particularly targeted against any US individuals trading with Sudan and preventing Sudanese directly involved with the war in Darfur from entering the USA. Khartoum retaliated by kicking out the senior UN official in the country, Jan Pronk, but also offered an olive branch. The government said it would hold unconditional talks with the National Redemption Front, the joint alliance of those who had rejected the earlier agreements. To underline the complexity, some Arabs groups started fighting the Sudanese army. The latest Arab formation was dubbed the Popular Forces Troops, which then allied with the National Redemption Front. Meanwhile, fighting between Arab groups, along traditional nomadic versus pastoralist lines, added to the mayhem. The latest was the feud between the Terjem and Mahria tribes in South Darfur.

While some SPLA officers had been involved with training rebels in Darfur, former SPLA commander Lam Akol, now the new foreign minister in the joint administration in Khartoum, took the government line and argued that the UN presence should be minimal and restricted to technical support. Meanwhile, the AU forces on the ground complained of a new Sudanese army offensive. The UN Commissioner for Human Rights reiterated the claim that the army and militias were targeting unarmed civilians. The Save Darfur Coalition in the US became the most vocal lobby in condemning Khartoum. Well-known Hollywood stars, the most famous being George Clooney and Mia Farrow, became prominent media commentators, demanding more intervention. The first Save Darfur Coalition mass rally was held in Washington DC in April 2006. It was attended by hundreds of thousands of people. According to one journalist there, 'It was a wonderfully eclectic mix of orthodox rabbis, scruffy students, bible-belt Christians, New York intelligentsia, black activists and film stars.' A few of the celebrities crossed illegally from Chad to visit refugees in the border areas. Access via Chad, although arduous, was a means for journalists to enter the war zone. Khartoum sometimes made it difficult for reporters to get to Khartoum or then from the capital on the few civilian flights to El Fasher.

Pressure was mounting on Khartoum: in April 2007 President Bush gave a speech at the US Holocaust Memorial Museum in which he threatened even more sanctions if the human rights situation in Darfur did not improve soon. The military options, such as a naval blockade of oil exports from Port Sudan and no-fly zones in Darfur, especially with French jets stationed in Chad, were extensively debated in public, and extensively rejected in private in the UK Ministry of Defence and the US Department of Defense. Both departments were up to their necks in the quagmires in Iraq and Afghanistan. Even the AU took notice of the international furore over Darfur; the planned Sudanese presidency of the AU was stalled. The Chinese were now inclined to shift slightly in their hardline support for Khartoum. They softened on the UN involvement, not least because the Western lobbies on Darfur had touched a vulnerable nerve: the 2008 Olympics in Beijing. The lobbies mass-produced slogans about the 'Genocide Olympics' because of Beijing's relentless support for Sudan. Al-Bashir could not ignore Chinese nudges and so some concessions were made on setting up the UN-AU hybrid force (UNAMID – African Union UN Mission in Darfur). Beijing allowed Khartoum, however, to impose many restrictions on size, composition and equipment. The lobbies were calling for NATO-style troops, but the new force was essentially a re-hatted AU. The few capable Western officers were sometimes not given visas by the Sudanese government. Al-Bashir insisted on African troops with a sprinkling of Asian contingents. The force never reached its projected size of 27,000 soldiers and police and never secured the mobility it needed, especially helicopters. Like its predecessor, it could monitor and report, but it did not have the resources or mandate to protect more than its own troops and, perhaps, some IDP camps. Above all, it could not be a peacekeeping force, for there was no peace to keep.

The ICC then intervened for the first time in the conflict. Ahmed Haroun, Sudan's minister for humanitarian affairs, and 'Ali Kushayb', a prominent militia leader, were charged with fifty-one counts of war crimes and crimes against humanity. This was a prequel to a major international controversy.

The government of national unity in Khartoum was still functioning despite its many frictions – the SPLM withdrew from the joint administration for a few months in late 2007 – but the siege mentality among the northerners was mounting because of the drumbeat of world condemnation. Just as his government had acted to assuage foreign pressures on previous occasions in the 1990s, al-Bashir set out to mend diplomatic fences, this time with Chad, the key western neighbouring state. The domestic conflicts in Chad were highly complex and also strewn with an alphabet soup of rebel groups. The neighbour had a long history of north-south/Muslim-Christian animosities, but it also shared many kinship ties with Darfur; at one time hundreds of thousands of Chadians were employed in Sudan, especially in the cotton industry. Both sides meddled in each other's affairs by backing rebel movements that regularly crossed the 600-mile largely unmarked border. Khartoum had supported Muslim rebels in the 1960s. In the 1970s, relations improved because both feared Gaddafi's expansionism and destabilization. Libya had long claimed a large section of northern Chad.

When al-Bashir came to power, relations had already deteriorated as Chad was supporting the SPLM. In May 1990 a column of Chadian soldiers raided El Fasher to rescue wounded colleagues held in a local hospital. This set a precedent for the fashion for daring long-range raids using columns of 4x4s, often driving cross-country. Chadian forces continued to strike across their border in pursuit of Chadian (and Darfuri) rebels operating out of Darfur. When a stage of the civil war ended with Idriss Déby's final defeat of his opponent, Hissène Habré, in December 1990, al-Bashir visited Chad for talks to improve bilateral ties. Déby, however, declared a 'state of belligerence' with Sudan in December 2005. That was resolved, but diplomatic relations were broken off twice in 2006. This was because Sudan was arming, training and equipping Chadian rebels based in Darfur, southern Chad and the Central African Republic. One of Sudan's favourite Chadian rebel chieftains was Abbogro Nour Abdulkarim, a charismatic young tribal leader born in Gereida, eastern Chad in 1971. He led or participated in a number of diverse political fronts and fighting units. He was, however, a man of action rather than a talker. He was in the vanguard of a daring long-range advance on the Chadian capital, N'Djamena, in April 2006. The rebels captured parts of the city, but failed to seize the presidential palace because of the last-minute intercession of French troops. Abdelkarim was later made minister of defence in the peace deal that followed. Undeterred, after three attempts on his life, he quit his government post and, in 2008, led another major invasion from the south that also reached the capital, but failed to displace Déby. Tanks and French gunships and Mirage F1s were too much for the Chadian rebels. Thereafter, Abdelkarim went into exile, although still supported by Libya. Gaddafi was backing a number of sides in the Chadian civil war. I interviewed Abdelkarim twice while he was in exile in Paris and Dubai. Highly articulate, he proclaimed his ideals of social democracy in elegant French. [4]

Al-Bashir signed a number of peace agreements with Chad's leader, Idriss Déby, usually soon overtaken by local fighting. The core of the deals promised not to support rebel movements in their respective territories. Déby was a Zaghawa himself and had close kinship ties with the Zaghawa leaders in the Darfur rebel movement. The Saudis were significant players too, because they were alleged to be paying for one of the main anti-Déby groups in the south of Chad.

In Darfur, the crisis deepened. Another Sudanese splinter, of the Sudan Liberation Movement, was blamed for attacks on, and car-jacking of, Oxfam aid workers; the charity threatened to pull out of Gereida which succoured over 130,000 refugees. Starvation and sickness were causing more deaths than military action. Now that Chinese diplomacy had softened, European Darfur lobbies helped to precipitate British and French diplomacy to boost the AU-UN hybrid force that could effectively police a ceasefire and ensure that aid agencies could operate. The Security Council finally approved, in July 2007, Resolution 1769 that stated that UNAMID was to take over from AMIS, the AU force, by the end of the year. The number was supposed to be nearly 27,000 troops and police.

At the beginning of 2008 four times as many UN troops, police and military observers were based in Africa than there had been in all UN peacekeeping operations around the world for the ten years previously. Africa took up 65 per cent of UN deployed troops, including three of the four biggest missions. Sudan had two large missions: UNAMID in Darfur and around 10,000 troops in the south (UNMIS), following the Naivasha accord. Next door was the troubled UN mission in the Congo. Darfur pushed worldwide deployment to 90,000. This was mainly internal security work, not the classic border operations (an exception was the UNMEE mission separating Eritreans and Ethiopians). The EU also set a precedent with a small military mission in Chad and in the CAR, although this was second nature to the French Foreign Legion. At the same time, an AU force was mandated to operate in the chaos that was Somalia. And the AU even became involved in an amphibious assault on a secessionist island of the Comores in March 2008. All the optimistic talk of a so-called African renaissance was an ironic contrast with the numerous international peacekeepers busy in some but not all of the messy wars on the continent. The recent 'First World War in Africa'— in the Congo — had killed perhaps as many as five million people.

Even Darfur's tragedy paled in comparison, but Hollywood seemed little interested in the original heart of darkness in the Congo. Meanwhile, foreign diplomats tried to resuscitate the Darfur peace efforts at Arusha, Tanzania, in August 2007. Most of the top Darfuri rebels came, except for Abdul Walid al-Nur, who represented a large part of the Fur people through his SLA splinter. Western diplomats bemoaned the fact that Darfur had not produced its own version of John Garang – one powerful leader who could speak for most of the insurgents. The senior leaders, especially the military boss of JEM, Khalil Ibrahim, did attend. Harangued by foreign diplomats, the fractious Darfuris reached a joint set of proposals regarding power sharing, security and humanitarian needs that were not that much different from previous peace arrangements. One difference was the increasing demand for independence, now championed by JEM, which threatened to go the whole hog if Khartoum did not grant effective autonomy on the Juba model. While the predominantly African leaders were parleying, many of the armed Arab militias fell out among themselves over grazing rights, especially in the Bulbul River valley. It was assumed they were grabbing land before the arrival of a big and effective UN force that might curb their annual feuds.

On 30 September 2007 heavily armed JEM forces overran an AMIS base at Haskanita, in North Darfur, killing ten peacekeepers and injuring many more. The seven Nigerians killed were later found to have malfunctioning rifles; they had not been cleaned and had not been zeroed since leaving Nigeria. Soldiers from Mali, Senegal and Botswana were also killed. The rebels returned shortly afterwards to loot and met only limited resistance. The biggest loss of life for the AU, it was the final blow to their confidence and morale (and low reputation among Darfuris).

The next 'breakthrough' peace talks were scheduled for the end of October 2007 in Sirte, Libya, under the aegis of Gaddafi. Many of the more potent fighting groups did not attend, so the talks were re-branded as 'advanced consultations' to save face. Even the Darfuri rebels realized that their endless splintering was undermining their cause. Some groups, seeking cash and kudos, did a bit of banditry and village-burning and then called themselves this or that liberation front to be invited to some travel and accommodation at posh hotels. The behaviour of some attendees at peace talks matched people just let out of prison. At the Abuja talks, for example, one hotel recorded 8,000 visits by prostitutes – they had to be signed in. The nocturnal activity may well have affected the delegates' political acuity in the long diplomatic sessions. Even a number of genuine long-term insurgents, especially those who had been in exile in Europe, were dubbed 'hotel guerrillas' because they had lost touch with their fighting cadres in the desert.

Six factions of the SLM coalesced with other groups and the official JEM to work as two groups apparently to negotiate with Khartoum. Instead, in May 2008, the Darfurian resistance movement staged the most dramatic action of the war. It was of course a long-range commando raid. It was a return to the first success of the war, the raid on El-Fasher, and it was partly a revenge for Khartoum's backing for two invasions of the Chadian capital. So, according to the rebels' thinking, only a major strike on Khartoum was proportionate.

Around 1,200 JEM troops in a convoy of 130 all-terrain vehicles drove through nearly 600 miles of bush and scrub to reach Omdurman on 10 May 2008. Until then many residents of the three towns had tried to ignore what was happening in Darfur; now fighting returned to the streets of the capital for the first time since 1976. Intelligence had completely missed the convoy. One of the first to react was a Russian helicopter pilot, working as an instructor for the Sudanese air force. The pilot positioned his Mi-24 gunship to strafe the column, but was shot down by a heavy-calibre machine gun on one of the technicals. The chopper was brought down and the pilot killed. The Russians did their best to keep this incident a secret, but failed. The JEM convoy split up to take the Arba'een military base and nearby police HQ, and then moved to seize the TV and radio buildings in Omdurman. The army responded with artillery, tanks and gunships, but much of the resistance was organized by NISS officers, some distrustful of the army's loyalties. They managed to stop the rebels just short of the parliament building, alongside the Nile, and before they could cross the bridge to Khartoum proper. JEM was supposed to be making for the presidential compound to overthrow al-Bashir. The government said that its forces had killed or captured all the rebels by the end of the first day, though locals reported some fighting the next day. Later, JEM asserted that forty-five of their men had been killed, while the government claimed double that number. Khartoum admitted that ninety-three of its soldiers and twelve policemen had been killed as well as thirty civilians. The government immediately rounded up the usual suspects, including Hassan al-Turabi, but they released him the same day, citing lack of hard evidence of complicity (although he later said the JEM invasion was a 'positive' move). Over 100 captured JEM fighters were tried for treason and sentenced to death, although al-Bashir pardoned and freed a small number of JEM child soldiers.

A JEM spokesman said that 'it might have lost the Khartoum battle and pulled out in dignity, but it has not lost the war'. Khartoum once more broke off diplomatic ties with Chad, but there was no hiding the intelligence failure and the political humiliation of a major raid on the capital. According to US intelligence, the army was now largely commanded by the NISS. Only 4,000 trusted elite army paratroopers were left in the capital.

JEM had brought the war to the three towns. The 2003 raid on El Fasher and the 2008 brazen assault on Khartoum bookmarked the Darfur war. Low-level insurgency and banditry continued as well as a humanitarian crisis. From now on – and until the time of writing – Darfur's war was mentioned in the international media only when peace talks, usually in Doha, failed – again. In 2009 General Martin Agwai, the Nigerian head of UNAMID, said that the 'real war' was effectively over. Nevertheless, playing to domestic lobbies, President Obama promised more forceful action in Darfur during his presidential campaign, especially as only 15,000 of the projected 26,000 UN troops were in place. Obama again raised the issue of no-fly zones.

Al-Bashir worked once more on the diplomatic route. He invited the Chadian president to visit Khartoum in February 2010. Déby pledged to stop aiding JEM and both countries set up joint military border patrols. In December 2010 the renamed coalition of the 'Liberation and Justice Movement' made progress with the Sudanese government representatives in Doha. Part of the discussion was about installing a Darfurian vice president. As the talks continued into 2011, compensation for victims and trials for those accused of human rights abuses were discussed. A long-term issue was the anger at Khartoum's previous arbitrary separation of Darfur into three states; the government was not keen to accept a unified Darfur with a single vice president. That smacked too much of the southern deal which, in early 2011, was speeding towards independence. Another Darfur peace agreement (of sorts) was signed on 14 July with some of the senior rebel leaders. Yet real peace did not come. The IDP camps became even more permanent and donors' conferences came and went. Banditry and general lawlessness rather than armed revolution were the issues. 'It's now a Wild West,' said Amin Mekki Madani, a leading NGO-ista. 'Only those with money and weapons survive.' The few banks and many stores were targets, not national liberation.

The low-level war peaked again when SLA and JEM units captured a town in North Kordofan, thus extending the spread of the fighting. In North Darfur Arab tribal warfare intensified. After hundreds were killed the Rezeigat and Beni Hussein tribes signed a peace deal, as did the Missiriya and Salamat clans. The introduction of so much modern weaponry meant that minor disputes could soon heat up into pitched battles. This happened between the Maalia and Rezeigat over a dispute about stolen cattle. Land disputes caused heavy fighting between Arab groups in the south of Darfur, again.

The overall civilian death toll in Darfur has been much debated. The government figure of less than 10,000 killed in the fighting in the first few years is far too low. Eric Reeves's claim that over 450,000 were killed in the first three years is far too high. Far more died from disease and malnutrition (and natural causes) than combat, cross-fire or atrocities, while millions have been displaced. The issue of genocide has also been much debated. In March 2005 the Security Council formally referred Darfur to the ICC. In April 2007 the ICC issued arrest warrants for two Sudanese citizens, but Khartoum, not a final signatory of the ICC treaty, said the Court had no jurisdiction and would not surrender the two men to The Hague. On 14 July 2008 the ICC prosecutor filed ten charges of war crimes against the Sudanese president. Was the ICC intervention helpful in containing the war or did it prolong the crisis in Darfur – and Sudan?

Chapter 9

The ICC and Sudan

The indictments

No one thought that the ICC would actually indict President al-Bashir for war crimes. It would be the first example of a sitting head of state being arraigned. The US lobbies had generated so much celebrity attention to bringing peace to Darfur, so why indict the president and derail the DPA and probably the CPA? It would be pressing the nuclear button. In a Western analogy, it would be like arresting Martin McGuinness during the negotiations that were about to end the thirty-year Northern Ireland civil war, the longest insurgency in Europe. In Khartoum the gossip coalesced around whether rivals might use the ICC as a justification for another palace coup. Even if he survived, how would a proud president react? Would he feel backed into a corner and strike out, or would he try to appease his enemies in the West?

Al-Turabi of course could not resist an intervention. He called on the president to surrender to the ICC, while holding al-Bashir responsible for the war crimes in Darfur. The president's patience finally snapped with his persistent tormentor. The Iman was sent back to Kober prison and then shifted to the more austere prison in Port Sudan.

In New York the UN Security Council had referred the Darfur issue to the ICC in The Hague. China and Russia had not vetoed the move. In September 2004 a UN commission of enquiry was set up. The following January it reported on serious human rights abuses, but found no evidence of genocide. Khartoum also created its own enquiry into allegations of war crimes. The man driving the ICC on Sudan was Luis Moreno Ocampo, an Argentinian judge with a flair for publicity. He had once hosted a popular legal show on Argentinian TV. As the ICC's chief prosecutor, it was his responsibility to decide if there was a case to answer. He never visited Darfur himself, although ICC teams were sent three times to Khartoum. They rarely left the Hilton, although for once Sudan's famed hospitality did not extend fully to the ICC visitors. On 27 April 2007 arrest warrants were issued for

Ahmed Haroun, the former minister of humanitarian affairs, and 'Ali Kushayb', a militia leader. President al-Bashir responded by saying that he would never hand over any Sudanese to the Court, even those Darfuris who had taken up arms against him. The media speculated about others who might be charged. There was talk of up to fifty or even eighty names in sealed indictments. British and American intelligence made sure that Saleh Gosh and Ali Othman Taha were excluded from any lists. It was a payback for all their security co-operation.

At a press conference in The Hague on 14 July 2008, Ocampo accused the president of crimes against humanity, war crimes and genocide (and also incidentally of corruption, by salting away $9 billion in European banks). Ocampo emphasized genocidal intent and a formal plan to exterminate the Fur, Masalit and Zaghawa tribes. Many experts on Darfur were shocked by the intemperance of language and fact displayed by Ocampo. As Alex de Waal said: 'In the absence of law and evidence, we have the theatrics.' In November 2008 three rebel leaders were also indicted for the attack on the AU base at Haskanita. On 4 March 2009 an arrest warrant was issued for al-Bashir. The warrant had left out, on this occasion, charges of genocide. Later, he was charged with that crime as well.

How did the president react personally? Probably the most accurate account came from a senior government official, who confided in me at the time, deploying his good command of American vernacular: 'The Boss went apeshit.' The official presidential response was slightly more measured on the reaction to the warrant: 'It is not worth the ink it is written with – they can eat it.' The president's family later told me he was 'hurt and angry', although his second wife, Widad, insisted on being diplomatic: 'I would prefer "upset" as a description.' That was no doubt an understatement. The president later told me that he considered the indictment 'a political issue and double standards because there are obvious crimes, like Palestine, Iraq and Afghanistan, but they do not find their way to the ICC.'

In the heat of anger, al-Bashir ordered thirteen major NGOs to quit Darfur, blaming them for providing inaccurate and defamatory data to the ICC. They were accused of being 'spies for foreign agencies'. Thousands of aid workers had to leave almost immediately, but not before the Sudanese Humanitarian Affairs Council, staffed by more intelligence than aid experts, ensured that the local employees were paid six months' severance pay, and much of the NGO data and electronic equipment were handed over. Roughly 6,500 – 40 per cent of Western aid workers – had to quit, sometimes abandoning patients in clinics and hospitals. It was a hammer blow to the humanitarian programme in Darfur. Publicly, the Sudanese health authorities announced that local agencies such as the Red Crescent and Khartoum's doctors could easily replace the expelled foreigners. Behind the scenes, Sudanese officials, caught off-guard by the president's sudden statement, told me that they 'were tearing their hair out', as they just did not have anywhere near the number of skilled personnel to replace the departing experts at such short notice. Eventually, many of the famous charities and NGOS were allowed to return, sometimes re-badged. But the ICC intervention had caused much disruption both to the humanitarian and peace effort. And because the ICC was so inter-related to the UN, the role of the UN-led forces in the country also hung in the balance. It was once more a classic example of the law of unintended consequences. Presumably, George Clooney or Mia Farrow had not foreseen the diplomatic results of their full-throated advocacy.

Unintended consequences

The ICC was arguably a noble endeavour, set up in 2002, eight years after the genocide in Rwanda. The ICC's mission was to improve international justice for victims of major crimes. The government in Khartoum saw the court as an instrument of Western political power. The object was regime change, not justice, said al-Bashir. The ICC was designed as a court of last resort, when national jurisdictions failed to implement justice. It was seen by some as a complement to local justice, whether formal courts or traditional African reconciliation methods such as the semi-successful Truth and Reconciliation process in South Africa. States were supposed to invite the ICC to assist. In Sudan's case the UN Security Council mandated involvement, albeit controversially.

Western intervention in Africa had rarely made things better and usually made them worse. Khartoum said that the ICC had no legal right to intervene in Darfur, not least because Sudan was not a signatory to the Rome treaty that had established the Court. Defenders of al-Bashir pointed out that all the ICC indictments had been in Africa. They were playing very successfully to the anti-colonial sentiments, not only in the African Union and the Arab League, but throughout the developing world. Khartoum's diplomacy prompted Sudan to be elected leader of the G77 in February 2009, in a deliberate snub to the ICC.

Thirty-four African states joined the ICC and many came to regret it when all thirty-six people publicly indicted all turned out to be African. In April 2014 the AU held an international conference in Addis to discuss what it perceived as ICC bias. Terence McNamee, a Canadian, summed up the proceedings:

> The ICC's sharpest critics claim that international law does not apply to the powerful, only the weak – hence the focus on Africa, the new court's 'laboratory'. The major powers have become, in essence, both players and referees, formulating the rules of the game but refusing to play by them.[1]

Opposition to the ICC's African ventures was often not ideological but pragmatic: would it make conditions better or worse? In Darfur, or Uganda, or the Democratic Republic of the Congo, or the Central African Republic, countries where the ICC had become entangled? Nor was Khartoum's fury entirely ideological: a delicious fervour would have erupted there from an ICC arraignment of an Israeli leader. The arrest warrants undermined peace efforts in Darfur, and prolonged the tragedy. Khartoum's hasty response of ejecting impeccable Western non-government organizations such as *Médicins sans Frontières* also made the suffering worse in Darfur. The ICC and Khartoum were being sucked into an action-reaction cycle, which was intensifying, not resolving, conflict.

The many critics of Khartoum said: if al-Bashir is innocent, why not go to The Hague and prove it? I did not raise that point when I visited the president's official Khartoum home in April 2009; that might have been a bit like fondly reminiscing about a favourite Jewish grandmother to the Führer. Al-Bashir outlined his sense of grievance, though he couched it diplomatically. The president said: 'When Morgan Tsvangirai raised his hand to take the oath of office in the government of national unity – with Robert Mugabe – all the international pressures and legal threats were forgotten. Maybe I should ask Tsvangirai to raise his hand here as well?' Al-Bashir felt victimized. His advisors constantly made the point that the Comprehensive Peace Agreement did not include specific judicial claims to punish the numerous war crimes on both sides. The 2005 agreement was threatened with disruption. That is why the SPLA ministers, then a part of the national unity government in Sudan, fretted to me about a possible return to war because of ICC destabilization. Sudan was often projected as a tough authoritarian 'Islamo-fascist' state. It was certainly authoritarian, but also potentially fragile. The implosion of Sudan would mean its removal as an ally in Washington's 'war on terror'.

The most persuasive argument against ICC involvement was the threat to peace, but Khartoum – while not recognizing the ICC – also mounted an elaborate legal counter-offensive, employing the best Western lawyers. A part of this defence was that President al-Bashir had national immunity because he was head of state, and *inter alia* the arrest warrants contradicted international law. Khartoum insisted, however, that the real challenge was political not legal, part of a long plot to dethrone another Islamic leader in an oil-rich country.

From the seventeenth century – through the Nazi war trials – until today, trials of senior political leaders have usually been a result of defeat in war (from King Charles I via Slobodan Milosevic to Saddam Hussein). The trials confirmed defeat, and often victors' justice rewrote laws. Not a single head of state indicted for major crimes has ever been acquitted; because the legal verdict had always been pre-ordained by a political verdict. In this view, political trials are, to adapt Clausewitz, a continuation of war by other means. Al-Bashir, an elected head of state, had not been defeated. Arguably, he was at the top of his game. To quote the Queen in *Alice in Wonderland*: 'Sentence first – verdict afterwards.'

International law evolved for good practical reasons as well as negative political ones. Many of the ecological challenges facing the planet are no respecters of international boundaries, nor is AIDS. So legislation on health or climate change are evolving to cope with planet-wide crises. Similarly, war crimes – for example, atrocities in Yugoslavia, or genocide in Cambodia and Rwanda – have inevitably transformed decrepit ideas of national sovereignty. The African Union itself had moved from non-interference in other African states to non-indifference to major crimes. In short, international law was evolving to cope with crises that the Westphalian concept of 1648 could not deal with. This was inevitable, and beneficial. But was this evolution to be used for humanitarian benefit, or short-term political goals?

The ICC, while claiming universal jurisdiction, was simply not international. More than half the world's population was not in its jurisdiction. The US, Russia, China and India, among many other countries, were not members of the ICC. Khartoum insisted that because it was a non-signatory of the 2002 Rome treaty, the Court was acting beyond its powers in pursuing a state which had not signed up. Nor does the Court have any police powers. By asking a signatory state to detain al-Bashir (in international air space, it had been suggested), the arresting state could also be violating international law, if it complied with the request. Air piracy could compound the struggle with sea piracy.

Publicly, Khartoum said that the president was free to travel to any friendly state and, just in case, in the local region, Sudanese jet fighters would escort him. Privately there were several scares for the president. In 2011 a flight to Beijing was apparently aborted, and in 2013 al-Bashir left Nigeria very early because of rumours that he might be arrested. In August 2013 he was apparently barred from Saudi air space. Even in next door Addis, the presidential protection unit got wind of an attempt to arrest him. Mostly, however, al-Bashir appeared to travel around Africa and the Middle East with relative ease, even to countries that were signatories of the ICC treaty.

Meanwhile, Khartoum also attacked Britain and France for funding and provoking the ICC to pass 'crazy laws', though it should also be noted that the other permanent members of the Security Council, especially Russia and China, let alone the US, did not wield the veto on the Darfur referral to the ICC. Khartoum's defenders argued that the ICC had chosen not to criminalize waging 'aggressive' war, a charge at the heart of the Nuremberg war crimes trials, and which more than one legal authority had compared with the 2003 Anglo-American invasion of Iraq. A war cry echoed throughout Arabia and Africa: if al-Bashir, why not Blair or Bush?

Legal experts also suggested that, in its first case, regarding the alleged use of child soldiers in the Democratic Republic of Congo, the ICC had ridden roughshod over key legal procedures, violating many of the main defendants' rights. Nor had it commented on the JEM's use of child soldiers, some of them captured in the 2008 raid on Omdurman. In sum, are the processes of the ICC undermining the development of sound international law?

The ICC had actively pursued cases only in Africa. For years, the Court decided not to investigate any Western involvement or complicity in alleged war crimes, crimes against humanity or genocide, whether in Iraq, Afghanistan, or Gaza. It was true that Africa had had more than its fair share of despots. Some of the arguments for deploying African national courts, or traditional tribal reconciliation, were often unconvincing. Many of the traditional rites were patchy, inauthentic and most African courts systems were deficient, even in relatively successful countries such as Kenya – as failure to process captured Somali pirates demonstrated. Moreover, concepts of international humanitarian rights, as defined by the UN, should be universal. Suggesting African exceptionalism – that Africa should use its own methods, such as Mozambique's national reconciliation after its civil wars, or Zimbabwe's former national unity government – could smack of racism; that Africa was not ready for advanced legal systems.

Nevertheless, the targeting of only African leaders – Charles Taylor, Joseph Kony, etc. – did imply white racism. It had been suggested that arresting African leaders was simply easier than taking on Western leaders. And the Court's actions in this regard were often seen as enforcing the ICC's credibility: that it was actually seen to be doing something. This was macho politics, not law. The Court's African focus fired up a continental paranoia about a new form of neo-colonialism. So far, however, the ICC had not produced a single unchallenged conviction. The ICC's timing had never been good. Just as the Lord's Resistance Army leaders were about to make peace directly with the Ugandan government, the Court's arrest warrants for those same leaders prompted them to return to war. And in February 2009 Khartoum's peace talks with JEM rebels were prospering. One fatal mistiming might seem an accident, but a repetition in the arrest warrants for al-Bashir might appear a conspiracy to some in Africa.

There was a long history of forceful action against Sudan backfiring. By 1996 the US had succeeded in isolating Sudan. The regime was fighting wars on several fronts and its back was against the wall. Then, in August 1998, the Clinton administration attacked a medical facility in Khartoum, claiming the factory was making weapons of mass destruction. Washington's claims were subsequently shown to be false. Almost overnight, Sudan was embraced by the developing world. African states and the Arab League, previously hesitant about the Khartoum regime, kicked out against a perceived injustice. The Africa group at the United Nations nominated Sudan to take the African seat on the Security Council (ultimately blocked, with difficulty, by Washington). Diplomatically – even taking Darfur into consideration – the Sudanese had not looked back. And, in a further twist, the US economic sanctions against Sudan, in place since 1997, largely insulated Sudan from the Western economic meltdown that began in 2008. The cranes dominating Khartoum's skyline were evidence of Sudan's booming oil-based economy.

Likewise, the ICC action now made al-Bashir a poster-boy for the Sudanese nation, almost regardless of party, just as he was standing in the presidential election of 2010. Many Sudanese, both opponents and allies, were likely to rally around him. Another unintended consequence was that, like Mugabe, fear of the ICC could have made al-Bashir president for life. He might not have risked retiring, even if he had wanted to, after twenty-five years in power. No one expected the ICC to entrench dictatorships. Except for the insurgents in Darfur, the ICC action was seen domestically as an assault on Sudan. Nationalism was fired up. The ICC action was presumably supposed to weaken President al-Bashir; it had the opposite effect.

Internationally, those Africans supporting al-Bashir over the ICC were not necessarily doing so because they admired him – many disliked him. They did so because Sudan was the lightning rod of a growing African impatience with diktats from the West and their former colonial masters in Europe. In the interlude between the ICC's original indictment in July 2008 and the issuing of arrest warrants, Sudanese diplomacy (and others hostile to the ICC) had succeeded in positioning the issue as a Eurocentric, Franco-German-British court embracing the old 'White Man's Burden' of civilizing savage Africans by forcing white man's magic on them; in this instance Western legal structures alien to traditional African reconciliation mechanisms, let alone cultural norms.

Richard Dowden, the director of the Royal African Society, summed it up nicely: 'The ICC cannot hand out justice in Sudan as if it were Surrey [England].' More robustly, The Hague had also been dubbed 'Europe's Guantánamo Bay for Africans', where it administered sub-prime justice. Therefore the ICC was seen to ignore those African voices, be they Ugandan, Sudanese or in the AU, who said that the Court's arbitrary pursuit of African leaders was impeding or delaying peace. It can be argued that the ICC had inadvertently prolonged the horrific war in northern Uganda by aborting seemingly fruitful peace talks by issuing warrants against rebel leaders. In the case of Darfur, the ICC warrants against al-Bashir merely bolstered rebel intransigence regarding peace talks. They claimed they would hold out, until al-Bashir was arrested. This would mean an indefinite prolongation of the Darfur war.

The ICC intervention had the effect of making Sudan Africa's spokesman on issues such as the ICC. Many African countries and leaders were happy for Sudan to make the sort of stand which they supported, but were politically unable to make themselves. Also, the Arab League and other Islamic states rallied behind Khartoum because the ICC was seen as another Western intervention in a majority-Muslim state. The ICC action had not improved Western relations with the Arab and African worlds.

Internationally, the ICC issue had also manifested itself at the worst possible time. As the Western economic meltdown worsened by the minute, confidence in 'white man's magic' was at a historic low in the period 2008-12. For Africa, the only possible bright spot was the election of the African-American Barack Obama as US president. He also faced difficult choices regarding Africa and the ICC, not least in satisfying domestic lobbies, such as the Save Darfur Coalition, which had peddled misinformation on an industrial scale, not least about allegations of genocide.

Washington had long declared its opposition to the ICC, arguing that it would be used to exact 'political' justice, and that states and individuals would be pursued for political reasons under the façade of justice. Paradoxically, the American position on Sudan and the ICC had proved this to be absolutely the case. While attacking the ICC in the strongest terms, Washington nevertheless acquiesced in the UN Security Council referral of Darfur to the ICC (while demanding immunity for its own citizens); and had urged Sudan to submit to ICC demands. To many observers this was precisely the sort of political vendetta the US had itself warned that the ICC might be used for.

The ICC action may have served as a warning shot across the bows of other regimes, not least Mugabe's destructive presidency. But, in a war-ravaged continent, peace must precede justice, whether defined as African or European. Compromise was possible. There did not have to be a head-on clash between peace versus justice – they could be complementary. Nor was a collision inevitable between national versus international approaches, punishment versus conciliation. A middle course might begin with the ICC also focusing on criminal leaders in other continents. Otherwise, to its many African critics, the ICC's arrest warrants for al-Bashir would look like the twenty-first-century equivalent of old-fashioned nineteenth-century gunboat diplomacy – but minus the gunboats. Meanwhile, the suffering went on in Darfur. And that's what the ICC was designed to relieve.

Low-level insurgency continued at the time of writing in 2014 and no comprehensive peace plan had been fashioned. The whole ICC manoeuvre had not worked for a number of reasons. The legal processes were utterly flawed or, as one commentator derided it, 'Keystone Kops meets Alice in Wonderland'. The Sudan indictments had cost millions of euros and the procedure, led by Ocampo, had been a shambles, despite or because of his showmanship. More and more African states pulled away from the ICC, not least after another head of state, this time a Kenyan, was indicted. Al-Bashir generally travelled freely throughout Africa and the Middle East, as an honoured guest, not as a fugitive. The much bigger tragedies in Africa, for example in the DRC, were largely ignored, even though the scale of fatalities there – maybe five million – did start to approach the numbers of a real genocide, the Jewish holocaust. Only the US government, under immense internal pressure from domestic lobbies, used the genocide term about

Darfur; whereas impartial experts, many very hostile to Khartoum, thought the ICC's judgements were legally autistic and factually incorrect.

At the start of the war African as well as Arab militias were armed by Khartoum, hardly the action of a government intent on exterminating African tribes. Millions of Darfuris fled *to* the safety of government-garrisoned towns and cities. Jews in the early 1940s did not usually flock to the *Wehrmacht* for refuge. The over one million Darfuris in the Khartoum area went about their business unhindered. The government co-operated in a vast humanitarian system, the biggest in the world, with thousands of Sudanese aid workers in support of foreign charities and UN aid agencies. The most impeccable of them, the MSF, was in attendance for the whole of the heavy fighting of the initial stage of the conflict. They saw no signs of genocide, although they had boldly attacked it in Rwanda. Many of the troops in the regular army were Darfuris and, although there were cases of coercion in enforcing the scorched-earth policy, it was unlikely that they would consistently follow genocidal orders against their own kin. The first two Sudanese officials to be indicted were themselves of African, not Arab, descent. The war was very nasty and atrocities were committed on both sides, but the ICC's claim of a planned extermination on the Nazi model was simply very wide of the mark. Most of what the ICC said and much of the Save Darfur Coalition's propaganda were just that – propaganda. In bringing attention to the crisis it did prompt massive humanitarian aid, which did save many lives. Overall, however, external intervention prolonged and exacerbated the war – a lesson learned throughout the continent.

Ultimately, the ICC intervention unintentionally bolstered al-Bashir's position. He now had to enter the endgame of the long north-south diplomacy – the national election of 2010 and the southern referendum on independence in 2011. Omar al-Bashir had weathered many storms since his coup: 2010 and 2011 were to be perhaps his most challenging years, not least in keeping his country unified.

Chapter 10

The Fall of the Republic

So much of Khartoum's political energy had been used up by the crisis in Darfur. Nevertheless, Khartoum still had to make the new government of national unity function. Getting old enemies to work alongside each other was never going to be easy. The CPA itself, a set of highly complex and sometimes ambiguous documents, established over forty joint commissions and committees made up of SPLM and largely NCP northerners. Often the southerners lacked the experience and capability to populate these power-sharing arrangements, some of which rarely met. When they did, usually the northerners ran circles around the southerners, as in the old days. Often NCP ministers made decisions without consulting their southern colleagues. The MPs from both parties sat in parliament, in roughly proportionate numbers to their respective populations, so they could talk to, or at, each other. The southern ministers now had smart cars and offices. What really mattered, though, was money and security.

The northern government remained in charge of calculating and distributing the oil revenue; southerners estimated that they were being short-changed by at least 20 per cent. In the case of military integration, the CPA said 21,000 troops from joint units from both forces would create the nucleus of a future unified army. Only one fully functioning joint unit was formed, and it was under-resourced, partly because Khartoum was reluctant to expend too much money and energy on arming their former foes. The two sides came to blows in the field and, in a few cases, such as in Malakal in February 2009, they got caught up in a major fire-fight (although most of the continued fighting in the south was caused by inter-tribal warlordism). The national security apparatus was still tightly controlled by Saleh Gosh, but some genuine operational integration did take place. The real decisions, especially on security matters, were made in a small coterie around al-Bashir – his long-term allies in the NCP such as Ali Othman Taha, Nafie Ali Nafie and Dr Ibrahim Ghandour.

The new government of South Sudan (GoSS) in Juba, led by President

Salva Kiir, appeared to have earnestly adopted all the bad habits they learned from Khartoum. The wealth was centralized in Juba among fat-cat commanders-turned-politicians and most of the oil money was spent on weapons. The SPLM officials were quite open about this – they said it was a prudent policy of insurance against the north should the CPA fall apart. As in Pakistan, the SPLA was an army that happened also to run a country. By 2009 GoSS had received about $6 billion in oil money, but perhaps as much as 90 per cent was spent on re-equipping the SPLA. Amid a sea of corruption and cronyism, very little was left over for funding education, health and agriculture as well as infrastructure, which was largely provided by foreign donors.

Despite its good intentions the CPA had bequeathed a winner-takes-all system that entrenched power in Juba and Khartoum and left very little power to the states in both north and south. This mattered especially in the south, where the states received just 2 per cent of oil revenues. Nor did the CPA introduce term limitation for the respective presidents. It had long been accepted, though not enacted, that the main advance in African politics would be limitation on the terms a president could serve, to avoid the too-common habit of presidents for life.

Salva Kiir had frequently tackled Garang about his authoritarianism. It came to a head in a leadership meeting in Rumbek in November 2004. He accused Garang of carrying the movement 'in his own briefcase'. But Kiir refused to split the leadership, after the trauma of 1991, and gradually won around his colleagues to the concept of a greater collective leadership. After Garang died, Kiir did not purge the leadership of senior Garang supporters. Instead, he tried to embrace some of the former dissident commanders as well as civilian critics of Garang. So there was optimism in the SPLM that the new leader would continue to avoid some of the Stalinist traits perceived in Garang.

Unity was required not least to begin the shift from army politics to the development of the country. One visiting Western economist told me he thought Juba was 'a scrap heap built on a rubbish dump'. To be fair, it had been under siege for over twenty years. The standard yardstick usually quoted was that only thirty miles of tarred road had been built by GoSS, and these roads were in the capital, around the new high-walled villas owned by senior politicians. Smart new government buildings had been erected, with carefully marked-out white lines in the car parks for the fleets of government Land Cruisers.

Outside Juba, the country was starving and wrecked. In early 2010 I stopped off at a small village halfway between Juba and Torit. I was invited to take tea with the headman, who introduced me to the sole teacher in the village school. The teacher pointed at the dirt track – supposedly a main highway – and complained of no road-building.

'Nor have we been given any schoolbooks,' he said. 'We have none at all.' He listed other things that he'd asked Juba for, but not received. 'There is not a single tractor for miles,' he added.

What have five years of your own government brought you then?

'Nothing – but we'll all vote for the SPLA, for freedom next year.' And he smiled.

Entrepreneurs had moved in from Uganda, Ethiopia and Kenya and developed small businesses in and around Juba, including the occasional hotel. For thirsty travellers from the *sharia* north, a new South African brewery had been built as well. The local Equatorians, however, felt doubly squeezed – by the Dinka dominance in the new government and job competition from foreign workers. Overall, South Sudan had developed very little in five years, despite the often tireless efforts of foreign NGOs and lots of American money. In the words of one British financial journalist, 'Southern Sudan was beginning to resemble a new African phenomenon, a pre-failed state – prostrate and enfeebled before it was born.'[1]

The three towns in the north had enjoyed boom times, however. The oil bonanza, championed by Chinese, Malaysian and Indian companies, had created lots of new infrastructure, from the massive Merowe dam scheme to roads and power stations as well as the sparkling new international airport. When I asked President al-Bashir in early 2014 what he considered to be his main legacy, he immediately replied: 'All the economic and infrastructural developments.' He then listed all the new universities and hospitals built during his rule. He also added that Western duplicity, broken promises and, above all, sanctions had made him turn east, to Sudan's great advantage. As he told a colleague on *Time* magazine, Sam Dealey:

> From the first day, our policy was clear: to look eastward, toward China, Malaysia, India, Pakistan, Indonesia and even Korea and Japan, even if the Western influence on some of these countries is strong. We believe that the Chinese expansion was natural because it filled the space left by Western governments, the United States and international funding agencies. The success of the Sudanese experiment in dealing with China without political conditions or pressures encouraged other African countries to look toward China.

Despite the UN arms embargo on Darfur, China and Russia continued to supply the bulk of imported Sudanese weapons; both nations insisted nothing was going to Darfur – although it was the main centre of fighting once the CPA was agreed with the south. China had built factories in the industrial belt around Khartoum which made Sudan one of the biggest arms manufacturers in Africa, after South Africa and Nigeria (for details see Appendix).

Armed by China, Russia, Ukraine and Belarus, and boosted by new investments from, especially, Qatar and Turkey on top of Beijing's financial largesse, Khartoum had less need to bend to American diktats. Paradoxically, massive amounts of food aid from the West, especially America, were going not only to the south and Darfur, but also to the north, not least for the large refugee camps around Khartoum. An American UN worker told me that he had questioned a Dinka tribesman from the south who was wearing a cross, but standing at a Red Crescent feeding centre in the capital. The American asked the Dinka about the cross. The man laughed: 'I might be a Muslim in the morning, a Christian in the afternoon, but at night I pray to my own [Dinka] god.' In the absence of a synagogue, I used to make a point of visiting church services in Khartoum and saw no problems, just as I have visited mosques freely throughout the world.

* * * *

Al-Bashir still had to deal with the West over Darfur and UN engagement. But other diplomatic resources, such as increasing support from the AU, the Arab League and support from the Gulf states (but not the Saudis), added flexibility to the Asian economic and political alternatives. In particular, al-Bashir drew very close to Thabo Mbeki, the South African premier, who later acted as an AU envoy to Sudan. 'Mbeki was a wise man – a real African,' the President told me. 'He wanted to keep out foreign intervention from outside Africa.' Unlike Mbeki, whose policy on AIDS proved highly ignorant, stubborn and disastrous at home, al-Bashir took a far different line towards AIDS by spending money on education and health programmes to combat the disease, an unusually enlightened policy for an Islamic government.

Even before the ICC intervention, al-Bashir had despaired of working with the West – he constantly felt betrayed by their broken promises, not least on sanctions and removal from the terror list. US sanctions did make life difficult. One senior finance minister told me that removal of

Washington's restrictions would improve the economy by perhaps 40 to 50 per cent. Because nearly all Western credit cards worked through a central system in New York, it forced northern Sudan to be a totally cash economy. Paying for everything in wads of US dollars created numerous problems, not least for visiting foreign businessmen and diplomats; and it encouraged corruption inside the country. It also led to actual shortages of dollars, not always provided by the Chinese who often preferred barter deals – oil for projects. The cauterization of the Sudanese economy did, however, prove a boon when the Western economic depression hit in 2007-2008; by accident, Khartoum was largely immune. Nevertheless, al-Bashir chafed at America's economic and political restrictions. Then came the final break: the ICC indictment, which he blamed largely on the Americans for encouraging the Security Council to mandate The Hague.

Yet Khartoum still needed to work with the West, not least the American, British and Norwegian co-architects of the CPA. They played an important role, for example, in keeping the IGAD members and the southern army in line. By 2010 Darfur had been largely contained as a military problem. There was no peace, but the conflict was low intensity, and the food programmes were working. Health, education and nutritional standards had surpassed pre-war levels and were often higher than the east and south of the country. Yes, the scorched-earth tactics of both sides had driven hundreds of thousands into camps, now increasingly looking like the permanent semi-towns inhabited by the Palestinian diaspora. Few could expect to return to their villages, destroyed or re-settled by nomadic tribes. The IDP camps would store up anger for the desert intifadas of the future.

In the east, al-Bashir had done a deal with the Beja Congress (and the Free Lions from the Rashaida clans) in 2006. Eritrea had been the main fixer. It covered the states of Kassala, Gedarif and Red Sea. Like the western deals it involved a figurehead post – a membership of the team 'assisting' the president, but not a vice presidency, plus assembly seats and absorption of some rebels into the national army. The deal took four months. Khartoum also set out to buy peace with the promise of big injections of development aid through the Eastern Sudan Reconstruction and Development Fund, although few of the promised millions ended up in infrastructural improvements outside the thriving area around Port Sudan. The government also made deals with the exiled politicians in the NDA and encouraged them to come home to take part in the first internationally supervised elections, which were delayed until 2010.

The Elections

The presidential elections in 1996 and 2000 were highly controlled affairs with limited electorates, although the government made much of al-Bashir's popular mandate. The last reasonably democratic elections had been held as far back as 1986 when the lacklustre Sadiq al-Mahdi became premier. Now, under the aegis of the Western-backed CPA, a free and fair election had to be held in the whole country, despite the NCP dominance in the north and the equally dominant SPLM in the south as well as trying to run elections in the devastation that was Darfur. It was a tough call and worrying for Khartoum because lots of foreign busybodies had to be allowed in as election observers.

I included myself as a 'busybody'. I was head of mission for fifty independent British observers, organized by the Centre for Foreign Policy Analysis, a small London think tank of which I was director.[2] The team comprised experienced British civil servants, mainly from the Ministry of Defence, former British officers, lawyers, academics, and local government officials with election expertise, as well as observers from previous EU and UN missions. Some were long-term observers serving in the country for two to three months, but most were short-term observers who were placed throughout the south and partially in the north. We were excluded from Darfur. On the eve of the arrival of the main body of my foreign observers, plus the larger influx from the EU and American Carter Center, President al-Bashir made an ill-tempered and ill-judged intervention. He warned any foreigners who tried to delay or interrupt the elections that 'we will cut off their fingers and put them under our shoes'. I had some trouble explaining to my teams about to leave from the UK that this was mere hyperbolic Arab rhetoric and could be dismissed. They would be met by hospitality, I said, and they were. What could not be so easily dismissed were the many obstacles that could prevent a free and fair election: inaccurate census numbers, gerrymandering (especially in Darfur), censorship and limiting air time and rallies for opposition politicians in the north. In the south, the SPLM were intimidating their much smaller rivals.

My teams traversed the country and were generally met with friendliness and co-operation, not least from the UN. One female member of a team in Wau was assaulted by an SPLA policeman and we came across many irregularities, for example, often party members – innocently or maliciously – tried to 'help' people to cast their ballot, especially among the vast majority of the illiterate voters in the south. The voting method – for national president, regional president, governors, state and national assemblies – was very complex, based on a mixture of US, French and British models. Twenty-five per cent of seats in the assemblies were reserved for females, and women – especially in the south – were vocally enthusiastic voters.

Al-Bashir did a lot better than his own party expected – he won 68 per cent of the vote for national president, although most of the northern challengers were straw men and women, and some dropped out because of the government's restrictions on campaigning, especially free and equal access to radio and TV. Salva Kiir took 93 per cent for the southern presidency, although the old warhorse Lam Akol complained to me personally, regularly and bitterly, by phone and email, about how he and his candidates were bullied by the SPLM. In the end, in north and south, the elections confirmed the existing domination of the two leaders. The results were predictable, but were they fair?

The larger EU and Carter Center observer teams basically said 'good try, but you didn't meet international standards'. Nevertheless, the earnest and affable former president, Jimmy Carter, said the elections were 'relatively peaceful, calm and orderly'. Of course, the AU and Arab League, many of whose representatives would not recognize a free election if it bit them on the backside, raved about the election process. The verdict produced by the Centre for Foreign Policy Analysis came somewhere in between the two extremes. Its final report said:

> After continuous disaffection or war since 1955, the fact that a national election was held in Africa's largest country, with few traditions of democratic contests, widespread illiteracy and poor infrastructure, especially in the south, is to be commended. We consider the election to be a credible and important step on the road to political pluralism.

The centre's team did offer a number of recommendations to improve the process for next time, especially the forthcoming referendum in the south. To temper what some might judge to be the patronizing tone of the centre's final verdict, it was also noted that these elections would have confused even a sophisticated Western electorate. In the concurrent UK national election, foreign electoral observers in Britain noted failures, not least in postal voting, lack of IDs, shortage of ballot papers and closure of some polling stations while angry queues remained outside. In South Sudan, the fact that the presidential candidate, Salva Kiir, had to go to three polling stations to find his name could be forgiven, perhaps, in the first and most inclusive and free elections ever held in the south. The Brits, on the other hand, should have known, and done, better.

The all-volunteer team I led worked hard to help the electoral process in Sudan. They were just about to fly home from Khartoum airport, when suddenly all flights to and from much of the northern hemisphere were stopped because of the ash cloud erupting from an Icelandic volcano. After forty years of working in conflict zones, I faced my toughest challenge: keeping fifty irritable and homesick Brits happy, occupied, housed and fed in an expensive city where they could not use credit or alcohol. Most eventually got home to Britain ten days later.

The UN had done an impressive job – their separate mission in the south (UNMIS or UN Mission in Sudan) had pulled out all the stops, despite their usual lack of resources, especially air transport. The large (and occasionally imperious) EU mission, however, complained of a failure of UN co-operation. As Mission Head, I attended some of the top-level meetings. I was astounded at the vituperation I sometimes witnessed: the most remarkable was the dressing down the deputy head of the EU delegation gave to the UN chief. The EU representative angrily and repeatedly waved and collapsed her fan – she was Spanish – and then used it to metaphorically jab the startled UN man, accompanied by a loud Latin torrent of criticism. The urbane Indian brigadier present had to try to calm the meeting. And they would have to do it all again the following year, for the referendum.

President al-Bashir felt vindicated – he had held an election under intense international scrutiny and he judged that he had won the approval of the north.

Al-Bashir knew that the south would vote the same way again – overwhelmingly for Salva Kiir, who was committed to separation from Sudan. John Garang had been dead for five years. The SPLM would always revere him, but the vast majority of his followers had fought for independence, not federalism. And what had the north fought for? If the south broke away, what had all the lost lives been for? And could the north survive if southern oil was turned off or diverted? Perhaps the majority of northerners had had enough of war and jihad and prayed for that rare thing, an amicable divorce. Some hardliners in the military and intelligence services, however, grumbled that their president had gambled and lost. The potential coup plotters would bide their time and wait for the referendum results and the immediate aftermath of the likely independence. It might all depend on how the new rulers in Juba behaved.

The southern referendum

South Sudan was set to become the fifty-fourth African state in July 2011 – would premature and triumphalist celebrations prompt the resumption of the long war? This time I was there with a film crew, not as an observer. We were rarely obstructed in our travels in the south, but media registration was a nightmare. The UN had repeatedly told GoSS that this was a unique opportunity to attract positive publicity and possibly investment by welcoming the hundreds of hacks who had expended the time, trouble and expense to get to inaccessible Juba. Rip-off prices for accommodation and transport were to be expected, but the expensive obstacle race – $100 per person per stamp, around various government offices to pay cash for a permit to travel, report, write and possibly breathe – angered the most seasoned of old Africa hands. GoSS's corruption and inept bureaucracy were vividly showcased. My team received some of the required permits and accreditation via urgent UN intercession. It was a bad start for the world's coverage of the referendum, and the new country.

The referendum was held over seven days in January 2011. Previously, 3.9 million of the estimated eight million southerners had registered to vote. And nearly every registered voter turned out, with over 99 per cent opting for an independent south Sudan. Except for isolated incidents, the voting was peaceful. The fighting in the village of Makir Abior, about six miles north of Abyei town, part of the disputed border, killed more than thirty people. Al Jazeera, which had over forty personnel in the south, played up the possibility of border clashes and northern intervention, but this did not materialize. The referenda were 'delayed' in the three large disputed border areas, however. They remain delayed.

Elsewhere in the ten southern states, the voters showed patience and commitment as they queued in the heat after walking miles to isolated polling stations. According to Western international observers, the polling was largely free and fair. Voting by southerners in the north was very low compared with the south, though an estimated 180,000 southerners made their way back, by road or river, to vote in their homeland.

While endorsing the process, international observers did note problems with voter registration, especially eligibility to vote, and a lack of voter education. As in the previous year's election, many enthusiastic would-be voters could not find their names even when they found the correct polling stations. Much assisted voting was witnessed, though this was again usually well-intentioned because of the very high levels of illiteracy. Many examples of security officials, especially police, being present inside the polling centres were also recorded. Nevertheless, it was absolutely clear that southerners voted en masse and freely – often passionately – for independence.

The referendum may have demonstrated the passionate desire for independence, but it also showed the shortcomings of the fledgling government of south Sudan. Southerners living in the north – two to three million had fled there during the decades of war – were urged by the southern government to return home. Thousands came by river along the White Nile. The gruelling journey usually took two and a half weeks. When they reached Juba port many were exhausted and some, especially children, were ill. In a few cases clergymen brought their whole congregations with them. Stephen Taban, of the Episcopalian church, had lived for twenty-two years in Khartoum. He pointed at the numerous people camped around him at the port: 'Some had relatives here, others don't. Some don't have food to eat. They really need help.' Some came for individual patriotic reasons. One blind 84-year-old lady was crying with joy to come back to the land she had last visited in 1949. Despite having to squat at the port, most were glad to be home, but complained about the lack of support from GoSS. The government responded by setting up mobile clinics, although the medical reception for the returnees was generally inadequate. Jobs and homes for the many returnees would still have to be found in one of the poorest regions of Africa. Nevertheless, none of the southerners I interviewed said they left because of northern pressure on them.

Many northerners – often Muslim businessmen – chose to return to the north either temporarily during the referendum, fearing rioting or looting, or in some cases left permanently. Many shops in the Muslim business area of Juba had shut during the referendum. The businessmen said that no local pressure had been put on them, though some had returned to Khartoum because of concerns among their relatives in the north. Yet other northern businessmen – many who had lived in the south for their whole lives – claimed that up to 5,000 merchants – in the countryside *outside* Juba – had not been allowed to get back their farms and shops which had been seized by the SPLA, despite promises from the ruling party. Siddig Mohamed Korak, a spokesman for dispossessed businessmen, said he had grown up in the south. Interviewed in Khartoum, he said: 'I lost US$ 50 million [in farms and plantations]. They [the SPLA] are looting everything – goods – cars and tractors. They are looting since the war.'

Southern Sudan was desperately underdeveloped. Approximately 90 per cent of the inhabitants lived on less than a dollar a day. Half required food aid. Corruption was endemic. The prime issue was still a settled border. Disputes, particularly over Abyei, festered. Thabo Mbeki, the AU mediator, had not done any better here than he did in Zimbabwe, said local critics. Arguments over sharing the national debt had not been reconciled. Nor had citizenship been resolved – this was paramount to prevent the mass exodus of southerners in the north and vice versa. Bosnian-style forced transfers of people threatened to destabilize both north and south. After the referendum result, the usually cool President Mbeki, as AU envoy, did heatedly complain that the north was pushing out southerners if they could not prove a patrilineal descent from the north. And the NCP elite – many of whom also held British or US passports – would not allow dual nationality to southerners. The official slogan was 'four freedoms' – including the right for southerners to live and work in the north – but many felt compelled to sell up and move south.

Besides aid, Southern Sudan was almost totally dependent on oil – 80 per cent of proven reserves were in the south, but the pipelines to the sea from the landlocked south ran through northern Sudan. Peaceful co-operation made sense. Talk of building alternative pipelines, through difficult terrain, to the sea via Kenya did *not* make sense, because of the high costs and the probability that southern oil output would soon peak and then decline rapidly. Border disputes could have sparked off war *by accident*. Tribal clashes spawned by dissident warlords were also to be expected. Much depended on the attitude of Khartoum, which was about to lose one-third of its territory and much of its oil revenue. Some northerners were relieved to be rid of the burden of the exhausting southern war. Others feared that the north would become a harsh Islamist police state, whether or not al-Bashir survived the rumoured coup attempt or copycat mass demonstrations on the model of Egypt as part of the Arab Spring. Al-Bashir told local media in Khartoum, 'Those who are waiting for the Arab Spring to come [to Sudan] will be waiting a while.'

Even if a resumption of war were avoided, south Sudan had to contend with numerous other difficulties, not least the crisis of expectations of its own people. SPLM leaders insisted that their new country would be like South Africa. They were (understandably) irritated when I suggested it could be another devastated basket-case like Zimbabwe. So would South Sudan be a multi-party democratic state? That was asking a lot of the cocksure dominant party, the SPLM.

I spoke to Joseph Lagu, the veteran military commander, just after the referendum results were announced. He grew rather animated and waved his stick, when I asked about the country's poverty. 'I don't know why people call us the poorest people in Africa,' he said, 'when we have oil under the surface of our soil. And we have got other minerals and we have got green agricultural land.' Yes, the country had many prospects but, as the last decades had shown, nothing could happen without peace.

The referendum was peaceful – so would be the reactions of the north, it was hoped. The state would be recognized, not least by their African neighbours. Nevertheless, a successful breakaway worried the African Union, which faced separatist movements throughout Africa. The helpful role of the UN should be acknowledged in the referendum. And al-Bashir's visit to Juba and positive comments while in the south also helped to soothe tensions. He did not treat the south as an awkward stepchild; rather he would magnanimously be the first to recognize the new republic. Whether independence heralded peace in a very troubled region depended ultimately on the wisdom of the politicians in Khartoum and Juba – and not the diplomacy of the AU, EU, China or the US.

Khartoum displayed again a self-deceptive approach to American promises. Al-Bashir's intelligence advisers reckoned that the State Department had unofficially promised that President Obama would remove all sanctions if the southern referendum and independence went smoothly. In January 2011 the State Department did release a formal statement thanking al-Bashir for his cooperation. Sanctions remained.

Independence

The independence of the Republic of South Sudan on 9 July 2011 was the culmination of a complicated international peace process that consumed a decade of haggling and intermittent violence. The mood of celebration, especially in Juba, was understandable. The joys of statehood and freedom were tangible. Consignments of the new flag, based on the former emblem of the SPLA, were shipped in from a helpful China. The creation of the new national anthem, the words forged by a collective of poets and the music involving a national competition, was on everybody's lips. 'Oh black warriors, let's stand up in silence and respect, saluting our martyrs whose blood cemented our national foundation.' Not a Eurovision hit, though it went down well locally. Peace now promised so much, but also generated a crisis of expectation – a wish list as long as the Nile.

A new currency was yet to be produced to replace the Sudanese one. And a place had to be found in the UN. The hall of the General Assembly was full. When a place was created, because the listing is in English alphabetical order, the fledgling country would be placed next to South Africa, if it decided on just 'South Sudan'. There was, typically, still much dispute about what the country should be called – 'South Sudan' was seen as a British or northern construct and insufficiently African. Purists preferred 'Nile' somewhere in the title. Juba's UN diplomats had yet to set up an office in New York. When South Sudan became a full member of the UN, it could organize its own postal stamps through the Universal Postal Union. For the time being, the post had to work through the system based in Khartoum. There was even talk of relocating Juba, still a largely shanty development with little infrastructure. Would the money materialize to build a new more central – but tribally neutral – capital?

A new internet domain had to be agreed. One that was possible was 'SS', but that had obvious negative connotations. South Sudan also wanted to develop its own national football team and take part in the 2012 Olympics. So many grand plans and such a pitiful national infrastructure. Freedom was a heady brew, but in the 2011 drought South Sudanese could not eat freedom. Also, the country had one of the worst maternal mortality rates in the world. And over 84 per cent of women were totally illiterate. At least they could aspire to learn to read in English, the official language.

Technically, South Sudan was a rich country, full of very poor people. Around 95 per cent of government revenue came from oil. Agricultural potential was high, but the farms and estates had been devastated by war. Statistically the country was already a failed state, so how could it rebuild itself? Foreign aid could help to feed the eight million population in the short term, though aid is addictive, undermines local initiative and often fuels corruption and cronyism. The return of experts from the diaspora would help, as would the flow of professional people from the north (which might balance the exit of southern Muslim businessmen).

Mass population transfers and religious and ethnic cleansing were then a clear danger, which could have been resolved by a deal on dual citizenship, though even more pressing were tribal conflicts in the south. Border fighting in Abyei and in South Kordofan dragged on throughout 2011. Common sense dictated that the two new countries should settle on an amicable divorce to share the oil wealth. The sharing of the national debt had to be settled too. Many southern leaders tended to blame the Islamist regime in the north for nearly all their woes. This was the central myth. The northern armies had been brutal; they had stirred up ethnic discontent and supported rival southern militias. Most of the southern travails since 2005 were largely self-inflicted due to bad governance, however.

During the independence celebrations, with the UN secretary general in attendance, some southerners suggested arresting Omar al-Bashir, and handing him over to The Hague. That would have kick-started another war. The resumption of war – which Juba's new government was desperate to avoid – was still possible, especially if the bloody border disputes continued to fester. Khartoum, however, was likely to be pre-occupied with conflicts in Darfur, though it would not cede oil-rich Abyei without a big fight. Even if Khartoum did behave over the border disputes, and didn't make life too hard for its neighbour – not least because of the need to share oil – Juba looked set to create chaos all on its own. Just as Mugabe's regime blamed all its ills on foreigners instead of rectifying its own domestic follies, so too Juba developed the habit of blaming everything on Khartoum. Corruption, tribalism, military overspending, and autocratic one-party rule threatened South Sudan with another Eritrea or, worse, Somalia. This would justify African leaders' nervousness about secession.

Many of the SPLA leaders were good commanders, though some were feeble politicians. Too much power had been pulled into the centre, with precious little development or authority in the regions. Much of the war was about marginalization, yet this still persisted. The SPLA/M government – only a small opposition had been elected in the national and state parliaments – needed to stop scapegoating Khartoum and start putting its own house in order. Domestic security was much more important than border security. It was very easy to blame all domestic woes on 'tribalism'. The internal fighting was as much intra-tribal as inter-tribal. Security would be difficult while so many citizens were armed. Attempts to disarm local militias often made things worse, however, as everyone complained about their own disarmament, while claiming that rival groups were allowed to keep their guns. Many of the domestic fights had nothing to do with tribe, but all to do with politics, local grudges or access to resources in drought areas. Cattle-raiding by well-armed gangs of young men, often beholden to no authority, and frustrated, literally, by the surge in bride prices, were often the cause of friction, frequently outside the control of a tribal or clan base. Sometimes disgruntled local SPLA commanders co-opted these lawless bands.

The solution to marginalization did suggest more local autonomy, yet this fed ethnic cronyism. On the other hand, over-centralized control in Juba smacked of military authoritarianism. This was the development paradox that Juba and many other African states faced. Professor Tim Allen, of the London School of Economics, headed a large research team during the build-up to independence. His report, *Southern Sudan at Odds with Itself,* indicated that the main peace dividends expected were 'personal security and access to resources'.[3] Certainly, the usual squabbling and disharmony among the numerous layers of international aid from the UN and NGOs caused problems, said Professor Allen. But his main conclusion was that Juba had to put its own affairs in order. Even if northern Sudan did not, *in extremis,* invade to seize the oilfields, South Sudan had to energize every resource to escape being a failed state.

National freedom had come, but it was precarious on the border, but even more so *within* the borders. President Salva Kiir had been an able military commander. He had to become a statesman if he were to avoid a warfare state with one-party (or one-tribe) rule. Salva Kiir had won his war, but could he win the peace?

Chapter 11

Aftermath

Khartoum kept its title of the Republic of Sudan. Omar al-Bashir was still in power, although he had 'lost the south' according to his internal critics, mainly in the military-intelligence nexus. Some securocrats even quietly suggested that their president's ICC millstone was an impediment to his continuation in office. The majority of the NCP stalwarts stayed loyal to the president, however. Most of the senior leaders I spoke to felt that the president had shown courage in risking all for a southern peace deal. One of the most powerful party leaders, Dr Ibrahim Ghandour, told me: 'We never gave up trying for unity. We gave them what was in the CPA … We worked until the last minute, although half-way through [the CPA process] we felt they would go their own way'. He said starkly, 'They are not ready for government.' He also said that the president felt 'disheartened' by the breakdown of the CPA. 'But he went to Juba and stated publicly that he would accept the result of the referendum. We were the first state to recognize the new government.' The president's take was poignant. He told me: 'I saw the suffering of the people in the south and the famine. I decided it was better to have two Sudans with peace.'

Border fighting continued after southern independence, especially in Blue Nile State. Khartoum was blamed for air raids into the south. In October 2011 Salva Kiir made his first visit to Khartoum as head of an independent state. Al-Bashir and Kiir had always had a good military man to military man relationship. Al-Bashir said of their relationship: 'Personally, we're good friends, but sometimes he had some bad guys around him.' So they sat down alone to try to resolve their disputes on the border and oil revenues. Despite their personal rapport, the dynamics of the conflicts, especially in the south, now seemed almost beyond their control. And al-Bashir still had to contend with the ICC. A Kenyan judge issued an arrest warrant for the president and said if he visited the country again he would be arrested. At the same time, the ICC's chief prosecutor issued an arrest warrant for Sudan's defence minister for alleged war crimes in Darfur. The fighting continued there; in December 2011, the JEM leader, Khalil Ibrahim, was killed by government forces. But one source of turmoil in Darfur was removed. Using the oasis town of Kufra, Khartoum sent military support to the rebels in Libya and finally helped topple a bitter enemy, Gaddafi. Ironically, in this war, al-Bashir was acting as an ally of NATO.

Then the big north-south break erupted. In January 2012 South Sudan turned off the oil because of failure to agree on transit fees. This made little sense for the struggling new state. Nearly all its income came from oil and, although state spending was slashed, the shortfall could not be made up by foreign aid. The influential American *Foreign Policy* magazine graphically summed up the situation: 'World Bank to South Sudan — Are you out of your freaking mind?' The closure was costing at least $20 million a day.

Meanwhile, Juba's new administration was failing. Overstaffing with so much unemployment was understandable. But ninety ambassadors were appointed and, in typically African fashion, the cabinet grew in inverse proportion to the economy.

Corruption had become rampant and blatant in Juba. It was discovered that government payments were being made to individual cows. Although many of the wonderful lyre-horned cows in the country do have their own names, the money was intended for humans. Many SPLM members felt a sense of entitlement: cronyism and graft were dues for fighting in the liberation struggle and for long years in the bush. Even when caught with their hands in the till, the guilty party members would say brazenly to accusers, 'What were you doing when we were fighting?' Salva Kiir had to resort to writing letters to request seventy-five former and serving senior government officials to return an estimated $4 billion in stolen funds. Much of it had ended up in banks in Nairobi and the sums disclosed were just the proverbial tip of the iceberg. The former freedom fighters had become public looters. Graft and the new austerity because of the oil stoppage could not be easy bedfellows. Nor could the oil simply be turned back on – closing and re-opening the pipelines and refineries required months of repair and maintenance to get the black gold flowing again, even if the politics were sorted. Turning the taps off made no sense.

Despite renewed talks, border fighting continued. At the same time, in the southern Jonglei state, ethnic clashes caused 100,000 people to flee their homes. Things were beginning to fall apart. On 10 April 2012 the SPLA made a surprise push into the north around the Heglig oilfield. Unexpectedly, SPLA armoured units made rapid progress. According to Khartoum intelligence sources, the SPLA elite units were accompanied by elements of

JEM, SLA and SPLM-N. Mohammed Atta, the new NISS chief and successor of Saleh Gosh, said that he had intercepts to prove that JEM commanders had been ordered to destroy the installations, although Juba later claimed that it was Sudanese air force retaliation that caused the damage. The SPLA held the area around Heglig – which the south call Panthou – for ten days. The northern army, aligned with the South Sudan Liberation Army militia, fought back; over 100 SLA were wounded and sent to Khartoum for treatment. Several JEM troops were also captured in the hot pursuit. Although Khartoum had been taken by surprise, the northern army claimed to have killed around 1,000 SPLM-aligned troops. The Sudanese air force retaliated by bombing the Bentiu area in the south. In Khartoum there were calls for the defence minister, Abdel Rahim, to be sacked, but he was considered too close to the president. The official Sudanese military explanation was that they initially withdrew to avoid damaging vital oil installations, which may have been partly true, but the revitalized SPLA was now operationally more efficient. Enough American money had been spent on training it, after all.

For once, Khartoum was portrayed in the international media, especially in Africa, as the victim of the south. Lam Akol, the eternal survivor, was now leader of the opposition in Juba. He said, 'South Sudan, which was the darling of the international community, was overnight being seen as an aggressor.' The decision to shut down the oil production and then the occupation of Heglig upset even ardent supporters in Washington. The SPLM was now viewed as part of the problem and not just a victim of Khartoum. Barack Obama berated Kiir in a phone call to Juba. The frosty conversation was not helped by the fact that when the two men had met briefly in New York some months before the Heglig crisis, Obama had warned Kiir about the SPLA's military movements. Kiir made the gross mistake of telling Obama 'to check the accuracy of your satellites'. It is rarely a good idea to tell an American president that he is incompetent, or possibly a liar. The UN Secretary General also warned Kiir.

Khartoum's surprise diplomatic advantage was undermined by a characteristic bout of presidential demagoguery. In private al-Bashir was a reserved and affable man, but once he was in front of a big political audience, he would wave his trademark eagle-topped cane and indulge his gift for fiery rhetoric. At a speech on 18 April 2012, on the eve of the successful northern counter-attack, al-Bashir roused the faithful at the NCP HQ in Khartoum. It was reported in the local media that he used an ugly pun. He talked about crushing the Arabic for 'insects' which is similar to 'movement'. Typically shooting from the hip, he was referring to wiping out the SPLM movement. But even avidly non-PC critics picked up the insect reference in the context of the Rwandan crushing of cockroaches. In front of his close party supporters, he gave a direct warning to the SPLM: 'Either we end up in Juba and take everything. Or you end up in Khartoum and take everything.' Many foreign military experts predicted a resumption of full-scale war between the two states. Fortunately, the AU and UN acted quickly to get the SPLA to avoid a counter-attack against the successful northern recovery of Heglig.

To their domestic audiences both presidents depicted the Heglig crisis as a success. It boosted the nationalisms of both states and delayed an agreement on oil. Both sides had taken a beating either in the surprise advance or the bloody withdrawal. Riek Machar conceded, 'We are not a pariah state. We don't want to be isolated from the rest of the world. We don't want sanctions against South Sudan, so we decided to withdraw.' The fact the vice president mentioned sanctions was a stark indication that the fledgling state's honeymoon period was over.

A year after independence, the UN claimed that over 650,000 people had been displaced in the border regions, with most of them fleeing south. In the north the termination of oil supplies forced Khartoum to cut subsidies on fuel and other vital goods generating popular anger. In June 2012 students clashed with police and speculation mounted that the Arab Spring would spread from North Africa and the Middle East. The unrest was soon contained, partly because the unrest in Egypt in particular was caused by factors largely absent in Sudan. For starters, Sudan had undergone its own Islamist revolution as far back as 1989.

Al-Bashir and Salva Kiir met in Ethiopia to try once more to resolve the chronic economic problems facing both countries because of the oil cut-off. They agreed on a demilitarized border buffer zone, but failed – inevitably – to resolve the three main contested zones, especially Abyei. Abyei had become a parallel to Kashmir, likely to cause friction and war for generations. If al-Bashir had ceded more territory, he knew he could suffer a coup from his security chiefs already chafing at the economic setbacks inspired by Juba's demented decision to turn off the oil. The most that al-Bashir could do was to promise to pull out the regular army from Abyei. The northern security chiefs were already edgy over renewed fighting in Darfur and South Kordofan. Rebels in both states as well as Blue Nile had formed the Sudan Revolutionary Front, which acted with the SPLA-North. Parts of eastern Sudan along the border with Eritrea were restless too. In the far west and far east, many of the problems were connected more to genuine banditry and criminality rather than politics. As ever, the country was fraying at the edges, but attacks came in the centre too. Khartoum's intelligence chiefs were caught off-guard by a long-range Israeli air raid on an alleged Iranian arms factory outside Khartoum said to be making weapons for Hamas. In the eastern Sudanese desert, the Israeli air force also hit a convoy of arms destined for Hamas. Eritrea had leased one of its small offshore islands, not far from Djibouti, allowing Israel to create the largest air base outside its borders. Jerusalem, of course, made no comment about either attack, but a warning message had been sent to Khartoum.

The capital was on edge in November 2012 when a coup was thwarted at the heart of the security establishment. Saleh Gosh, head of the National Intelligence and Security Service until 2099, was arrested, along with twelve other serving senior military personnel. Gosh, for long the president's right-hand man, had retired, apparently on grounds of ill-health in 2009, but remained a presidential advisor. Khartoum was on alert, because of the positioning of tanks and armoured vehicles at strategic points. The security forces were still very largely loyal. Nearly all of the middle-ranking army officers commissioned since 1993-94, after the immediate post-revolution purges, were NIF/NCP loyalists. A handful of more senior officers – brigadiers and generals – had survived because of their competence, despite being former communists or socialists. The vast majority of the top brass were apolitical Islamists. The breakdown in the NISS was approximately 95 per cent loyal. The vast majority came from the Brotherhood or were sympathizers, with a handful of apolitical professionals. With such a small number of potential dissidents, the coup didn't quite happen. Despite the (very short) prison terms, either a deal was done to forestall the coup or it went off at half-cock. This palace coup didn't really get out of the palace. Nobody was hurt, but the opposition to al-Bashir from such trusted sources was a worrying development for the president. A considerable backlash had built up in the intelligence services because Gosh was seen to represent a consensus view on what was going wrong, especially in the south. Some of the jailed or suspended intelligence and army personnel were quietly rehabilitated for the sake of national unity. When I asked the president about the coup, he was understandably reluctant to discuss it, brushing me off politely with 'It's all sorted now'. But the mini-rebellion in his core constituency probably played a part in his stated desire to retire by 2015. Some of his old army comrades had tried to bend his ear about getting out of politics.

Besides disquiet in Khartoum's security community, the president had to face growing popular discontent with the deepening economic crisis. In March 2013 al-Bashir managed eventually to persuade Juba to turn the oil back on, fourteen months after the closure had rocked both economies. It would take months, however, to get the oil up to previous output. The southern economy was in meltdown, while the more diverse and advanced northern economy was in clear difficulties. In September 2013 waves of protests shook the north, because of more austerity measures. The nationwide protests were met with heavy-handed police counter-measures and at least thirty-six protesters were killed, according to official figures.

After the intelligence split, and in protest against the police crackdown, a small group of reformists in the ruling NCP broke away to form alliances with the old secularist and leftist parties or what remained of them, although by definition all the parties considered themselves Islamic. Younger political activists also set up *Girifna* ('We are fed up'), a new political movement outside the traditional parties. Although most of the NCP stayed intact, the departure of some of the (slightly) younger and abler politicians, such as the suave UK-educated surgeon Ghazi Salahuddin Atabani, meant that this was the biggest shake-up since the big split with al-Turabi. The shift towards a reformist direction perhaps also spelled the final death knell of the Islamist revolution. The president had already initiated a regeneration programme in the party. Some of his long-serving allies, such as Ali Othman Taha, wanted to retire (although others didn't). Al-Bashir also announced a 'dialogue' with his traditional opponents, including hereditary leaders such as al-Mahdi and his enduring nemesis, al-Turabi. Resurrecting these yesterday's men would not exactly satisfy the younger and especially female demands in the NCP for a party renaissance. Al-Bashir made the tough former defence minister, Lieutenant General Bakri Hassan Saleh, the first vice president and officially his successor, should the president suddenly die. General Bakri was not exactly the renaissance man the young reformers were hoping for. As one of the most senior NCP bosses confessed to me, 'Bakri is a man of the palace, not the people.' Despite the so-called 'dialogue' with opposition parties to create an atmosphere of national unity, the government was still prepared to crack down on protests and it again arrested Sadiq al-Madhi, prompting the moribund troika of British, American and Norwegian foreign ministers to issue a formal protest to Khartoum.

The northern party-political turmoil was nothing compared with what was happening in the south. In June 2013 President Kiir sacked two senior ministers to attempt to address the blatant financial corruption in his government. But the southern president faced fundamental political differences in his party, not least over his authoritarian style. The danger was that many in the SPLM felt that no democratic outlet for political change existed – except via the tribe. Nor had the CPA developed proper Truth and Reconciliation measures, especially for the south. The southerners spent more time and effort killing each other rather than fighting Khartoum, and probably would have done so even without northern manipulation.

In July 2013 Salva Kiir fired his *whole* cabinet, including Vice President Riek Machar. By year end, the contemporary political differences had degenerated into ancient tribal rivalries, especially in elite military units in the capital. It was assumed in Juba that the inveterate troublemaker Riek Machar was trying to stage a coup. According to northern intelligence sources, still very well-informed on the inner workings of the new state, there was no coup. For once, apparently, Machar was innocent of the charges. It didn't matter. Soon, fighting between the two main tribal wings of the SPLA – Nuer, led by Machar, and Dinka, led by Kiir, although the tribal distinction was never that precise – led to all-out civil war. Dissident warlords had already been active in the south before the December crisis. Now the two rival armies, as well as the inevitable militias, tried to occupy their traditional tribal constituencies, especially around the oilfields. Machar's forces initially captured three state capitals, Bor, Bentiu and Malakal. All were devastated in the fighting. Ugandan troops and aircraft came in on the side of President Kiir, who also appealed to al-Bashir. The northern president shuttled regularly to Juba on peace missions. He was back in the role of regional peacemaker. He knew Machar and Kiir well and tried to bring them together. Towns such as Bentiu were captured and recaptured sometimes two or three times in one week. It was a highly fluid semi-conventional war, with both sides well-equipped. Hundreds of thousands of southerners were again made refugees. The UN and IGAD pushed the rival leaders together, and a number of peace agreements were made, and broken almost the next day. In these Addis summits the divisions were not necessarily tribal; some of Garang's family were in Machar's negotiating team, for example.

By the summer of 2014 full-scale civil war raged unabated in the new state of South Sudan. Juba had spent some $1 billion on weapons since the start of the civil war in December 2013. In June 2014 China North Industries Group, the country's biggest arms manufacturer, shipped a large consignment of equipment, consisting of missiles, grenade launchers, machine guns and ammunition, to Juba via Mombasa. At exactly the same time humanitarian agencies were appealing for $1.3 billion to feed four million starving people in the country. Even the capital faced acute shortages of basic food. What food there was cost five times more than the same staples in next-door Uganda. Yet even the mass suffering of their own people did not stop the warlord class from re-arming and fresh recruitment. Besides the largely Dinka rump of the SPLA versus Machar's mainly Nuer supporters, a host of other gun-toting groups joined in the mayhem. Besides the Ugandan forces and existing southern militias, Sudanese intelligence reported on the heavy presence of Darfurian elements, especially JEM as well as, curiously, a detachment of M23 guerrillas from the Congo's East Kivu. M23 took its name from the 23 March Movement, which had been led by a colourful commander with the *nom de guerre* of The Terminator. South Sudan had enough terminators of its own – it didn't need more well-armed psychopaths. So far, independence had been a disaster.

Yet the northern elite were not in the mood to say 'I told you so'. They had genuinely believed that the south was not ready for independent statehood – and Khartoum's many critics would add that the north had helped to create the political, cultural, economic and tribal maelstrom that was South Sudan. Khartoum's press coverage on the south's new war was notable for its lack of censorship. A few examples of snide racism and *schadenfreude* were evident, but generally the mood was of compassion about the unfolding humanitarian crisis. Gloating was rare, not least because South Sudan's misfortune was hurting the north as well. Also, the self-evident impact on the north made it easier for Khartoum to justify the tough austerity measures.

A complete collapse of the southern economy could implode the north. The politicians and economists had done little long-term contingency planning for the oil crisis and had failed to diversify the economy sufficiently during the boom years. The intelligence and military chiefs in Khartoum now had to look at all the *immediate* options. No one wanted to re-occupy the whole south. The military challenges were far too great, especially after the initial military drubbing by the SPLA at Heglig. And, of course, the diplomatic repercussions would bring down the wrath of the UN and AU on their heads. Nor would the Chinese let them get away with it; the US had little leverage left, except for even more sanctions. Khartoum was almost past caring what Washington thought. The optimal solution, said the intelligence people, was – in extremis – to re-occupy just the key oilfields and pipelines and hold them – temporarily. The PR line would be that they were safeguarding them for Juba once the civil war was resolved. Indeed,

Salvia Kiir had asked his northern counterpart for military support, and al-Bashir was prepared to help with intelligence, logistics and some air power and air transport. Khartoum, however, had caught the contemporary American disease: it was reluctant to put boots on the ground. The military in Khartoum were very irritated by what they considered to be the trigger-happy intervention of the Ugandans, especially their air force. The last civil war in the south had lasted for over two decades; millions were killed. If the current war within the SPLA continued for anything like that period, South Sudan would run out of people.

Both parts of the former Sudan faced an uncertain future. South Sudan was already a failed, devastated state at independence; then it became far worse. Visitors to Khartoum would see gleaming office blocks and fancy hotels. Brand new 4x4s jammed the streets. Behind the façade, the inheritor state of the old Sudan faced many of the problems of rapid growth suddenly halted – unemployment, rapid price rises caused by inflation and hidden poverty in the shanty towns on the edge of the capital. Unlike many African cities things by and large worked – even the traffic lights and lifts. And Khartoum was still the safest and friendliest, if also one of the most boring, capitals in Africa. The two parts of Sudan could not survive without peace and each other. They were destined to live or die in each other's economic embrace.

Omar Al-Bashir's Legacy

The Western media has often portrayed Omar al-Bashir as a ruthless thug in the mould of another Arab Field Marshal-President with a moustache who had been in power for over two decades: Saddam Hussein. I have tried to portray the Sudanese leader as a far more interesting, complex and, frankly, more humane character, although Saddam is hardly a cherished yardstick. Faced with the almost impossible legacy of keeping Africa's largest country together amid endless war, a better comparison might be with Marshal Josip Tito. I have worked extensively in Iraq and ex-Yugoslavia and al-Bashir – for all his many faults – had done, arguably, a better job than either his Iraqi or Balkan counterparts.

One of the most colourful and long-term critics of the Khartoum government, the prominent human rights lawyer Ghazi Suleiman, had always insisted that al-Bashir has been a moderate in the ruling party. In perhaps a deliberately crunched metaphor, he said, 'Al-Bashir is a pigeon, not a hawk.'

In his recent book on Sudan, *A Poisonous Thorn in our Hearts,* the BBC's James Copnall – certainly no friend of the president – commented on al-Bashir's charisma and the fact that he has more popular support 'than many in the West believe'. The ICC indictment certainly boosted his popularity among his own countrymen, even those who did not normally support him. As the NCP party boss, Dr Ghandour, succinctly put it: 'I'd rather him stay, but it's not a technical question of immunity as head of state. It is a question of national pride.'

Alex de Waal, one of the West's leading scholars on Sudan and a critic of the government, said of al-Bashir: 'He was often a puzzling figure: a simple soldier at heart, yet intensely proud; prone to fiery outbursts in public speeches, yet a good listener in private and open to discussion, even with Westerners.' Above all, de Waal said, 'he was a master of survival'. The president has indeed survived many potential threats to his rule, and life. He weathered the US storm about Osama bin Laden's sojourn. Washington rained down cruise missiles and also tried regime change by indirect leverage and direct sanctions. He resisted armed invasions from nearly all his neighbours. Despite a massive debt crisis, he funded his counter-insurgency campaigns for decades. The president fought wars in the east and west, and a major internationally supported insurgency in the south led by a charismatic and tough military commander, John Garang. Al-Bashir's greatest threats were internal, however. His arch-nemesis was his erstwhile mentor, Hassan al-Turabi. Despite years of plotting amounting to treason, al-Bashir refrained from imposing more than token and usually comfortable imprisonment or regular house arrest. Al-Bashir remained in power for over twenty-five years, while other politicians were worn down and defeated by the sheer intractability of the country's problems. He negotiated endlessly with the Americans and British, but felt in the end that the Chinese were more reliable allies. He came to a conclusion shared by many Africans: the Chinese build things that can be of use, while Westerners just bring ideas. Although to be fair, they – and especially the Americans – also supplied food and medicine for decades. Al-Bashir was hostile to UN intervention because he feared that the blue helmets might be part of the plot to depose his government. Two of the largest-ever UN missions, in Darfur and south Sudan, were allowed in, however. He withstood all the Western attempts to topple him directly or by proxies, while working endlessly with chameleon allies and enemies in the neighbouring states, especially truculent governments in Chad, Egypt, Ethiopia and Eritrea. Much of the time al-Bashir had also to keep a straight face and a sharp sword, while handling the madcap Gaddafi who at times posed a very serious threat to Sudan's territorial integrity.

Was survival a sufficient accolade? What did al-Bashir actually achieve with his twenty-five years in power? He did not keep the country together, although that was probably impossible even before the death of John Garang, who also believed in unity. The president himself would claim only one major legacy – the rapid development of infrastructure in the north. It is true that Khartoum changed from almost a medieval backwater to a modern city – albeit with many slums – in a remarkably short time. The developments, however, were largely confined to the riverine settlements; Darfur and the east outside Port Sudan were still under-developed. For too long the governments in Khartoum and, later, in Juba obeyed the traditional dictum that they would listen to the peripheries only when they were carrying guns.

I asked the president about his greatest regret. He said it was the breakdown of the Naivasha accord. Unless he was an Oscar-quality actor, al-Bashir showed great compassion about the lives lost in the south. He said in early 2014:

> More people have been killed since 2005 in the south than in twenty years of fighting. Now it is far more killings of civilians – five hundred were recently killed in Jonglei, for example. And the fighting between the Dinka is something new. Dinka never fought or looted cows from each other.

This was from a man who was an authority on tribal divisions, who was judged to be an expert practitioner of divide and rule when he was a military commander in the south and later as president determined to win a COIN war there. At the end of his career, he was again acting as a peacemaker – using all his expertise in tribal nuances to talk to the mercurial Machar and rather stolid Kiir to curb, not exacerbate, their war. Al-Bashir showed great statesmanship in signing the Naivasha peace accord, and laboured tirelessly to end the post-2013 civil war in South Sudan. He failed to curtail the Darfur uprising in 2003 by military means and has been savagely vilified by the West and indicted by the ICC for the conduct of that war, although it can be argued that the ICC prompted the Darfur insurgents to stall in negotiations and wait for Western-backed regime change, rather than settle.

Many of the atrocities inflicted by multiple sides in the numerous wars cannot be ignored. But the previous analysis of Darfur's war does not confirm the allegations of genocide, despite the carnival of celebrity accusations. The ICC has proved counter-productive in Sudan as in much of the rest of Africa, by delaying settlements and peace in the name of largely European 'justice'. It is often said that ICC indictments are likely to entrench authoritarian leaders because they cannot resign and risk their successors handing them to The Hague.

President al-Bashir has said he has had enough of power, or so he told me. Nearly all politicians pretend that they don't want to stay in power and only do so because their supporters insist on it. I believe that Omar al-Bashir, after twenty-five years in the hot seat of one of the most difficult jobs in the world – trying to stop Sudan's endless fighting – wants to retire and write his memoirs. Like Cincinnatus, he yearns to return to his plough, almost literally. He is genuinely passionate about developing his small farm just outside Khartoum. He was a proud host when I walked around the six-acre array of grapes, mangoes, dates, grapefruit, lemons and chickens. The NCP bigwigs insisted that he cannot stand down, but every single member of the president's family was passionate that he should retire, not least because of his failing health; and because, they said, twenty-five years in the army and twenty-five years as president is more than enough service to his country.

In October 2014 the NCP would decide whether al-Bashir should stand again for election in 2015. Whether the family or party will win the battle is unclear, although the presidential election may be delayed for a year. The Khartoum rumour mill was full of alternatives, preferably younger candidates or a radical but balanced ticket: the current official successor (if the president were incapacitated), the hard-line General Bakri teamed up with a reformist female vice president; a successful woman candidate is very unlikely, however.

Al-Bashir inherited the war in the south and spent most of his presidency trying to end it, first by military means and then diplomacy. Some statesmen earn their spurs by breaking the historical fetters that imprison their polities – for example Charles de Gaulle's granting of freedom to Algeria or Richard Nixon's rapprochement with China. Algeria's peace was largely tragic; China is now America's greatest challenger. In the famous Nixon-Zhou Enlai meeting, the Chinese leader was asked what he thought of the French Revolution, and replied, 'It's too early to say.' The remark, 200 years after the revolution, buttressed the image of a far-thinking, patient Chinese civilization compared with the short-termism of the West. Sadly, the story was a result of a mistranslation – the Chinese politician thought he was being asked about revolutionary protests in Paris in the late *1960s*. The translator at the time decided not to correct the misconception because it was so apt. It remains so. It all depends on the timeframe to make a proper historical judgement. In the immediate aftermath of South Sudan's independence and current chronic civil war there, a sound adjudication of al-Bashir's legacy might be premature. Many in the West would say they want the tyrant to go, unlike many of al-Bashir's own voters, and many regional leaders, who worry that chaos would follow his departure. *Après moi, le déluge.* The fear that no-one could follow successfully is often the curse and yet occasionally the truth of African and Middle Eastern politics. Nevertheless, al-Bashir has a proven track record over twenty-five years of keeping the lid on the cauldron of Khartoum politics. Far more privileged and educated men, such as Sadiq al-Mahdi, usually faltered after a few months. In the summer of 2014 a savage civil war was engulfing South Sudan, and even more barbarous conflicts raged in Syria and Iraq that are redrawing the maps of the Middle East. The elders of the ruling party in Khartoum would no doubt argue that they needed the old warrior even more than before.

Sudan's history has witnessed a tragic recycling of repetitive themes. The 'Turks' over-centralized and ruled by force. The British favoured the riverine Arabs, while treating Darfur as a distant and occasional security problem, and failed to make any real decision on the south. The imperial rulers could have created a southern independent non-Muslim state in an informal federation with the British colonies of Uganda and Kenya. Not without its pitfalls as a solution, true, but it probably would have saved millions of lives. When the Sudanese nationalists took over in 1956 they practised roughly the same policies as their colonial predecessors: centralized authoritarian rule, while ignoring the peripheries. Unlike the British, the new government in Khartoum enforced Islamicization and Arabization in the south, which was bound to cause perpetual conflict. Even if John Garang had lived beyond 2005 it was unlikely that he could have created a democratic unified state. After all, he had many authoritarian instincts himself. When the southern war almost inevitably led to independence, Juba repeated the Khartoum experience by concentrating on the capital and the army and failed to even begin dealing with the needs of the peripheries.

Since 1956 probably no Sudanese, north or south, has had sufficient vision or a sufficient following to forge a unified democratic state. The more powerful neighbour, Egypt, didn't manage it, despite boasting a potentate once reckoned to be the most charismatic of all modern Arab leaders. And, despite the large Coptic community, until recently Egypt did not have to suffer chronic Islamist versus Christian enmity; that was during the brief Morsi presidency in Cairo – to which, inevitably, the perpetual meddler, al-Turabi, offered advice. It is too easy for Westerners to blame most of Sudan's problems on excessive interference of religion in politics. The essence of Islam is the fusion of both while modern Western democracy demands the separation of Church and state. Also, many Arab nations have had to endure the fusion of military and politics, unlike the Clausewitzian model, common but not universal in (very) recent Western history. It is simplistic to assert that Islam and Western democracy are incompatible, albeit with a grudging nod to Turkey. Or submit to racism and say that Arabs are not ready, or fit, for democracy. Or that they simply don't want to slavishly adopt the model of late Western crony capitalism or tax-oppressed northern social democracy. The debate on poor Arab governance – is it a question of faith versus modernization? – could fill another book. So it might be more useful to take a short cut by making a brief comparison with an earlier European leader who had to balance religion, politics and soldiering.

It is often difficult for a Western audience, especially a secular or Christian one, to understand the context of Omar al-Bashir's Sudan. I do not want to argue for an Islamic or African exceptionalism – that Africa is different and that different standards, not least of human rights, should be applied. Clearly, UN definitions of individual rights are, or should be, universal. To make a comparison of Omar al-Bashir and Oliver Cromwell might be instructive, albeit controversial.

Al-Bashir might be considered 'Allah's general' by his more religious supporters. Cromwell, dubbed God's Englishman, was famous for being a passionately religious man and the leading general of mid-seventeenth century England. Born from fairly humble, if not peasant, stock, Cromwell spent his early life in obscurity. He was more interested in farming than politics. As the Protector of the Commonwealth (England, Scotland and Ireland) he believed that a religious revolution was required to reform the state and the army. Cromwell overcame the hereditary ruler, King Charles, by reluctantly executing him. The comparison with Sudan is al-Bashir's religious revolution against the equivalent of royalty, Sadiq al-Mahdi, the successor of the Mahdi. Both Sudanese and English generals were unprepossessing physically, but achieved national and international status. Both led their men from the front in combat and rose through the ranks on merit. Both Cromwell and al-Bashir had to fight constant wars on the peripheries of their central domains. Both were accused of genocidal conflicts and what we call today ethnic cleansing. Cromwell was exceptional in British history in being a parliamentarian and a serving general; nevertheless both generals were accused of excessive military intervention in politics. As a result, both men struggled to balance messy civilian politics with army discipline. Both were decisive in closing down their parliaments when necessary. Both were accused of ruthlessness in suppressing some of their own more radical supporters (the Levellers in England and the 'fundamentalists' under al-Turabi). They believed in providentialism – that God used them for the good of their people. Both were accused of sometimes allowing captives of their army to be sent into servitude. Above all they had to balance their political authoritarianism with their strong faith. Both have been castigated equally as hero or villain – or sometimes as brave bad men – in their own countries. Over 300 years separate their rule, and the context is, of course, different. The comparison may be instructive, however, even though it may need another three centuries for a true evaluation. And it may still depend on the eye of the beholder: perhaps a Catholic Irishman or Equatorian may see it differently from a Protestant Londoner or an imam in Khartoum, perhaps in 2314.

It's often said that countries get the governments they deserve. The Sudanese, for all their good personal qualities, have not been blessed by good governance. The lasting British legacy was not democracy, but a relatively efficient army. Sudan fell into the African trap of a big man leading a big army. The country also inherited almost intractable sectarian politics, firstly the Umma and DUP, both anachronistic feudal family operations; then the Brotherhood/NIF/NCP muscled in. They all tended to put party before national interest. This was also true of the south, as the current civil war tragically illustrates. Nobody could really answer the perennial question – what is Sudanese? The wrong answer for so long was Islamic inclusivity; that was bound to cause endless war and continuous growth of the diaspora abroad.

It could be argued that Omar al-Bashir – despite being an Islamist and a strongman with a big army – broke the mould. Finally, he cut the Gordian knot of *sharia* by allowing self-government and religious freedom in the south and the option of independence. And, unlike President Numeiri, he stuck to his word. Al-Bashir faced constantly the risk of defenestration from his own party. Critics will say he had no choice, that he was dragged kicking and screaming to the CPA final deal. Al-Bashir did not regard the CPA as a defeat, however. 'We did not sign it after we had been broken,' he said. 'We signed it while we were at the peak of our victories.' That might be an overstatement, but the oil money was paying for a more modern army, which was not defeated. Obviously the battlefield played a part, but al-Bashir genuinely was sick of the killing in the south. He told me this repeatedly. In my view, al-Bashir was playing a straight bat. Andrew Natsios, the American special envoy to Sudan, was a relentless critic of the al-Bashir government, but he said, 'In my dealings with Bashir, he has been straightforward and never misled me.' I share that opinion. That is why I believe that the president took great risks for peace. And, for once in Khartoum's black history of governance, put country before party.

In my conversations with him, it was clear that the president felt that he was a wronged and misunderstood man. Perhaps he will be judged by history rather than the ICC. And history's verdict may be that Omar al-Bashir sincerely tried to keep his vast quarrelsome country together. He was doomed to fail almost regardless of what he did, although maintaining Islamicization in the south was bound to inflame tensions. Ultimately, he was guided by his faith and patriotism, even if they sometimes tugged in different directions. Perhaps Sudan was simply unworkable in the borders inherited from the British. It was al-Bashir's bad luck or misguided sense of destiny that he chose to lead an ungovernable country, at probably an ungovernable time. His father cautioned him against a political career because he thought Sudan was impossible to rule. Omar al-Bashir's father may have been correct.

Appendix

A Short Guide to the Internal Armed Forces Fighting in Sudan's Civil Wars

This is a rough guide as Sudan has always tended to be a statistics-free zone. As a regular force, the northern-led army was more standard. The insurgents formed a sometimes competing mosaic of irregular forces and militias that switched sides, although during the course of the civil war the SPLA became the dominant southern player. When the south became independent in 2011, in effect the army became the government. The sizes and equipment also varied widely according to the flow of the conflict, deliveries of foreign weapons and battlefield attrition. Also, from 2005 to 2011 the northern and southern armies set up joint forces, although this was often a theoretical paper exercise. In 2011, on independence, the south set up its own army and spent far more on weapons than welfare. Some of the new imported equipment was destroyed in the civil war that began in 2013. It would be useful to provide an order of battle (orbat) at a set date, for example, 2005, the signing of the Comprehensive Peace Agreement, or southern independence in 2011. Because of the shifting patterns of the wars and sometimes inaccurate official or non-existing statistics, I will provide a general summary of the structures that operated in the period from 2003 to 2013.

THE NORTH
Sudanese Armed Forces
Army
The forces have been designated by a variety of names in the north and south. For ease of description, I shall call the northern forces the Sudanese Armed Forces. The modern structure originated in the Sudan Defence Force set up in 1925 (I have described this in more detail in the historical section of this book). Sudan developed its own forces after independence in 1956. The new state inherited an experienced and well-trained army from the British, but it was small, around 5,000 to 6,000 after it was reduced

following the Second World War. It was volunteer, professional and apolitical. Years of coups and endless wars changed the nature of the army, as did the later introduction of conscription and the incorporation of ill-trained paramilitaries. The army roughly doubled in size in the decade following independence. By the end of the first round of the civil war in 1972, the army had reached about 50,000 to 60,000 men. When the second round began, conscription, militias and paramilitary forces further boosted its size. The regular army was still essentially a light infantry force, supported by specialized units.

Most estimates, such as by the International Institute of Strategic Studies (IISS) in London, put the northern armed forces at between 100,000 and 105,000 by the time of southern secession. This included 20,000 conscripts, liable from 18-30 to serve for two years. This estimate does not include militias and paramilitaries.

The army was headquartered in Khartoum with six regional commands. Each command was supposed to be of divisional strength, but this was often a paper estimate. The 6th Division was based in El Fasher (the Western Command), for example, but it was usually at half-strength, 2,500 personnel. The commands were often drained of manpower to stem an operational disaster or two in the south. And sometimes the stationing and manpower were related to coup preparation or deterrence, especially for the 7th Armoured Division at Shajarah, south of Khartoum, and the Airborne Division based at Khartoum International Airport.

The army officially had one armoured division and six divisions of infantry, supported by mechanized units. The Special Forces Battalion, with five companies, was based in Khartoum, both as a praetorian guard and as support to the special anti-terrorist unit that could deploy rapidly in the three towns. Special reconnaissance units and engineer brigades could also support SF operations. In addition the army relied on artillery and general engineering formations. The army also had a brigade of border guards in its complement.

The army inherited the Sandhurst and Staff College training system from the British. A military college was established just outside Omdurman in 1948 and ran a two-year officer cadet programme, leading to a commission as second lieutenant. In the post-independence period about sixty graduated each year; this reached an average of around 150 in the 1980s. This could be much increased by political pressures – not so much the war, but foreign officers being inducted. Some sixty Ugandans were trained in 1982 after Idi Amin's removal from power.

The Sudanese started off with surplus British stock, for example the Saladin and Ferret armoured vehicles. The IISS reported that, in 2011, the army boasted 360 main battle and light tanks. Russia and Ukraine provided much of the early armour which had been upgraded. China replaced Soviet largesse and the latest Chinese Type 96 tanks were reputed to be in the Sudanese arsenal. In 2012, when South Sudanese armour penetrated the north near Heglig, a Chinese Type 96 was reported to have knocked out a Russian T-72 manned by the SPLA. The Sudanese were said to deploy over 400 armoured personnel carriers as well as seventy-five older Russian infantry fighting vehicles. Over 100 Egyptian versions of Russian armoured vehicles, including the Walid, were ordered in the 1980s – but nobody has recorded how many arrived or survived. Constant war and often poor servicing hollowed out the Sudanese inventory.

The Sudanese had a standard array of towed and self-propelled artillery. They also deployed a psychologically devastating system, despite its age and inaccuracy: multiple rocket launchers, variants of the Soviet 122mm BM-21, NATO codenamed Grad (meaning hail). Sudan also had a small range of surface-to air-missiles, including the Strela-2 and SA-7 Grail.

Air Force

The air force manpower complement was estimated to be 3,000, with eighty-four combat-capable aircraft. It had an official front-line strength of thirty-nine fighters, of which the majority were Russian-built MiG-29s types (Fulcrum in NATO reporting) as well as Chinese export variants of the Chengdu F-7s. A-5 Fantans were used for ground attack. The inventory also included Chinese/Pakistan-built Karakorums for training and as light attack aircraft. For transport, the air force used AN-26s, some of which were used as bombers – throwing out barrel bombs from the back. This has been castigated in the current civil war in Syria, and publicized with lots of video phones around; it was more hidden in Darfur (although I witnessed its effects in 2004). Four C-130 Hercules were also said to be in the air force.

The fleet included over thirty Mi-24 attack helicopters, codenamed Hind by NATO. This is one of the most deadly COIN weapons in the world (as I can personally attest from being on the receiving end, daily, in 1984 in Afghanistan during the Soviet occupation). Sudan also deployed over twenty Mi-8 transport choppers.

The two main air bases were at Khartoum International Airport and Wadi Sayyidna, north of Omdurman. The air force also freely used civilian airports, for example during operations in Darfur, mainly El Geneina, Nyala and El Fasher. Plane crashes were common, often because of accidents, caused by poor maintenance or pilot error rather than enemy action. Sometimes senior personnel were killed during VIP flights.

The Navy

Fighting with armoured steamers along the Nile had been a regular part of colonial history in the region. Shipbuilding in Khartoum had developed before independence. The British conducted naval operations initially from Suakin, with its charming if ruined old city built from coral. By the mid-1920s Britain had switched operations to Port Sudan, thirty miles away. Busy with policing on the Nile, the navy was slow to develop any kind of blue-water strategy to control its 530-mile coastline. The Iranians supplied two 70-ton coastal patrol craft and later some inshore craft. The 2011 naval complement was around 1,300. The two main bases were Port Sudan and Flamingo Bay on the Red Sea.

Paramilitary

Popular Defence Force (PDF)

The standing force of the PDF was around 20,000, with perhaps 85,000 reservists. Set up in November 1989, it became a provisional military wing of the Islamist movement. This 'paramilitary revolution' was intended not only to create *mujahedeen* fighters in the holy war in the south, but to also galvanize a cultural revolution in the north. The whole nature of security systems was changed after 1989. With Islamist mobilization, the former authority of the army and police were diffused with the PDF, community forces and a wide array of tribal militias. Moreover, the Sudanese regular forces, hard-pressed in the south, needed a range of paramilitary auxiliaries to plug the many holes. If paramilitaries relieved overstretch in the rural areas, the PDF also served a vital function in the three towns: the highly politicized and ideologically committed PDF elite could act as a praetorian guard against the coup-prone military. Originally inspired by the spiritual campaigns of Hassan al-Turabi, after his political decline the PDF was placed under the direct authority of the president. The professional army, despite a number of purges which removed a third of the officer corps, often opposed the PDF, because of its sometimes poor combat record or simply because of the diffusion of scarce resources.

The origins of militias preceded the 1989 revolution. The British had used them in Darfur, for example. An attack on the village of al-Gardud in Kordofan state in which sixty Missiriya Arabs were killed in July 1985 prompted the Umma party to later form a militia under Sadiq al-Mahdi's premiership. This led to the arming of a number of Baqqara tribes by the state. Right from the start the line was blurred between pro-government and informal paramilitaries. The irregular *murahileen* militias were often armed by the state and came under state protection from legal persecution when militias sometimes ignored government directives by indulging in traditional pillage and cattle-raiding.

After the 1989 coup, when the PDF was officially boosted, Khartoum set a target of 100,000 volunteers. TV appeals and propaganda in the schools and universities for volunteers did not always work. Technically, all youths between 16 and 30 could be conscripted or press-ganged. Students were sometimes given deferment and wealthy or politically powerful families sometimes bought exemptions. On the other hand, *pour encourager les autres,* some wealthy urbanite sons were conscripted as well as the jobless tribal levies.

Resentment within the regular army continued as military offensives often included regular troops, PDF 'volunteers' and existing tribal militias. Also, individuals could choose to join military units as volunteer jihadists. All were deemed *mujahedeen* in the holy war and the tame media encouraged a cult of martyrdom, even though the regular army sometimes accused the PDF of being combat-averse. Nevertheless, thousands of PDF were killed, occasionally in their emulation of futile Iranian-style human-wave tactics against entrenched SPLM machine guns. An easy route to paradise perhaps, but demoralizing for regular professional soldiers who witnessed the PDF sent ahead as cannon fodder.

The revolutionary government planned a paramilitary defence of the northern border lands, especially in Kordofan. Besides this Islamist 'tribal belt', 5,000 university students in the three towns were enrolled at the al-Qitaina PDF camp in March 1990. Although they did basic military training during the standard three months' course, much of the induction consisted of interminable Islamic lectures on how to be worthy of a citizen army of *mujahedeen*; and to be alert to any civilian or especially regular army threat to the new government. Four coup attempts were rumoured in the first years of the revolution. The urban militia units were issued with smart Land Cruisers to patrol the three towns. Gradually, regular army units were moved out of the capital. Some officers were sacked or, if senior or influential enough, offered comfortable jobs in government-controlled businesses.

Heavy mobilization of the PDF occurred during 1992 to 1997 to bolster the army trying to contend with the increased tempo of fighting in the south.

A small volunteer elite PDF leadership was trained by pro-NIF officers to act along the lines of the *Pasdaran,* the Iranian Revolutionary Guards. Some of these PDF personnel received advanced military training, including tank and artillery instruction. A second group was coercively conscripted – they included students, civil servants and recalcitrant army personnel – and sent for political indoctrination and re-education. The first two groups tended to be from urban areas. Their urban backgrounds often did not match the rigours required for southern bush combat. Technically, on the three-month courses, the PDF member could ask *not* to be sent into combat, especially students who had been forced to disrupt university courses. Another group of PDF was recruited from rural areas where the *ghazi* warrior tradition persisted. Some of these men needed no instruction on small arms, but were usually very keen indeed to get their hands on, and keep, modern automatic weapons. The PDF also recruited a national network of informers to safeguard the revolution.

The PDF was intended to galvanize Islamist volunteers and indeed the whole of society, but by the mid-1990s high battlefield casualties led to low recruitment, foot-dragging and occasional rebellions in the PDF training camps. In April 1998, according to reports in Western media, hundreds of secondary-school-age conscripts broke out of the Eilafoun PDF camp, fifteen miles from Khartoum. A number of them were reportedly shot for mutiny; a few months later, another more successful and bloodless mass escape happened at the same camp, according to Sudanese media. Children of well-off professional classes in Khartoum were sometimes conspicuously conscripted and many of the student exemptions were rescinded. A recommendation from the PDF often became a prerequisite for state employment or permission to travel abroad. A certificate of service in the armed forces was also sometimes required for government employment, for example in medicine. Technically, front-line combat was voluntary but the media, nightly on the TV, and at rallies and mosques played a key role in urging the Islamic obligation of jihad. A martyrdom cult was developed. By mid-1993 it was claimed that the PDF combat volunteers matched the size of the regular army in the south. The PDF were also active in 'cleansing' operations in rebellious regions such as the Nuba Mountains, where, in the period 1992-93, thousands of locals were killed, including Muslims who were declared apostates. Fourteen Nuba mosques were destroyed, damaged or looted, alleged Western reports.

According to professional army officers, some tribal PDF elements were more interested in looting than fighting. Even eager urban volunteers often proved to be second-class soldiers. Poorly trained and sometimes indoctrinated for martyrdom, as well as enduring numerous examples of 'friendly fire', they occasionally marched into the entrenched gun-sights of astounded SPLA guerrillas. Moreover, the coercive recruitment and high casualties alienated many northern Sudanese, including conservative Islamists who did not share al-Turabi's proselytizing programme.

The waning of al-Turabi's influence, the reaction to mass casualties and the anger in the army at the sometimes poor performance of the PDF led to a decline in the PDF and, by the end of the 1990s, a re-assertion of the primacy of the professional army. Although jihad was never abandoned, under President al-Bashir's influence a more pragmatic approach was introduced. The army effectively took over the PDF during 1997. General Saleh Gosh, reporting directly to the president, took charge of all security and military organizations including the PDF. In 1998 compulsory military service in the professional army, from age 18, was introduced. The fall and then imprisonment of al-Turabi tended to confirm the general view in northern Sudan that the PDF was a political not religious cause. Despite calls for disbandment, the PDF morphed into tribal militias and its armed tribesmen were recruited into more deadly militias in Darfur, later called the *Janjaweed.*

Other paramilitaries
Hundreds of pro-government militias, some permanent and others temporary, were formed in the north and south. Some were more or less autonomous. Some were anti-government forces that had come over to Khartoum, such as Minni Minawi's faction of the Sudan Liberation Army (based in Darfur), or the South Sudan Defence Forces, based in the Nuer territories of the south. Some were less formal groups, armed but not controlled by Khartoum such as the Meidob forces of northern Darfur.

Legally constituted paramilitaries with central government direction were the PDF, discussed above, but the Border Intelligence Guards and Central Police Reserve should also be included, although they did not have the prominence, or size, of the PDF. There were also tribal police, especially for nomadic groups.

Procurement
Sudan had a long history of local small-arms production, but protracted war and sanctions encouraged Khartoum to develop further its indigenous defence production. Also, being treated as pariah or rogue state by Western

arms suppliers forced Khartoum into numerous illegal forays in the international arms bazaar. Poor equipment and lack of standardization had been one of Omar al-Bashir's pre-occupations as a soldier, especially as the commander of an armoured division. In 1994 the Military Industry Corporation (MIC) was set up under the ministry of defence to co-ordinate the wide range of weapons suppliers. It absorbed a complex array of manufacturers. Alshagara Industrial Complex, for example, had been long established as a manufacturer of small-arms ammunition. The idea was to create dual-use products. In the massive GIAD complex, started in the mid-1990s, twenty-five miles outside Khartoum, Sudan's largest employer had developed a range of vehicles and engines. In 2002 the MIC co-ordinated the manufacture and maintenance of armoured vehicles, as well as commercial heavy vehicles. It did the same with electronics for the military as well as the commercial telecommunications market through Sudatel. In 2005 the Safat Aviation Complex was set up to support military aviation.

Sudan is a wonderland for defence equipment geeks and a nightmare for politically correct arms controllers. Sudan proved very adept at smuggling or buying equipment under licence, then cloning the machinery and producing its own clones. Its friends in China, Russia and Iran often turned a blind eye. The Marra pistol was a clone built on Chinese machinery that was originally designed and built in the Czech Republic. Often high-quality German designs were pilfered and then produced on Iranian machinery, for example the Dinar G3 assault rifle. Machine guns were vital in the defensive entrenched and mined warfare fought in the south. The Mokhtar was a PKM machine gun built from machinery bought from Russia/China; the Khawad was a DShK machine gun with the same provenance. Sudan often paid for the licences for the machinery or equipment; at other times its sanctioned status and cash-only economy gave it an edge in the arms bazaar. That was the case with a fancy range of clever clones of MBTs (main battle tanks). The Al Basheer MBT (Type 85 M-11) was an unlicensed copy from China. The Al Zubair 2 MBT was also an unlicensed copy from China, and it was suspiciously similar to the Type 59 D. Presumably the Chinese were taking so much oil, and paying often in kind not cash, that it was easy to turn a Nelson eye to such minor sleights of hand as cloning big tanks. It is not clear what Russia or Iran thought about unlicensed production. The MIC also built unlicensed Russian howitzers; and unlicensed Russian armoured vehicles derived from the BTR-80A. The MIC was even-handed – it built unlicensed copies of Iranian and Chinese infantry fighting vehicles. And so it went on.

The artillery cloning resulted in a long list of stirring Islamist names such as Khalifa and Mahdi. One wonders what the Prophet would have said. Presumably anything goes in a jihad.

It was also one of the many unintended results of sanctions. Arms sanctions inspired ingenious piracy and import substitution in Rhodesia and South Africa, and in the latter case it prompted a world-beating arms industry, especially its artillery pieces.

The Sudanese procurers were often swashbuckling, but the armed forces still struggled with spares and standardization problems, besides the surcharges for purchasing on the black market.

SOUTHERN FORCES

The initial guerrilla forces were called Anya-Nya, but they often splintered into regional or tribal militias or, conversely, absorbed them. After the first peace agreement under the Numeiri government in 1972, some insurgents fought on and later formed Anya-Nya 2. The Sudan People's Liberation Army and its accompanying political wing, the Sudan People's Liberation Movement, usually written as SPLA/M, was founded in 1983. It was the dominant southern resistance force in the second round of the war from 1983 to 2005. It was led by John Garang de Mabior until his accidental (though this is disputed) death in 2005. Garang was succeeded as commander in chief by Salva Kiir Mayardit, who became vice president of Sudan as well as president of the southern autonomous region in 2005, and then president of the new state of the Republic of South Sudan in 2011. Kiir had joined the integrated army in the 1972 peace deal, and worked in military intelligence. He was one of the founders of the SPLA in 1983. Later, as its chief of staff, he forged a strong support base throughout the guerrilla army. As both Garang and Kiir, as well as other senior offices in the SPLA, had served in the northern army, the structure of the guerrilla army was modelled to a large extent on the Sudanese armed forces. This included an internal security branch, which conducted Garang's various purges.

Estimates vary of the SPLA size on independence, but some put it as 200,000 troops, along with a small air force. Many of these would have been part-time. The US spent a lot of time and money training the SPLA, especially after 2005. American sources estimated the SPLA total to be 300,000 at independence, with 125,000 regulars. When the southern civil war broke out in December 2013, the regular army fractured largely along ethnic lines, although the causes of the war were political and constitutional disputes that then played into pre-existing ethnic divisions and the legacy of betrayals in the long war against the north, when some of the senior officers defected to Khartoum.

The initial southern rebellion was sparked by a mutiny in Torit in 1955 and the second stage of fighting was ignited by another mutiny, in Bor, in June 1983. The majority of southern leaders believed in secession for the south, but the dominant political and military personality, John Garang, argued that the search for democracy should be in the whole of a secular Sudan, to include marginalized people in the south, west and east as well as the Nuba peoples in the north. One of the main *causi belli* was the imposition of *sharia* law in the south, when the majority of people were animist or Christian. The debate on secession versus the struggle for democracy in a unified state was a part of the internecine fighting between the SPLA and Anya-Nya 2. One of the prominent Anya-Nya holdouts was Commander Gordon Kong Chuol, who eventually joined the SPLA in 1987.

The main sanctuary for the SPLA was Ethiopia, led by the Derg. When this government collapsed in 1991, this helped to precipitate a split in the SPLA. Commanders Lam Akol and Riek Machar encouraged, respectively, the Shilluk and Nuer peoples to break away because of Garang's alleged authoritarianism and human rights' abuses. This new movement, called the SPLA-Nasir, advocated southern independence. The two SPLAs fought for supremacy against each other and the northern army. Despite the schism, the rebels made progress against the northern army, although SPLA-Nasir also did deals with Khartoum.

The rebels received arms and training from the Israelis in the beginning, then extensively from the Ethiopians. At one stage Colonel Gaddafi provided cash and guns. Uganda and Kenya were generally supportive, and the USA provided funding. American aid and training were extensive in the transformation of the SPLA into a much more professional force after the signing of the 2005 Comprehensive Peace Agreement. Immediately after independence in 2011, border tensions flared with the north and disputes over the sharing of the oil wealth. In 2012 the southern army invaded the north and, surprisingly, their new armour pushed back the Khartoum forces near Heglig, a key oil installation. International pressure forced a pull-back. An uneasy ceasefire lasted for over a year, as IGAD and Chinese and American as well as UN officials tried to prevent the return to full-scale war. Then, somewhat unexpectedly, political differences in Juba burst out into a major ethnic civil war in December 2013. Regional powers, the US and UN as well as China, worked hard to secure a number of ceasefires, which were repeatedly broken by mid-2014.

After 2005 the SPLA was re-organized along more conventional lines as it transformed from a guerrilla to a more professional conventional army. It was reformed as six divisions and four independent brigades.

1st Division (Upper Nile state)
2nd Division (Equatoria region)
3rd Division (Northern Bahr el-Ghazal and Warrap states)
4th Division (Unity state)
5th Division (Lakes state)
6th SPLA (elements of the joint integrated units set up by the CPA)

The four independent brigades were stationed in Southern Blue Nile, Bor (Jonglei), Raja (western Bahr el-Ghazal) and, controversially, north of the border in the Nuba Mountains in South Kordofan. Some of the units were re-organized after 2011 and the units in the north officially left the mainstream SPLA to become SPLA-North. Khartoum also repatriated 30,000 southerners in the regular army after 2011. The SPLA set up an SF or Commando brigade of approximately 3,500 men, which was activated at the end of 2007.

The SPLA deployed a number of captured and reconditioned tanks, including T-55s and T-72s, the latter seeing action in the incursion into the north in 2012. It also deployed captured BM-21 Grad rocket launchers. Large supplies of small arms came originally from Ethiopia then via Kenya and Uganda. In September 2008 a Ukrainian-flagged ship, *Faina*, was seized by Somali pirates. It had on board thirty-three Soviet-era tanks, anti-aircraft (AA) guns, RPGs, etc., as well as ammunition and spares. It was officially bound for Mombasa. After a series of deals, the ship finally arrived in Kenya in February 2009. The Kenyans swore blind that the ancient equipment was for them. They didn't need it, and the cargo manifest said it was for South Sudan. In 2013 reports came out of modern equipment, aircraft and tanks, sourced from Uganda. The air force operated mainly a small fleet of Mi-17s.

The military high command was unstable in 2012. President Salva Kiir purged a large number of senior officers, including forty generals, in early 2013. Fearing a coup, he also sacked his entire cabinet in July 2013. Opponents accused him of establishing a dictatorship, despite his undoubted popularity, as evidenced by his winning over 90 per cent of the vote in the 2010 national election throughout Southern Sudan.

Pro-government southern militias
Numerous pro-Khartoum militias sprouted in southern Sudan. In 1997/8 the main ones were:

> Riek Machar's South Sudan Independence Movement/Army (SSIM/A) (later renamed the South Sudan Defence Force (SSDF)
> Kerubino Kuanyin Bol's SPLA-Bahr el-Ghazal
> Theophilus Ochang Lotti's Equatoria Defence Force
> Arok Thon Arok's Independence of the Bor Group
> Muhammad Harun Kafi's SPLA-Nuba
> Kawac Makuei Mayar's Independence Movement for Southern Sudan
> Lam Akol's SPLA-United
> Paulino Matip's South Sudan Unity Army (SSUA).

Some of them were formally allied with, others took money or arms from, Khartoum, and some entered into temporary ceasefires. They split and renamed themselves frequently, though usually the regional or tribal/clan bases were consistent.

Darfur etc.
Darfur produced, inevitably, over twenty different insurgent groups, which were mainly Darfurian, let alone the groups connected to the civil war in Chad or south Sudan. The breakdown of the various insurgent groups in Darfur is outlined in Chapter 8, which also discusses the Chadian forces. Details on other fighting groups, such as the Lord's Resistance Army, can be found in the text, by using the index.

The main and most cohesive Darfur groups were:

> SLA (Sudan Liberation Army), led by Minni Minnawi. This splintered several times. Another prominent SLA leader was Abdul Wahid al-Nur.
> Justice and Equality Movement, led by Khalil Ibrahim.
> Various coalitions were formed from these groups, the most influential was the NRF (National Redemption Front).

Militias in South Sudan after independence
Besides the south Sudanese groups mentioned above, after 2005 a number of groups opposed the Dinka dominance of the government in Juba; some continued after 2011. Juba did persuade some of the followers of four militia groups to join the regular army:

A militia led by Peter Gadet (a Bul Nuer);
One led by Gatluak Gai (a Jagei Nuer);
One led by David Yau Yau (a Murle);
And one led by Gabriel Tanginya (a Nuer).

Three groups remained outside the initial amnesty programme: the militias of George Athor (a Padeng Dinka) in Jonglei; Johnson Olonyi (a Shilluk) and Ayok Ogat (also a Shilluk), both operating in Upper Nile. Athor was killed in December 2011, and his successor, Kuol Chol, led around 1,000 men into the government's amnesty programme. David Yau Yau defected back to Khartoum and was made overall commander of the South Sudan Liberation Army (SSLA) and the South Sudan Democratic Army in Jonglei State.

Endnotes

Chapter 1: The Historical Background

1. Robert O. Collins, *A History of Modern Sudan* (Cambridge University Press, New York, 2010) p.19.

2. Gordon's death has prompted literally hundreds of fictional and non-fictional books, most of them hagiographies. A recent impressive revisionist account is by Fergus Nichol, *Gladstone, Gordon and the Sudan Wars* (Pen and Sword, Barnsley, UK, 2013).

3. Ataf Lutfi Sayyid-Marsot, *A Short History of Egypt* (Cambridge University Press, Cambridge, 1985) p.75.

4. Slatin Bey, *Fire and Sword in the Sudan,* 1896 edition, p.158; see endnote 5 below.

5. I would again recommend Nichol's book *Gladstone, Gordon and the Sudan Wars* for the best short revisionist account of Gordon. It is interesting that in the foreword to Slatin Bey's book, *Fire and Sword in the Sudan,* the head of military intelligence in Cairo, Colonel Reginald Wingate, adds a personal note on transliteration in the original 1896 edition. One would have thought that, in funding and promoting of the book, British intelligence would have been more discreet.

6. See Paul Moorcraft and Philip M. Taylor, *Shooting the Messenger: The Politics of War Reporting* (Biteback, London, 2011) pp.19-22.

Chapter 2: British Rule

1. For more detail on Wingate's time in the SDF, see Simon Anglim, *Orde Wingate: Unconventional Warrior* (Pen and Sword, Barnsley, UK, 2014).

2. For a short summary of this war, and references for the figures, see Paul Moorcraft and Philip M. Taylor, *Shooting the Messenger: The Politics of War Reporting* (Biteback, London, 2011) pp.53-55.

3. Cited in Collins, op. cit., p.65.

Chapter 3: Failed Democracy — Failed Coups (1956-1989)

1. Cited in Richard Cockett, *Sudan: Darfur and the Failure of an African State* (Yale University Press, London, 2010) p.62.

2. Lam Akol, *Southern Sudan: Colonialism, Resistance and Autonomy* (Red Sea Press, Asmara, 2007).

3. Cited in Gérard Prunier, 'Sudan's Regional Relations', in John Ryle *et al, The Sudan Handbook* (James Currey, Woodbridge, Suffolk, 2011) p.154.

Chapter 4: The Makings of a President

1. The phrase was quoted to me by Hadiya Mohamed al Zein, Omar al-Bashir's mother, January 2014. Most of the quotes in this chapter came from interviews in Sudan in January 2014.
2. *Shura* means council or the practice of consultation in Arabic. The implication is that al-Bashir is collegiate in his approach.

Chapter 5: The Duopoly

1. Cited in Collins, op. cit., p.195.
2. Cockett, op. cit., p.119.
3. Douglas H. Johnson, *The Root Causes of Sudan's Civil Wars: Peace or Truce?* (James Currey, Woodbridge, Suffolk, 2011) p.122.

Chapter 6: The General Takes the Reins

1. The quote came from Hassan Ali, the Secretary General of Sudan's Ministry of Energy and Mining, cited in Luke Patey, *The New Kings of Crude: China, India and the Global Struggle for Oil in Sudan and South Sudan* (Hurst, London, 2014) p.65. Patey's book provides a comprehensive account of China's oil politics in Sudan.

Chapter 7: The Road to Peace in the South

1. For a powerful dramatized version of a true story of one such boy, see Dave Eggers, *What is the What* (Penguin, London, 2006).
2. For a detailed summary of the group, see Rebecca Hamilton, *The Wonks Who Sold Washington on South Sudan* (Reuters special report, 11 July 2012).
3. Richard Dowden, *Africa: Altered States, Ordinary Miracles* (Portobello, London, 2009) p.164.
4. The main components of the NDA at this time were:

   1. The Democratic Unionist Party (DUP).
   2. The Umma Party.
   3. The Sudan People's Liberation Movement (SPLM/SPLA).
   4. The Union of Sudan African Parties (USAP).
   5. The Communist Party of Sudan (CPS).
   6. The General Council of the Trade Unions Federations.
   7. The Legitimate Command of the Sudanese Armed Forces.

8. The Beja Congress.
9. The Sudan Alliance Forces.
10. The Federal Democratic Alliance.
11. The Rashaida Free Lions.
12. The Arab Baath Socialist Party.
13. Independent National Figures.
14. Representatives of the Liberated Areas.
15. Sudanese National Party.

5. According to Collins's account, op. cit., p.253.

Chapter 8: The War in the West: Darfur

1. Rob Crilly, *Saving Darfur: Everyone's Favourite African War* (Reportage Press, London, 2010) p.219.
2. Julie Flint and Alex de Waal, *Darfur: A New History of a Long War* (Zed, London, 2008).
3. Cockett, op. cit., p.218.
4. For a poor translation in English of his views, see his *Chad in a Changing World (*No publishing details, c. 2012).

Chapter 9: The ICC and Sudan

1. Terence McNamee, *The ICC and Africa* (Conference Proceedings, Brenthurst Foundation, Johannesburg, April 2014).

Chapter 10: The Fall of the Republic

1. Cockett, op. cit., p.257.
2. As Director of the Centre for Foreign Policy Analysis, I had organized six London conferences on Sudan and especially Darfur, usually in tandem with the Royal United Services Institute, Britain's oldest and most distinguished security think tank. It was amazing how bitter enemies at home would take tea together in London and reminisce fondly about old times at school or college. I was invited to lead an observer team by a range of government and anti-government politicians, some of whom had found the conferences useful.
3. Mareike Schomerus and Tim Allen, *Southern Sudan at Odds with Itself: Dynamics of conflict and predicaments of peace* (Development Studies Institute, LSE, London, 2011).

Select Bibliography

Akol, Lam, *Southern Sudan: Colonialism, Resistance and Autonomy* (Red Sea Press, Asmara, 2007).

Allen, Tim, *Trial Justice: The International Criminal Court and the Lord's Resistance Army* (Zed, London, 2006).

Cockett, Richard, *Sudan: Darfur and the Failure of an African State* (Yale University Press, London, 2010).

Collins, Robert O., *A History of Modern Sudan* (Cambridge University Press, New York, 2010).

Copnall, James, *A Poisonous Thorn in our Hearts: Sudan and South Sudan's Bitter and Complete Divorce* (Hurst, London, 2014).

Crilly, Rob, *Saving Darfur: Everyone's Favourite African War* (Reportage Press, London, 2010).

Flint, Julie and Alex de Waal, *Darfur: A New History of a Long War* (Zed, London, 2008).

Johnson, Douglas H., *The Root Causes of Sudan's Civil Wars: Peace or Truce* (James Currey, Wodbridge, Sussex, 2011).

LeRiche, Matthew and Matthew Arnold, *South Sudan: From Revolution to Independence* (Hurst, London, 2012).

Moorcraft, Paul, 'Sudan: the Bin Laden Connection' in Paul Moorcraft, Gwyn Winfield and John Chisholm, eds, *Axis of Evil: The War on Terror* (Pen and Sword, Barnsley, UK 2004).
 – 'Sudan: End of the Longest War?' *RUSI Journal,* February 2005.
 – *Inside the Danger Zones: Travels to Arresting Places* (Biteback, London, 2010).
 – and Philip M. Taylor, *Shooting the Messenger: The Politics of War Reporting* (Biteback, London, 2011).

Moorehead, Alan, *The White Nile* (Penguin, London, 1983).

Natsios, Andrew S., *Sudan, South Sudan and Darfur: What Everyone Needs to Know* (Oxford University Press, Oxford, 2012).

Nichol, Fergus, *Gladstone, Gordon and the Sudan Wars* (Pen and Sword, Barnsley, UK, 2013).

Patey, Luke, *The New Kings of Crude: China, India and the Global Struggle for Oil in Sudan and South Sudan* (Hurst, London, 2014).

Royle, Trevor, *Orde Wingate: A Man of Genius* (Frontline, London, 2010).

Salmon, Jago, *Paramilitary Revolution: Popular Defence Forces* (Small Arms Survey, Geneva, 2007).

Schomerus, Mareike and Tim Allen, *Southern Sudan at Odds with Itself: Dynamics of conflict and predicaments of peace* (Development Studies Institute, LSE, London, 2011).

Scroggins, Deborah, *Emma's War: Love, Betrayal and Death in the Sudan* (Harper Collins, London, 2003).

Waddell, Nicholas and Phil Clark, *Courting Conflict: Justice, Peace and the ICC in Africa* (Royal African Society, London, 2008).

Wolff, Steffan, 'South Sudan's Year One: Managing the Challenges of Building a New State', *RUSI Journal*, October/November 2012.

Young, John *The Fate of Sudan: The Origins and Consequences of a Flawed Peace Process* (Zed, London, 2012).

Index